THE FRENCH CRITICAL RECEPTION OF AFRICAN-AMERICAN LITERATURE

Recent Titles in
Bibliographies and Indexes in Afro-American and African Studies

Index of Subjects, Proverbs, and Themes in the Writings of
Wole Soyinka
Greta M. K. Coger, compiler

Southern Black Creative Writers, 1829–1953: Biobibliographies
M. Marie Booth Foster, compiler

The Black Aged in the United States: A Selectively Annotated
Bibliography
Lenwood G. Davis, compiler

Àshe, Traditional Religion and Healing in Sub-Saharan Africa and
the Diaspora: A Classified International Bibliography
John Gray, compiler

Black Theatre and Performance: A Pan-African Bibliography
John Gray, compiler

Health of Black Americans from Post Reconstruction to
Integration, 1871–1960: An Annotated Bibliography of
Contemporary Sources
Mitchell F. Rice and Woodrow Jones, Jr., compilers

Blacks in Film and Television: A Pan-African Bibliography of
Films, Filmmakers, and Performers
John Gray, compiler

Daddy Grace: An Annotated Bibliography
Lenwood G. Davis, compiler

African Studies Thesaurus: Subject Headings for Library Users
Freda E. Otchere

Chester Himes: An Annotated Primary and Secondary Bibliography
Michel Fabre, Robert E. Skinner, and Lester Sullivan, compilers

A Bibliographical Guide to African-American Women Writers
Casper LeRoy Jordan, compiler

Invisible Wings: An Annotated Bibliography on Blacks in Aviation,
1916–1993
Betty Kaplan Gubert, compiler

THE FRENCH CRITICAL RECEPTION OF AFRICAN-AMERICAN LITERATURE

From the Beginnings to 1970
An Annotated Bibliography

Compiled by MICHEL FABRE

With the assistance of Rosa Bobia,
Christina Davis, Charles Edwards O'Neill,
and Jack Salzman

Bibliographies and Indexes in Afro-American and African Studies, Number 33
Henry Louis Gates, Jr. and John W. Blassingame, Series Advisers

GREENWOOD PRESS
Westport, Connecticut • London

Library of Congress Cataloging-in-Publication Data

Fabre, Michel.
   The French critical reception of African-American literature :
from the beginnings to 1970 : an annotated bibliography / compiled
by Michel Fabre, with the assistance of Rosa Bobia . . . [et al.].
      p.   cm.—(Bibliographies and indexes in Afro-American and
African studies, ISSN 0742–6925 ; no. 33)
   Includes bibliographical references and index.
   ISBN 0–313–25368–4 (alk. paper)
   1. American literature—Afro-American authors—History and
criticism—Bibliography.   2. American literature—Appreciation—
France—Bibliography.   3. Criticism—France—Bibliography.
I. Title.   II. Series.
Z1229.N39F33   1995
[PS153.N5]
016.8109′896073—dc20   95–12543

British Library Cataloguing in Publication Data is available.

Library of Congress Catalog Card Number: 95–12543
ISBN: 0–313–25368–4
ISSN: 0742–6925

First published in 1995

Greenwood Press, 88 Post Road West, Westport, CT 06881
An imprint of Greenwood Publishing Group, Inc.

Printed in the United States of America

The paper used in this book complies with the
Permanent Paper Standard issued by the National
Information Standards Organization (Z39.48–1984).

10 9 8 7 6 5 4 3 2 1

Copyright Acknowledgments

The author and publisher are grateful for permission to reprint excerpts from the following copy-
righted materials:

Keneth Kinnamon, Michel Fabre, Joseph Benson, and Craig Werner. *A Richard Wright Bibliography:
Fifty Years of Criticism and Commentary.* Reprinted with permission of Greenwood Publishing Group,
Inc., Westport, CT. Copyright © 1988.

Michel Fabre, Robert Skinner, and Lester Sullivan. *Chester Himes: An Annotated Primary and Secondary Bibliography.* Reprinted with permission of Greenwood Publishing Group, Inc., Westport,
CT. Copyright © 1992.

Contents

Introduction

At least some French readers have been aware of literary productions by blacks in the Americas since the mid-eighteenth century, before there was talk of Phillis Wheatley in England. Jean-Jacques Rousseau quoted a song in creole in a manuscript he wrote in 1740. It was sung in Saint-Domingue at the time, and in 1831 a French visitor, Pierre Forest, reproduced this song, "Lizette," the text of which he had been given by a *griffone* near Lake Pontchartrain, Louisiana.

> Dempé mo perdi Lizette
> Mo pa sochié calinda,
> Mo pas bram bram bamboula,
> Quand mo contre l'antre négresse
> Mo pa gagnié zié por li,
> Mo pa souchié travail pièce,
> Tant que chose à moé mourir .

> Since I lost Lisette
> I don't care about calinda,
> I don't dance the hectic bamboula;
> When I come across another Negro girl,
> I have no eyes for her;
> I don't care any more about work
> So much so that my things die.

Black productions in the English language originating in the United States had to wait until the early nineteenth century to find a French reaction. When Abbé Henri Grégoire, one of the founders of the Société des Amis de Noirs, published, his volume *De la littérature des nègres, ou recherches sur leurs facultés intellectuelles, leurs qualités morales et leur littérature,* he selected the poetry of Senegal-born and Boston-bred slave Phillis Wheatley (which Thomas Jefferson considered "beneath the dignity of criticism") as one of the signal proofs that the black race could elevate itself to civilization. The book was translated in 1820 as *An Enquiry Concerning the Moral Faculty and Literature of Negroes, Followed with an Account of the Life and Works of Fifteen Negroes and Mulattoes Distinguished in Science, Literature, and the Arts.*

Originally an attempt was made to collect in the present volume all citations to published items relevant to the impact of African American literature in the French-speaking world from the beginning to the present time. Yet apart from Henri Grégoire's favorable reaction to the achievements of Phillis Wheatley hardly anything in French could be found to exist before 1900, except in Louisiana itself.

To *Les Cenelles*, the anthology of poetry by young men of color edited by Armand Lanusse in New Orleans in 1845, no Paris-based reactions have been found. Nor were any found to Camille Thierry's volume of poetry *Les Vagabondes*. Although it was printed in Bordeaux and Paris in 1874, *Les Vagabondes* was apparently not reviewed there. In a few Louisiana-based publications one can find references to the literary production of local free people of color, but this takes us outside French territory.

The first real reviewing of African American literary productions in France began in 1844 when audiences welcomed the romantic dramas of Victor Séjour. As a result, the reactions of leading Paris theatre critics to Séjour's twenty-odd plays constitute the bulk of the "Pre-1900 section" in this volume, thanks to the essential collaboration of Charles Edwards O'Neill.

Ideally, all criticism of African-American literature printed in French should have been considered. However, the gathering of items published outside of France and its immediate neighbors, Belgium and Switzerland, could not really be attempted with the limited means at our disposal.

The bulk of the items selected were published between 1900 and 1970 and they were all printed in French. There are references to a few translations of texts not published in English, like Richard Wright's preface to *La Croisade de Lee Gordon* by Chester Himes or Langston Hughes' introduction to his *Anthologie de la littérature négro-africaine*, as well as to a few articles by U.S. authors reprinted in translation in French periodicals. These are important if only because those periodicals were widely read by the French-speaking audience. They were ideologically oriented publications most active during the Cold War, either pro-communist periodicals like *Europe,* or the USIS-sponsored reviews, *Informations et Documents* and *Profils.* A third, different case is the publication in *Présence africaine* of literary essays written by African-Americans themselves.

This present selection has been limited to works printed before 1970, excluding mimeographed dissertations and theses, which were far fewer than one may think The selection has also been limited to responses to the works of creative writers. The inclusion of autobiographical entries concerning Frederick Douglass and Booker T. Washington, who were political leaders more than literary figures, has seemed to warrant an exception for historical reasons. This has also been the case for Malcolm X, Martin Luther King, and Eldridge Cleaver, because French reactions to their writings became extensive and their popularity great in the late 1960s. We have not listed reactions to political, sociological, historical, and other studies, except when written by primarily creative writers (e.g. LeRoi Jones' *Blues People* and *Black Music*).

Even within the present selection, there are lacunae. Notably, most of the reviews pertaining to Frank Yerby's numerous best-sellers have not been found because they were published in dailies or weeklies, not in the more serious periodicals, and the available clippings in publishers' files have been destroyed.

Our search has been painstaking because indexes to French periodicals are rare, and indexes to daily and weekly newspapers are practically non-existent for the period covered. A search was conducted in Paris libraries and publishers' files, but several collections of journals and periodicals are incomplete while whole runs of newspapers are unavailable even at the Bibliothèque Nationale. Much information was rescued from publishers' archives although many of these files are systematically destroyed after a decade or two. Also, the clippings in such files usually bear no page numbers, no issue or volume number and sometimes no indication of the title of the periodical. The references to such items were retrieved, when possible, by subsequent searching which was done mostly by Patrick Salès and Rachida Chbihi. This search could by no means be completed, if only because most of the newspaper runs concerned remain unavailable.

The end result is therefore far from exhaustive, but all the items listed and annotated here did exist at one time and they were read by one or more of the researchers even when their location in newspapers or reviews could not be indicated in full. We decided to publish this bibliography, however incomplete and imperfect, because we feel that a more systematic search would not yield much more information and the years and labor needed to locate pages are not worth the waiting. As it stands, we are persuaded this volume can help researchers interested in charting the critical reception of a specific body of literature abroad. Going beyond the bibliographies of specific authors, it also reflects the often unforeseeable course of international literary influences. Perhaps it can help provide foundations towards the building of a working model.

In the case of the reception of African-American creative literature in France (or by the French-speaking audience) up to 1970, one can note the following features:

1. This critical reception of literary works reflects the general attitudes the French have vis-à-vis black Americans. Richard Wright, among others, was surprized, upon arriving in Paris in 1947 by the "wild notions" held by French people concerning the Negro and his influence upon the American scene. Their conceptions were out of date. He noted in his essay "French Preconceptions about Negroes" that "the Negro of 1946 is unknown in France, and the image of the Negro of 1922 is the one cherished." This was the result of a long isolation from the American scene, as well as a longing for reality as it once was, i.e. "glamorous and thrilling."

2. Especially after World War II, French attitudes have included most of the political implications of racial issues, not only as fuel to anti-U.S. propaganda during the Cold War, but also out of sympathy for, and in support of, the black liberation struggle during the Civil Rights movement and the Black Power period.

3. Conversely, French critical responses, even when ideologically slanted, have placed great emphasis on aesthetic perspectives and artistic achievement. It should be noted that African-American writers have been translated, and reviewed proportionately as often

and as earnestly as "mainstream" American authors.

4. The authors who are best-known, admired and cherished in France are not necessarily those who are successful in the U.S., as is notably the case with Chester Himes. French residence or the expatriation of these writers played a certain role in shaping their reputation but was not determinant.

5. There seems to be a constant trend among French critics to link written literature by African Americans and their oral cultural production (the blues, spirituals) which is held in high esteem, probably because of the earnest acknowledgment of early African-American musical performance in Europe.

6. Fiction occupies the forefront, followed by poetry and drama.

7. Many reviewers and critics have a tendency to specialize in areas of writing and the same names often recur. These "specialists" often include comparisons of different black authors within their reviews, although many also resort to comparisons with white American and French authors.

8. With the passing of time, African-American works have become increasingly known in France, where they are now translated almost as soon as they come out in the United States. Yet, until the 1950's, they were dependent upon a handful of deeply-concerned enthusiasts, like Frank L. Schoell, René Maran, or Georges-Albert Astre to popularize this literature. As a whole, French academics were more conservative and made far less room for black writing than they tend to do now.

An early exception was Claude McKay's acquaintance, Sorbonne professor and Whitman translator Léon Bazalgette; another notable exception was Professor Jean Wagner, the author of the major dissertation, *Les poètes nègres aux Etats-Unis,* whose role was most important in the 1960s. The following letter, which Professor Wagner wrote in 1961 to Marc Saporta, the Editor of a Paris-based USIS magazine, is included here to show a typical example of his integrity:

The Editor
Informations & Documents
4, Avenue Gabriel, Paris

Dear Sir:

A year ago, you were kind enough to ask me, through Mr. C. Rudolph Aggrey, at the time Director of the American Cultural Center of the rue du Dragon, for an article on Langston Hughes, together with a selection of representative poems of this author.

Permit me to express my astonishment at the way in which you have just published, in issue No. 135 of *Informations & Documents*, dated January 15, 1961, the different parts of the manuscript which I handed over to you.

I shall say nothing about the minor re-writing which you deemed necessary to undertake within the body of my article. Nor do I hold against you the fact that you did not publish all of the poems submitted to you, within the exact limit of the number of lines you requested.

But I can positively not accept that you should publish under my signature, without warning your readers or myself, curtailed versions of the poems accompanying my article. You have cut off the last stanza of "Negro" (p.31) and the last seven lines of "Pride" (p.33). Out of this operation, the poet Langston Hughes, whom you requested me to present objectively to your readers, comes forth emasculated. As a member of the teaching body of France, I have too high a sense of the honesty I owe to those who it is my duty to inform, for me to stand by in silence as you distort, not mere words, but the thought of a human being.

I therefore beg you please to insert in your very next issue to be published the text of the present letter by way of rectification.

In the meantime, I am, yours sincerely.

Jean Wagner

[The lines suppressed at the end of "Negro" were:
"The Belgians cut off my hands in the Congo
They lynch me still in Mississippi

I am a Negro
Black as the night is black,
Black like the depths of my Africa."

The Editor did not comply with Professor Wagner's request. He was known for eliminating any word which might imply criticism of U.S. policy, as Professor Simon Copans, himself a enthusiastic supporter of African-American culture in France has personally confirmed to me.]

A few words should be added about the format of this bibliography.

The order is chronological by year, and then alphabetical within each section. The references follow standard MLA procedure. English-speaking readers should be aware of discrepancies and complexities in spelling which may seem due to carelessness but which, in fact, reflect French usage. Capitalization in French titles is more complex and less abundant than in American English. As a rule, the first noun in a title (plus the adjective when it *precedes* the noun) begins with a capital in short titles (i.e. two or three words) of published works. In longer titles only the initial word and/or noun begin(s) with a capital. To complicate matters, the few words which begin with capitals in French are not the same as in English, e.g. French adjectives indicating nationality, race, or religion are not capitalized.

Dates are indicated in English. Volume numbers for periodicals are not preceded by "vol.," but issue numbers are preceded by "No." whenever volume numbers are not provided. Whenever page or issue numbers are not indicated, the reason is that they were not available.

We have tried, when needed, to clarify a number of points which may be misleading for the non-initiates. For instance, there are two Jean Wagners.The "other" Jean Wagner, by the way, wrote mostly in *La Quinzaine littéraire*, and is a perceptive literary and musical critic but not an academic.

The use of "Negro," "black" (capitalized or not), "Afro-American" and "African-American" roughly corresponds to the French author's intentions and to the historical usage of those terms.

This project was initiated two decades ago and like many enterprises of this kind, its outcome is the result of collaboration and team work. At the initial stage, I benefited from the help of my M.A. students at the Sorbonne Nouvelle. The following were especially involved in checking publishers' archives in the mid-1970s: Marième Ndiaye, Christine Bédouelle (on the treatment of African-American literature in *Présence africaine*), Sylvie Marchand, Eric Surpin (on Langston Hughes), Catherine Blanchard (on Malcolm X and Martin Luther King), Aminata Diop, Claude Grimal (on pre-World War II items), Mohammed Kadri (on Chester Himes), Michèle Sandiressegarame (on Margaret Walker), Geneviève Dary, and Lydia Fernandez. Additional checking and completing of references was done by Patrick Salès in the 1980s and by Rachida Chbihi in 1991.

In the course of this research two questionnaires were prepared with the help of my students. The first was sent to one hundred and fifty French writers in order to gauge their acquaintance with African-American literature. A second questionnaire, prepared with the help of computer-expert Jean-Pierre Turbergue, was administered to French students in order to evaluate the respective knowledge of Afro-American writers and their image of black music. Part of the findings were published in *Studies in Black Literature* (Autumn 1973) in a translation by Stephen Rubin. They were included in my book, *French Approaches to Afro-American Literature* (Paris: Université de la Sorbonne Nouvelle, 1980).

Other scholars generously provided help. Dr. Rosa Bobia (now on the faculty of Kennesaw College) was in the process of writing her dissertation on "The Critical Reception of James Baldwin in France" when she shared with us her findings as we shared ours with her. Similarly, all the items concerning Ralph Ellison listed by Jacqueline Covo in her June 1973 *CLA Journal* article, "Ralph Ellison's Critical Reception in France," were used. A selection of my own contributions to *A Richard Wright Bibliography : Fifty Years of Criticism and Commentary*, compiled by Keneth Kinnamon with the help of Michel Fabre, Joseph Benson and Craig Werner (Greenwood Press, 1988) and of Kinnamon's own findings has been included. Also the relevant items contained in *Chester Himes: An Annotated Primary and Secondary Bibliography* by Michel Fabre, Robert Skinner and Lester Sullivan (Greenwood Press, 1992) have been incorporated into this bibliography. Last but not least, Charles Edwards O'Neill kindly allowed the many reviews of Victor Séjour's plays which he cites extensively in his forthcoming biography of the Louisiana Creole author to be included here, which enabled us to have a nearly exhaustive 19th-century section.

Most of the annotations were done by me, with the exception of items borrowed from bibliographies and lists already prepared by the several collaborators acknowledged. All translations of quotations are mine and/or Christina Davis', except in the case of items about Victor Séjour, which were all annotated by Charles E. O'Neill.

The preparation of the final manuscript from the card files was due, at a first stage, to Christina Davis who corrected annotations and typed many of them in an acceptable format. The first computerized version was made possible thanks to the collaboration of Jack Salzman, director of the Center for American Culture Studies at Columbia University, who provided advice as well as editorial and technical help. The typing and editing is especially due to the care of those in his Center who entered the items into a database I later established the final version, meanwhile benefiting from the editorial advice provided by Nick Nesbit, who corrected the annotations of about one hundred additional items

I thank all of them for their collaboration and I am pleased to acknowledge their work and contributions. I am solely responsible for the remaining errors.

Finally, I thank Lori Blackwell, Marilyn Brownstein, George F. Butler, Maureen Melino, my editors at Greenwood Press for their patience and valuable advice.

Michel Fabre

Bibliography

1844

1 Anon. Review of *Diégarias* by Victor Séjour. *Journal des théâtres* (July 28, 1844), p. 1.
Victor Herbin may be the author of this article which cheers "the debut of a young writer, a happy beginning full of promises." He sees talent and artistic consciousness in the work presented and rates Séjour's style and delineation of character higher than his intrigue-woven plot. Struck by the high drama that Séjour can bring off, he is disappointed by the slowing down of tense action as the play moves through its final act. Young as the playwright is, he seems, like many others, to use touches of old-time melodrama. Séjour's lines are described as "nervous, incisive, flowing." A few verses are declared defective, nothing seriously wrong, merely imperfections to be polished away by a closer prosodic examination.

2 Anon. Review of *Diégarias* by Victor Séjour. *L'Illustration* (August 1, 1844), p. 556.
"The author is a young man of 25 years of age. It is only fair to attribute to taste and youthful inexperience the melodramatic core of his work, the borrowings from predecessors, the incomplete portrayal of the characters. But there are qualities that must be accepted as a sign of precocious talent and of a good future: a style often clear, energetic and concise; feeling expressed with sensitivity or with vigor; and two or three dramatic confrontations."

3 Bayon, Charles. Letter from Paris. *Courrier de la Louisiane* (January 5, 1844), p. 2.
On November 16, 1843, the script of Victor Séjour's *Diégarias* was accepted by the Théâtre français. The Paris correspondent of the *Courrier de la Louisiane* told of the unanimous final vote. No mention is made of Séjour's race.

4 Cellier-Dufayel, N. Review of *Diégarias* by Victor Séjour. In *Mission dramatique*. Paris, 1844. Clipping in Bibliothèque de l'Arsenal. Ref. 48019.
"This play contains not one single fine sentiment, not one great thought. On the contrary, we are constantly shown a development of instincts, of evil passion." Suicide seems casually accepted by the author. The play, lacking didactic purpose, breathing only "disgust of humanity," is "therefore dangerous in several ways."

5 Furgy, Julien de. Review of *Diégarias* by Victor Séjour. *Le Voleur* (July 30, 1844). Clipping in Bibliothèque de l'Arsenal. Ref. 48018.
The critic lambasts *Diégarias*. The play is "long, heavy, improbable and boring." The melodramatic secrets are worthy of the out-of-date Victor Ducange and René de Pixérecourt.

6 S., J. Review of *Diégarias* by Victor Séjour. *La Revue de Paris* No. 57 (1844). Clipping in Bibliothèque de l'Arsenal. Ref. 48018 (1).
"Twelve or fifteen years ago, *Diégarias* would have stirred the crowd's feelings as much as any play of the time; today it's a cannon fired after the battle." The play smacks of 1829, yet there are several qualities which make for good and beautiful works. "We would willingly say what M. Hugo said one day of a book by one of his friends, 'The fruit is unripe, but the fruit is there.' "

1849

7 Anon. Review of *La Chute de Séjean* by Victor Séjour. *La Semaine* (August 1849). Clipping in the Bibliothèque de l'Arsenal. Ref. 48018.
The reviewer commends Séjour's knowledge of the historical period. Séjour's "style also is remarkable for its precision, its elegance, its

unity... a style which is distinctively his." He has advanced --"a giant's step"-- beyond his *Diégarias*. He has succeeded in portraying *les grandes passions* --jealousy, ambition, scorn, fury-- especially in the scene where Séjan spurns Livia after, and, indeed, because of their amorous complicity in murder. Séjour's verse "is correct, elegant, concise," and is not encumbered in this "epoch-making drama."

8 Anon. Review of *La Chute de Séjean* by Victor Séjour. *La Semaine* (September 1849). Clipping in the Bibliothèque de l'Arsenal.
See item 7.

9 Janin, Jules. Mention of *La Chute de Séjean* by Victor Séjour. *Le Journal des débats* (August 2, 1849), p. 2.
Janin suggests that Rachel turned down the main role in Séjour's play because it was the work of an unknown author.

10 Janin, Jules. Review of *La Chute de Séjean* by Victor Séjour. *Le Journal des débats* (August 27, 1849), pp. 1-2.
Séjour dedicated the play to the highly esteemed theater critic, who in turn praised it highly. Janin is won over by the playwright's artistry: "This drama is the offering of a true talent. To understand Rome -- and human nature-- Victor Séjour has studied with exceptional care the heights and slips of the interesting career of Sejanus." Séjour guides the action "with rare felicity: no useless noises, no idle efforts. He is sober in ornamentation and outcry." Janin compliments Séjour for poetic creativity in having Séjan retreat to the arms of his wife for courage in his last hours. Each aspect of the play is lauded: "the style is energetic, the passion is vibrant... the action is swift, the dialogue is animated." Going further, Janin finds a political lesson: Tiberius and Robespierre were tyrants who ruled by terror. Words of caution for the Second Republic?

1852

11 Busoni, Philippe. Review of *Richard III* by Victor Séjour. *L'Illustration* (October 9, 1852), p. 226.
Séjour is commended as "a man of integrity and talent," who did not yield to the temptation to take over the possession of Shakespeare, which he could easily have done. Instead, "he made himself the architect of his house, and decorated it according to his inspiration

and fantasy: inspiration a bit sombre, fantasy a bit violent. But when you choose Richard III, it is not precisely to amuse your audience, but rather to make them tremble." This ability of Séjour to put together a well-built plot structure is recognized. *Richard III* is "one of these great engines solidly built," designed "with a great deal of care, dexterity and talent."

12 Cyrano (pseud.). Review of *Richard III* by Victor Séjour. *La Revue de Paris* (December 1852), p. 174.
The successful run of the play was brought to a close in mid-December because of another contractual obligation of actor Ligier. The theater columnist feels that the "victorious" Richard could have gone on much longer: *Richard III* finished "as it began--before an audience that was numerous, eager and pleased."

13 Deschamps, Théo. Review of *Richard III* by Victor Séjour. *Le Théâtre* (September 29, 1852), p. 3.
In 1852 Marc Fournier, the brilliant theatrical entrepreneur, brought Séjour's *Richard III* to the redecorated Théâtre de la Porte Saint-Martin. Opening night, September 28, was awaited with great expectation. Deschamps, judging from the dress rehearsal, predicts a triumph; he considers the work "one of the most splendid expressions of modern dramatic literature."

14 Janin, Jules. Review of *Richard III* by Victor Séjour. *Almanach de la littérature, théâtre et beaux-arts* (1852), pp. 39-40.
Janin feels that his young Creole friend is "one of the young poets of our times who gives the greatest expectations. He is, first of all, an inventor. He combines rushingly the most varied scenes and the most terrible emotions." From Shakespeare he borrows only the man Richard III. Then, leaving the English tragedy in place, Séjour composes an "entirely new drama."

15 Plouvier, Edouard. Review of *Richard III* by Victor Séjour. *Le Théâtre* (October 2, 1852), pp. 1-2.
The critic vividly describes the first night when the audience "was on its way to appreciate the daring attempt of this young poet who is among the most beloved of the younger literary generation." Maybe Séjour has tried too hard to show that he was not imitating Shakespeare's phrases. This detail aside, he "has created a magnificent drama, written in a style that is firm, muscular, warmly colored. Grandeur of conception, logical and well conducted

developments, stirring situations, profound conclusions, -- all are there to justify a truly triumphant success."

16 Plouvier, Edouard. Review of *Richard III* by Victor Séjour. *Le Théâtre* (October 6, 1852), p. 3.
Richard III was played by Ligier "who alone could enact the fearful role. Gesture, gait, eye, voice and physiognomy are in marvelous harmony to render the feline caresses, the sinister recoiling, the tiger rages, the sudden about-faces, the ferocious obstinacy, that the role is full of." Séjour is as fortunate in having Ligier for Richard as he has been in having Beauvallet for Diégarias. The role of lovely Princess Elizabeth was given to Lia Félix, the sister of Rachel.

17 Plouvier, Edouard. Review of *Richard III* by Victor Séjour. *Le Théâtre* (October 17, 1852), p. 1.
The critic thinks that the play continues to merit "daily receipts of four thousand francs, constant and enthusiastic attention of the public from orchestra to the highest balcony, and repeated ovations for the great situations of the play and their performers."

18 Plouvier, Edouard. Review of *Richard III* by Victor Séjour. *Le Théâtre* (November 27, 1852), p. 2.
The critic salutes author and cast again when the sixtieth performance is given. "It is rare that a truly literary drama has so brilliant a career, but too often also, in those plays called literary, style has replaced action." That is not the case with *Richard III*. In this work everything is proportional, in harmony. "What a Gloucester Ligier makes! How this eminent actor has well captured each touch of that wild majesty!"

1854

19 Busoni, Philippe. Review of *L'Argent du Diable*. *L'Illustration* (April 8, 1854), p. 211.
The play is found too serious for its lighthearted stage: "M. Victor Séjour is a conscientious and talented man, who has made a clear mistake in regard to genre, setting and scene. He is too intelligent to do it again--at the Variétés." However, Busoni acknowledges, the playwright and his ill-chosen stage are making "a devil of a lot of money."

20 Anon. Mention of *L'Argent du Diable*. *Le Théâtre* (April 29,

1854), p. 3-4.
After the play closed in Paris, it was promptly staged in Brussels --
on April 22, 1854-- and is reported "a complete success."

21 Masquelier, Albert. Review of *L'Argent du Diable*. *Le Théâtre*
(March 29, 1854), pp. 2-3.
The critic describes the audience's attention as eager, the applause as
enthusiastic. "There are very pretty scenes in [the play]. The plot is
simple, touching, natural; the interest is real and powerful." Some
passages, he feels, seem as if from the hand of George Sand.

22 Masquelier, Albert. Mention of *L'Argent du Diable*. *Le Théâtre*
(May 17, 1854), p. 2.
Whatever early apparent success *L'Argent...* enjoyed, it was short-
lived: the play survived only two weeks. According to Masquelier
the blame was to be laid up to the playwright, for Deshayes had
given all one could to the role of old Loriot.

23 Masquelier, Albert. Review of *L'Argent du Diable*. *Le Théâtre*
(April 1, 1854), pp. 2-3.
Masquelier is favorable but not without reserve. "Yes, *L'Argent du
Diable* is a happy success, an honorable success, to which an author
ought to be proud to sign his name. The play of M. Séjour is, no
doubt, not irreproachable." In the analysis the critic regrets that the
dénouement has not been worked out better.

24 Thierry, Edouard. Review of *L'Argent du Diable*. *Le Moniteur
universel* (April 4, 1854).
Thierry reproaches Séjour for having Loriot fall --after the author had
presented him as thoroughly generous and self-sacrificing. That he
should be tempted, yes; but that he should fall, no. After making
this point of plot and characterization, Thierry praises the play.
"This vaudeville is good workmanship. It is boldly constructed.
Life and strength run through it."

1855

25 Danjeau, Léopold. Review of *Les Noces vénitiennes*. *Les
Modes parisiennes* (1855), pp. 2029-2040.
The critic likes the "beautiful drama," and judges it "an energetic
work... The effects are grand and terrible, the plot situations show

the hand of a master. The scenes are broadly drawn." It is, then, worthy of the author of *Sejanus* and of *Richard III*.

26 De La Rounat, Charles. Review of *L'Argent du Diable*. *La Revue de Paris*, 21 (April 1, 1855), p. 154.
The critic declares the play a success. The vaudeville theater has taken a chance in departing from its typical offering; the public has ratified the decision. "*L'Argent du Diable* is more than vaudeville; it is a comedy, almost a drama."

27 De La Rounat, Charles. Review of *Les Noces vénitiennes*. *La Revue de Paris*, 24 (March 15, 1855), pp. 947-948.
De La Rounat expresses his disappointment that the author of *Richard III* has not measured up to expectations: "...we experienced the greatest amazement in finding in this drama nothing that makes a work of art live." It has no spark. The playwright seems mistaken on the real causes of his success in *Richard III*, but the effect produced by the *Noces vénitiennes* will call his attention to "a system of composition which, if continued in, would lead him to grave grief."

28 Thibout, M. Review of *Les Noces vénitiennes*. *Le Théâtre* (April 21, 1855), p. 2.
Thibout observes that "For forty days already *Les Noces vénitiennes* is on the marquee, and still is far from closing. The powerful situations of the drama, whose grand effects are sustained in a solid and lofty style, the richness of the staging, the splendor of costumes and scenery are sufficient to assure M. Victor Séjour's work a long and productive career."

29 Thibout, M. Review of *Les Noces vénitiennes*. *Le Théâtre* (March 8, 1855), p. 2.
The critic treats the play respectfully in his review of the first night performance and promises to return.

30 Thibout, M. Review of *Les Noces vénitiennes*. *Le Théâtre* (March 14, 1855), p. 2.
In his second review, Thibout complains of flaws in the plot. The first three acts are solid, he judges; the last two, weak. It was a little too facile for Galieno Faliero to jilt Morosina and to cherish Albone Orseolo, also too facile for Orseolo to soften the vendetta, and for the

young couple to look forward to living happily ever after. Thibout reproaches Séjour for the weakening finale. "M. Victor Séjour is not a careless fabricator of plays; he is a poet. He works at it, he has a goal in mind, and consequently he merits our serious attention." Thibout predicts that the flaws will not stand in the way of success.

31   Thierry, Edouard.   Review of *Les Noces vénitiennes*.   *Le Moniteur universel* (April 28-29, 1855).
Thierry imagines the play a response to the question "What would have happened in *Romeo and Juliet* if old Capulet ... had had more tenderness for Juliet than hate for the last of the Montaigus?" "This drama, somber and terrible, is complete" with the Porte-Saint-Martin specialities: melodrama, dance, scenery, and romanesque adventures. This theater's traditions, dating back to 1830, are, after a temporary closing, enjoying new life. To the repertory of that "valiant and generous school" is now added the "vigorous dialogue" of Séjour. Thierry praises the stellar cast who move artistically through the terror, crime and violence.

1856

32   Anon.   Mention of *Le Fils de la nuit* by Victor Séjour.   *Journal pour rire* (September 20, 1856).   Clipping in Bibliothèque de l'Arsenal. Ref. 47992 (1).
The humorous *Journal pour rire* twits Séjour and Alexandre Dumas about the exchange of compliments about *Le Fils de la nuit*. Its parody reads: "I dedicated my first masterpiece to Charlemagne, my second to Louis XIV. O great Alexander, permit me to offer my third to you." Then comes the "beautiful response" from the Great Alexander: "That's okay, but I'd like to have something along with it." A drum is sketched over the quotations; a caption beneath the item reads: "Variations on the big drum." [In French, to beat the big drum means to advertise, and *caisse* (drum) also means cash register or box office.]

33   Anon.   Mention of *Les Noces vénitiennes*.   *Le Théâtre* (December 10, 1856), p. 3.
After the one hundred and fiftieth presentation --with the night's receipts down to 2,940 francs-- it was judged necessary to trim the play. Also, in place of the much acclaimed dancer Petra Camara, a ballet, unconnected with the drama, was placed on the program. This added attraction was a device commonly used to draw crowds

back to a hit whose popularity had begun to fade.

34 Cochinat, Victor. Review of *Les Noces vénitiennes*. *La Gazette de Paris* (July 20, 1856). Clipping at Bibliothèque de l'Arsenal, Ref. 47992 (3-4).
"Startling, prodigious, enchanting," raves the critic after first complaining of some structural defects in the composition of the drama. "Don't be surprised," he underestimates "to see M. Victor Séjour's play have a 100-production run."

35 D'Auriac, Eugène. Review of *Les Noces vénitiennes*. *Le Théâtre* (July 16, 1856), p. 2.
"The drama of M. Victor Séjour is well laid out, well developed, and indicates a profound understanding of theatrical resources. The situation, the characters are clearly drawn, and the scenes, perfectly sketched, are full of stirring details and captivating interest." The critic has bouquets for the actors as well: This remarkable play, which held the entire audience in suspense, was "not only perfectly conceived   and   composed,   but   also   was   admirably played....Especially Mmes. Guyon and Laurent are incomparable in the scene of the two mothers, a new, an original scene, admirably written, admirably rendered." Costumes and scenery, especially the ship in the storm, also received praise; indeed, the applauding audience called the ship back for a curtain call! The Theatre de la Porte Saint-Martin, D'Auriac feels, could go no further in prodigious magnificence.

36 D'Auriac, Eugène. Mention of *Les Noces vénitiennes*. *Le Théâtre* (December 20, 1856), p. 2.
In mid-December a benefit performance was given for M. Caron, chief machinist of the theater, and his associates. The feeling was that "never before certainly has anyone pushed so far the machinist's technique, and the tableau of the ship maneuvering at sea will certainly remain a most remarkable model."

37 Danjeau, Léopold. Review of *Le Fils de la nuit*. *Les Modes parisiennes* (1856), p. 2940.
Mentions that the royalties from *Le Fils de la nuit* had to be shared by Séjour in accord with an out-of-court settlement.

38 De Langey, Henri. Review of *Les Noces vénitiennes*. *La Presse théâtrale* (July 20, 1856), pp. 2-3.
The critic is worried by the very success of elaborate scenery and

mechanical technique. As for the ship and its maneuvers, were not "mischievous jokesters saying that *Le Fils de la nuit* [was] the greatest nautical event of the summer season"? Langey insists that "the machinist ... ought to obey the poet, and not give him orders." He moves on to analyze the specifically Séjourian style. "M. Séjour has read widely and reflected long. There is some Shakespeare, some Corneille and some Byron in his work." For all that, M. Séjour, in spite of his merit, is not a winsome artist. "In his best moments, he stirs you rather than moves you. At a given moment he grabs the spectator, but soon the spectator resists the embrace and slips back into passivity; in general, M. Séjour is a writer of emphasis and veneer. His lines have a clickety-clack that winds up very wearying." Still Langey acknowledges that the play is a "complete success." Regarding the dialogue of the two mothers, he knows of no "more beautiful scene in contemporary theater." Although he feels the play could have been improved by cutting the final tableau, he winds up subscribing to the poster's claim that *Le Fils de la nuit* presents "a fabulous, incomparable spectacle that all Paris will want to see!" The critic frankly expresses his reaction that "The day that dramatic art ceases to be amusement of the mind and the feeling of the heart in order to become the gross distraction of the senses, that art will degrade itself, will lose all its moral influence and all its grandeur: it will be no more than a pastime always frivolous and sometimes dangerous."

39 Gautier, Théophile. Review of *Le Fils de la nuit*. *Le Moniteur universel* (July 14, 1856), pp. 1-2.
Gautier applauds both play and playwright. "A brilliant success! The play of M. Victor Séjour is at the same time a poem, a drama and a ballet: a poem in the telling of the story, a drama in the power of the conflicts, a ballet in the splendid variety of staging." He marvels at the technical perfection of the Ben-Leil's ship--pursued by Donato's in a storm: "A ship sails and pitches on the backs of monstrous waves. Its prow dips and presses into the bitter troughs, soaking the forward sail, then rises and glistens. The pulleys scrape, the sails flap, the ropes quiver, the frame groans painfully and seems to beg for relief... The storm redoubles its fury, the lightning multiples its sulfurous flashes... Soon, the main mast cracks, totters and falls. The space between the ships lessens; they are linked with grappling hooks." Then the boarding and the battle on the moving decks!

40 Jalabert, Adolphe. Review of *Les Noces vénitiennes*. *Le Théâtre* (September 27, 1856), p. 3.

The critic writes: "*Le Fils de la nuit* draws countless crowds. The box office takes in daily five thousand francs; this figure dispenses us [the editors of *Le Théâtre*] from all commentary. Rendering justice all the while to the SHIP, which is the principal cause of this immense success, we ought not, however, forget Mme. Guyon, admirably beautiful in the role of Julia Favelly."

41 Jalabert, Adolphe.   Mention of *Les Noces vénitiennes*.   *Le Théâtre* (November 22, 1856), p. 2.
The editor of *Le Théâtre* notes with emphasis that the play has reached "*its one hundred and thirty-fourth PERFORMANCE,* and this hit seems to want to eternalize itself, for the crowd flows in as numerous, as enthusiastic as in the first days."

42 Mouton, Charles.   Mention of *Le Fils de la nuit*. *La Presse théâtrale* (October 19, 1856), p. 3.
Mouton notes briefly the continuing success of *Le Fils de la nuit*.

43 Tiengou, J.-M.   Mention of *Les Noces vénitiennes*. *La Gazette de France* (December 29, 1856).
The critic concurs with many others that the tableau of the ship maneuvering at sea in the play will certainly remain a most remarkable model.

44 Tiengou, J.-M.   Review of *Les Noces vénitiennes*. *La Gazette de France* (July 14, 1856), pp. 1-3.
In his favorable review, Tiengou tells how Donato and Ben-Leil's "instinctive hate followed its course, with diverse fortunes, amid emotions of every sort and through all the marvels that decorative art can invent. ... Gigantic ruins of an ancient palace..., a raging sea hurling its angry waves against a ship about to sink. ... Everywhere emotion and life." One scene above all, the scene of the two mothers, is a little masterpiece. The play from any point of view, is admirably staged. Rarely has anyone done better."

1857

45 Anon. Mention of *Les Noces vénitiennes*. *Le Théâtre* (January 14, 1857), p. 2.
States that for the final few early 1857 performances, Fechter, who had to move on to his next play, yielded the lead to Raphael Félix,

who had been chosen to play Ben-Leil in the tour *en province*.

46 Anon. Review of *André Gérard*. *Le Théâtre* (May 13, 1857), p. 3.
Mentions that *André Gérard* opened on April 30, 1857 at the Théâtre de l'Odéon. Napoleon III and Empress Eugénie attended the eighth night. At the express will of the Emperor, the play began before the arrival of their imperial majesties. The director, M. de La Rounat, went to their box to put them "au courant of the first scenes already played. The Empress appeared deeply moved during the course of the beautiful presentation and was pleased to join the Emperor several times to applaud the players of M. Victor Séjour's work." After the curtain their imperial majesties expressed their complete satisfaction to M. de La Rounat in very flattering terms.

47 Gautier, Théophile. Review of *André Gérard*. *Le Moniteur universel* (May 4, 1857), feuilleton.
Gautier has a problem with André Gérard's reticence when the cheating is discovered. "It's true that we would have lost three very beautiful acts, and that the same reproach could be addressed to many a play based on reticence or secrets." However, his overall judgment is favorable: "Definitely, here is a touching, poignant drama, with scenes that are bold and pathetic,--a play which helped the actor [Fréderick-Lemaitre] as much as he helped the play."

48 Louet, Ernest. Review of *André Gérard*. *Le Théâtre* (May 2, 1857), p. 1.
Louet in his first-night review challenges the consistency of André Gérard's behavior: why did he accept the hand of cards prepared by Truphème, why did he not denounce the cheat to General de Morand, why did he not confess the first time? In the play which intended a moral lesson, why was Truphème never unmasked? "Strange moral, which leaves to crime the enjoyment of all worldly pleasures." But, Louet acknowledges, "the playing of the actors carried us all along with them; the audience did not reflect, did not analyze anything, explain anything, it just applauded, and that first night, which ordinarily brings the most intelligent of the public, makes us believe in a great, an enormous success."

49 Saint-Victor, Paul de. Review of *André Gérard*. *La Presse* (May 3, 1857), pp. 1-2.
Frédérick-Lemaître's come-back--the second in a long career--is the

center of attention for the reviewer: never had he been "more simple, more pathetic, more naturally inspired." The drama has "the faults and the qualities of Victor Séjour: violently drawn beautiful scenes, striking and improbable situations, great impressions produced by exaggeration of contrasts. But the core of it lacks neither breadth nor power, and Frédérick has a warm, lively illusion-making authenticity that covers over any raw details." On one detail the critic voices an opinion: Truphème the traitor belongs in a melodrama of the Ambigu but is out of place in a play by Séjour.

1858

50   Busoni, Philippe.   Review of *Le Martyre du coeur*. *L'Illustration* (March 27, 1858), p. 196.
The critic rather likes the play but would have preferred it were much shorter. Its title awakens interest.

51 De Fère, Eugène. Mention of *Le Martyre du coeur* by Victor Séjour and Jules Brésil. *Le Monde dramatique* (April 15, 1858), p. 3.
The review is favorable.

52 Di Pietro, Albert. Review of *Le Martyre du coeur* by Victor Séjour and Jules Brésil. *Le Monde dramatique* (March 18, 1858), p. 3.
The review is implicitly favorable.

53 Gautier, Théophile. Review of *Le Martyre du coeur* by Victor Séjour and Jules Brésil. *Le Moniteur universel* (March 22, 1858), p. 2.
Gautier agrees with Guillemot and Saint-Victor that the play could well have ended when a humbled Clarisse welcomed Pierre's love and received her inheritance. He finds the title pretentious.

54 Guillemot. Review of *Le Martyre du coeur* by Victor Séjour and Jules Brésil. *Le Théâtre* (March 20, 1858), pp. 1-2.
The critic would have preferred a shorter, less cluttered play. But he stresses its commercial success claiming that the first six performances have grossed 17,800 francs. It is the biggest hit in years for the Ambigu-Comique.

55 Guillemot. Review of *Le Martyre du coeur* by Victor Séjour and Jules Brésil. *La Presse théâtrale* (March 28, 1858), p. 3.
Guillemot pens a witty theory on the joint authorship of the play: "Here's how I explain the collaboration of Messieurs Séjour and Brésil. The first, bearing a drama in three acts and four tableaux, must have met the second, bearing a drama in two acts and three tableaux, in the office of M. Chilly, the new director [of the Ambigu-Comique]; a stitching must have been done, right then and there, and the result would be this 'bilogy' in five acts and seven tableaux." Guillemot divides the play into two themes: that of proud Clarisse and faithful Pierre, who are aided by the arrival of Placide with money; and that of the sinister Lerdac who uses a forgotten crime to blackmail a husband into divorce for the sake of wife and mother. Proceeding as if his divided attribution were authentic, the critic praises Séjour and regrets that the two plays were merged. Séjour's drama is "full of emotions of love, of terror and of pity." The third act, Guillemot writes, "is almost a masterpiece, and when I say almost, I'm almost surprised at my reserve, [for] all the scenes of that act, tender but without exaggeration, are as delicately felt as they are poetically phrased." In this third act the beautiful, haughty Clarisse, suddenly aware of her penury, comes close to suicide but is inspired by Pierre to choose life over the sin of self-destruction.

56 Guillemot. Review of *Le Martyre du coeur* by Victor Séjour and Jules Brésil. *La Presse théâtrale* (April 18, 1858), p. 2; (April 25, 1868), p. 2.
Favorable comments on Séjour's play.

57 Saint-Victor, Paul de. Review of *Le Martyre du coeur* by Victor Séjour and Brésil. *La Presse* (March 28, 1858), pp. 1-2.
The critic finds the play too long; it should have ended after Placide brought Clarisse her patrimony. The further developments are "fillers, delays, useless complications." The play had gone from its clarity to obscurity because of roundabout mechanisms. "Nonetheless, it has succeeded; its exordium saved its peroration."

1859

58 Anon. Mention of *La Tireuse de cartes* by Victor Séjour and Jean-François Mocquard. *L'Ami de la religion* N. S. 124 (December 22, 1859), p. 867.

The paper shows its readers what use is being made of the play by simply quoting word for word from *Le Siècle*, which praised "the happy idea of bringing on stage the odious attack committed by the Holy See against the Mortara family." The *Ami*'s uncommented upon, matter-of-fact quoting of the Catholic but anti-clerical paper was felt by Séjour as quite a sting.

59 Anon.   Mention of *La Tireuse de cartes* by Victor Séjour and Jean-François Mocquard. *Le Monde illustré* (December 21, 1859). Clipping at Bibliothèque de l'Arsenal, Ref.48018 (9).
Report of the opening of the play. Napoleon III and Empress Eugénie graced the first night with their presence; that they would attend was known in advance. This patronage heightened the political significance of the play and drew the curious theater-goers in greater numbers. As the writer puts it, "public curiosity reached such proportions that it would make M. Marc Fournier [the Porte St.-Martin's manager] wish he had for a theater that night the Champ-de-Mars or at least the Palais de l'Industrie." The play has its internal faults, but "was written from start to finish with that ardor and conviction" which win the public, "especially the public of the boulevards."

60 Anon.   Review of *Les Grands Vassaux* by Victor Séjour. *L'Illustration* (February 19, 1859), p. 115.
The reviewer is led to a wry reflection on success and failure in the entertainment world. "At the Theater of the Porte Saint-Martin, you build a *grand vaisseau* with the lightest of construction materials, and you are hailed with waves of bravos for 200 consecutive performances. Then for the Odéon Theater you work at composing with much care, art and integrity the *Grands Vassaux*, and it's a complete fiasco."

61 Anon.   Review of *Les Grands Vassaux* by Victor Séjour. *Le Figaro* (February 13, 1859), p. 7.
The reviewer is not favorable to the play. He snickers that Séjour has been more fortunate with *grands vaisseaux* [great ships -an allusion to *Le Fils de la nuit*] than with *Grands Vassaux.*

62 Busoni , Philippe   Review of *Les Grands Vassaux* by Victor Séjour. *L'Illustration* (February 19, 1959), p. 115.
Busoni thinks "The problem with the *Grands Vassaux* is Séjour's legitimate attempt to rehabilitate Louis XI; the character portrayed is

too different to be acceptable to an audience taught by Walter Scott and Casimir Delavigne. Séjour's energetic stagecraft was doomed from the start."

63 Flamand, Jules. Review of *Les Grands Vassaux* by Victor Séjour. *Le Théâtre* (February 27, 1859), p. 2.
Flamand finds the crowds are still coming. With reserve he congratulates Séjour, but regrets that the play has been accepted at the Number Two National Theater. For Flamand, "the success is entirely in the role and the talent of Ligier."

64 Fournier, Edouard. Review of *Les Grands Vassaux* by Victor Séjour. *La Patrie* (February 14, 1859), feuilleton. Clipping in Bibliothèque de l'Arsenal. Ref. 48018 (8).
Fournier lectures his readers on the real, complex Louis XI that no novelist or playwright--including Séjour whose effort was superior-- has ever portrayed authentically. Yet the real history is more fascinating than the novels and the plays. Séjour went too far in exonerating Louis XI of egotism and in making him a man of liberating regeneration. Nonetheless, for style and study, you have to take notice of Séjour.

65 Gautier, Théophile. Review of *Diégarias* by Victor Séjour. *L'Art dramatique en France depuis 25 ans*. Paris, 1859. Vol. 3, pp. 236-238.
In a very balanced review the outstanding critic finds that Séjour's drama "showed tendencies and studies of romanticism." Although "many would find it an occasion for blame and reproaches," Gautier commends Séjour for imitating Victor Hugo. *Diégarias* is "skillfully structured. ... The style, which could be more proper and more poetic, has a quality most important in theater; it is clear and clean-cut, saying what it wants to say--without excessive concession to rime and hemistich." Gautier comments on how chancy indeed is a theater career. Most young writers prefer to write books or to be journalists. He congratulates Séjour "for preferring the theater to journalism and the piecemeal glory of serial narratives."

66 Gautier, Théophile. Review of *La Tireuse de cartes* by Victor Séjour and Jean-François Mocquard. *Le Moniteur universel* (December 26-27, 1859), pp. 1-2.
Gautier feels it is "a great drama, with a broad, strong structure full of sudden changes and high-powered scenes." He singles out for

attention the finale which went past the *crescendo* --Paula's collapse to conclude with a *diminuendo*--Paula at peace and the mothers reconciled. Gautier finds that this uncommon ending had "a gentle, pleasant effect."

67 Gebauer, Ernest   Review of *Les Grands Vassaux* by Victor Séjour. *Le Monde dramatique* (February 17, 1859), p. 2.
Gebauer is blunt in his negative judgment, but he writes not without some softening recognition of Séjour's talent: The play "lacks body, action, interest.... What places M. Séjour above vulgar hacks and writers who grind out more words to get more money is his style, which lacks neither color nor elegance." He is convinced that the author of *Les Grands Vassaux* will produce a remarkable work. "On that day I will clap my hands and will not hold back on praise. While waiting, I express my reserve and I conclude by saying that M. Victor Séjour limited himself this time to writing a play for Ligier. The return [to the stage] of the intelligent and vigorous Ligier, that was the real attraction of last Thursday night!" Gebauer is further displeased at the series of works that were transforming the wily, imperious Louis XI into a democratic monarch. The public, he insists, "refuses to swallow nightly that tyrant, whether Casimir Delavigne has concocted the gravy, or M. [Michel] Carré has garnished the dish, or M. Victor Séjour has prepared the stew."

68 Herlem, Louis. Review of *Les Grands Vassaux* by Victor Séjour. *La Presse théâtrale* (February 20, 1859), p. 1.
Herlem is weary of seeing another Louis XI play. He doubts that this will be the last since authors seem to like to exploit this monarch's character. Séjour's mistake, according to Herlem, was trying to take in the entire life of Louis XI; the result was a "formless drama." Then Herlem shoots at Séjour with the Ligier barb: "Anyhow let us admit that M. Victor Séjour had some reasons not to go to too much trouble in this work of his, since he was putting its destiny in the hands of the foremost tragedian of our time, M. Ligier, who by dint of genius and of dramatic power, ought to be able to bring it along to success." Herlem disapproves of the scene in which Louis XI allows his brother to drink poison, a whole scene given to this agony of brother being done away with by brother. "After this boldness of today, are you going to complain any more about the strictness of censorship [by the government]?" Taking the play apart act by act, Herlem concedes some beauty to the second act, and more to the fifth. The emotion of the final act will, he feels, continue to

draw the crowds.

69 Janin, Jules. Review of *La Tireuse de cartes* by Victor Séjour and Jean-François Mocquard. *Le Journal des débats* (December 26, 1859), p. 1.
Friendly Janin regrets that the time has passed for religious debates on stage, for witness to belief through drama, and for great poets and great souls. Séjour is not Corneille. The contemporary playwright, after setting the drama, has passed to fantasy for finale. "But fantasy lacks the power to untie Gordian knots." The pathos, however, contained in the play, Janin is convinced, would make it a success.

70 Roux, Georges. Review of *La Tireuse de cartes* by Victor Séjour and Jean-François Mocquard. *Le Théâtre* (December 25, 1859).
For Roux "the drama is written with the warmth and passion we find in almost all the other plays of the author. It contains that kind of duet in which the dialogue leaps forward, alive, swept along, brilliant, and in which M. Séjour excels." Yet Roux complains that the play keeps tension so high and steady that it produces a fatiguing monotony.

71 Saint-Victor, Paul de. Review of *La Tireuse de cartes* by Victor Séjour and Jean-François Mocquard. *La Presse* (December 25, 1859), pp. 1-2.
Saint-Victor calls the play "the most beautiful success that M. Victor Séjour has achieved." Although at first sight one might be shocked at the staging of a struggle of two religions, the point of the drama is rather of flesh and blood. "These women are mothers [not religions]; their theology is only their maternal love. ... Thus we are not at Jerusalem or Rome, but in raw nature. True sentimental feelings wipe away the irritation of current events." When Paula accuses the two mothers of self-seeking, the scene, full of tragic feeling, ends with a heart-rending burst of emotion,--"one of those moments when you can hear the audience's heartbeat." The critic finds the ending soothing after a harsh, intense, exhausting play: "The weary drama closes its eyes in a religious slumber." He recognizes its "vigor" as the distinguishing trait of Séjour's talent.

72 Veuillot, Louis. Review of *La Tireuse de cartes* by Victor Séjour and Jean-François Mocquard. *L'Univers* (December 28, 1859), feuilleton.

The ultramontanist *L'Univers* names Séjour as the "author in evidence," but then focuses on "the seemingly principal author, M. Mocquard, secrétaire de l'Empereur. The inside and the outside press compliments him with the most indiscreet flattery. That is as it should be. In the upper spheres of politics, the eagerness of flatterers gives a good estimate of the faults involved." Mocquard, *L'Univers* notes, is the author of several plays that have met with some success; for example, there was the *False Adulteress*--of questionable morality. The sharp-penned editor ironizes the Séjour-Mocquard team: "Currently people reproach playwrights for not creating anything. That's hard to do--create. There's less trouble and more profit in exploiting the old or in exploiting already made passion."

1860

73 Anon.   Mention of *La Tireuse de cartes* by Victor Séjour and Jean-François Mocquard. *L'Ami de la religion* (February 9, 1860), p. 235.
Notes that even before the Paris run ended, *La Tireuse* was staged in Strasbourg, whose percentage of protestants and Jews was higher than in most French cities.

74 Anon.   Mention of *La Tireuse de cartes* by Victor Séjour and Jean-François Mocquard. *La Gazette de France* (January 6, 1860), p. 2.
While journalists polemicized with Louis Veuillot of *L'Univers* and used the occasion to attack ultramontanes and clergy in general, Marc Fournier, director of the Porte Saint-Martin responded to the outcry by writing: "We are passing through a historic moment.... This play has been conceived with the intention of reconciliation, and not with the intention of proselytism." He is quoted here with irony by the critic.

75 Anon.   Mention of *La Tireuse de cartes* by Victor Séjour and Jean-François Mocquard. *Le Figaro* (January 15, 1860).
Judging the box office revenues to be exceptional for the era, gossipy *Le Figaro*, with a backward look at *Le Fils de la nuit,* claims that this Séjour play "without the smallest rope ladder, without the simplest ballet, without [actor] Fechter,... has rung up about 100,000 francs in twenty performances."

76 Anon. Mention of *La Tireuse de cartes* by Victor Séjour and
Jean-François Mocquard. *Le Figaro* (March 18, 1860), p. 5.
Touches upon the question of government censorship regarding a
play based on the delicate Mortara case. Approved in Paris, the play
was banned in Lyons and questioned in other cities.

77 Anon. Review of *Compère Guillery* by Victor Séjour. *Le
Monde dramatique* (March 8, 1860).
The critic of *Le Monde dramatique* is favorable. Describing the
Robin Hood-style play, he affirms that "the drama of M. Victor
Séjour was a very happy success, and his success will at least be
equal to that of *Fanfan la Tulipe*."

78 Anon. Review of *La Tireuse de cartes* by Victor Séjour and
Jean-François Mocquard. *Le Monde dramatique* (February 2,
1860).
While Mme. Laurent as Gemea reigned over the stage and the
reviews, actress Lia Félix was not far behind. The critic comments:
"As a great artist, she plays the role of Paula; she knows how to be
now gracious, now naive; she rises at times to the dramatic heights."

79 Bourquart, C. *"La Tireuse de cartes "* [by Victor Séjour and
Jean-François Mocquard]. *Revue catholique de l'Alsace* 2 (1860),
pp. 118-129.
The critic recalls Corneille's *Polyeucte*. The reference is followed by
a remark that, unlike the classic dramatist, Séjour seems to set
opposition between grace and nature. "At several points in the
course of the drama [Séjour] presented Christianity under a false,
odious light," the critic complains, "and the impression remaining
after such a presentation is no other than this: the differences of
religion and the resulting consequences offend both human nature
and reason." Séjour, the critic continues, seems to argue that, if
Noëmi --the child in the play-- was born into a Jewish family, she
must not become a Christian. This would be inconsistent with the
liberty of conscience proposed by the defenders of the Mortara
parents.

80 Bramtot, H. H. Review of *Les Aventuriers* by Victor Séjour.
Le Monde dramatique (April 14, 1860), p. 3.
Bramtot is not severe in tone but hardly favorable in judgment.
"This author has definitely taken over the monopoly of sombre
plays, and from the Porte Saint-Martin theater to the Gaîté theater,

his name shines out in triumphant letters on the posters.... He carries off success by assault." Bramtot has to admit: "This struggle of good and evil goes on for four hours amid the clink of swords, the cries of war, the chorus of orgies, as becomes any self-respecting melodrama. You find the 'mysterious ring' and the 'cross of my mother.' You hear long tirades declaimed. You see tears of pity become oceans of love. And, in spite of all that, perhaps because of all that, you are moved, you weep, you applaud." He expresses his regret that Séjour had abandoned the finer tendencies of his earlier career: Why has the poet betrayed his first love? Why has he preferred flashing, facile work over delicate artistry? "It is not my business to reproach him for this, but at least I have the right to regret it," Bramtot concludes.

81 Clary, Arthur. Review of *Les Massacres de Syrie* by Jean-Michel Mocquard and Victor Séjour. *Le Théâtre* (December 30, 1860), p. 2.
"Interest is sustained from beginning to end," Clary writes, "and you feel penetrated also by that loftiness of ideas that characterized last year's *La Tireuse de cartes* as different from the common run of melodramas that clutter up the theaters."

82 D., A. Review of *Les Aventuriers* by Victor Séjour. *Le Gaulois* (April 12, 1860). Clipping, Bibliothèque de l'Arsenal, Ref. 48018 (11).
"There are some beautiful lines,--correct, even elegant," writes A.D. "but all the rest swims in numbing pathos. It's two-penny romanticism."

83 Davidson, G. Mention of *La Tireuse de cartes* by Victor Séjour and Jean-François Mocquard. *Le Figaro* (December 23, 1859), p. 8. Clipping at Bibliothèque de l'Arsenal, Ref.48018 (10).
It was rumored that the idea of the play had been Mocquard's to start with. Audience applause for the named author had to be divided in two, as the *Figaro* playfully puts it, when "indiscreetly" naming the "high personage" involved.

84 De Hault de Lassus, Charles. Review of *La Tireuse de cartes* by Victor Séjour and Jean-François Mocquard. *Le Théâtre* (January 8, 1860), p. 2 ; (January 12, 1860), p. 3.
The Count de Lassus, writing in *Le Théâtre*, judges the play "rather poorly structured," but praises Madame Laurent for the tender power

shown in the title role. He acknowledges the chorus of praise the drama was winning, and foresees a long run.

85 Di Pietro, Albert. Review of *Les Aventuriers* by Victor Séjour. *Le Théâtre* (April 15, 1860), p. 1.
The critic censures Séjour for wasting his talent on this facile assemblage of pieces cut out, it seemed, from other plays. He calls the play "a long, monotonous, teary-eyed drama. ... You need fresh air, I swear, after all this mixture of the horrible and the false, laid out in overdone prose, puffed up to the point of popping or else of despairing insipidity,--in a word, of the kind M. Victor Séjour knows how to write."

86 Fournier, Edouard. Review of *Compère Guillery* by Victor Séjour. *La Patrie* (March 12, 1860), feuilleton, p. 1. Clipping, Bibliothèque de l'Arsenal, Ref. 48018 (12).
A book but not a play could be drawn from the story of Guillery; so thinks Fournier, who praises the sets, the electric lighting [sic] and the clever mechanical stage devices. He complains about confusing elements that turned up, disappeared and left him wondering. Yet "there are flashes of remarkable talent, spurts of well turned poetry, vigor of well struck blows, and above all ... a chivalric loftiness ... worthy to hover, not over scaffolding, but over a monumental work of art. You can see that M. Séjour frequented of yore the literary heights; at times you feel breezing through his new frameworks some gusts of the pure air he had breathed up there. Once he handled the gold of eloquence and of beautiful verses; some of it has stuck to his hands."

87 Gautier, Théophile. Review of *Les Aventuriers* by Victor Séjour. *Le Moniteur universel* (April 17, 1860), feuilleton.Clipping, Bibliothèque de l'Arsenal.
Gautier, while insisting that Séjour could do better, is benign. "Go see [*Les Aventuriers*]. It will entertain you more than a realistic play.... Séjour knows how to make these bandit characters live and move; with a sure hand he sketches their features, he colors their complexion with the sombre, bygone tone of old frescoes, and from their mustachioed lips he sends out words that have a sort of epic reverberation." Gautier calls the prolific Creole "the Lope de Vega of the Boulevard." Séjour, he writes, "who could have aimed higher is pleased to design with a bold, sure hand those plays in which he puts a lot of action for his public and a little style for the critics. The

"trade" (*métier*) sidetracks Séjour from his art.

88 Gautier, Théophile. Review of *Compère Guillery* by Victor Séjour. *Le Moniteur universel* (March 12, 1860).
Gautier thinks Séjour is still in the rich vein of his talent's gold mine. The drama, he writes, "full of movement and action, never drags for a moment." It is "fantastic as a dream, poetic as a legend." Gautier admires an author who can vary his style as Séjour has in passing from *La Tireuse de cartes* to *Compère Guillery*. Implicitly, though, the critic is warning the playwright not to produce cape-and-sword duplicates of the current success.

89 Gebauer, Ernest. Review of *La Tireuse de cartes* by Victor Séjour and Jean-François Mocquard. *Le Monde dramatique* (April 18, 1860), p. 2.
Gebauer, a critic who was severe on the dramatists and audiences of his time, applauds along with the audience. "I like M. Victor Séjour well enough indeed, in spite of his excessive ardor and the flights of his imagination. This writer rises above the series of common confectioners of plays." His language is "excellent, a little redundant at times, but faultless, elegant, warm." Redundancy, though, leads to ennui; so Gebauer is unwilling to rate *La Tireuse* higher than another popular new play *Le Roi des Isles* [by Ernest Rollin and Eugène Woestyn]. Mocquard's influence is "seen" in the theme and in the lofty style.
Gebauer mentioned the play again in the same newspaper on December 29, 1859 (p. 3), and on February 2, 1860.

90 Janin, Jules. Review of *Compère Guillery* by Victor Séjour. *Le Journal des débats* (March 19, 1860), p. 2.
Janin finds the play pleasant; the drama of love, to be found in simpler style and personages, "has exquisite grace and infinite charm," but the genre is now becoming dated.

91 Janin, Jules. Review of *Les Aventuriers* by Victor Séjour. *Le Moniteur universel* (April 22, 1860), p. 2.
Janin hits both the rival-playing *Roi des Isles* and the *Aventuriers* in the same review. After the *Aventuriers'* "battles, ambushes, betrayals and confusions," Janin quips, "it would be a real relaxation to hear the fifth act of *Rodogune*." These two current plays, Janin regrets, "will no doubt draw the easily pleased fan, but they pain and sadden people with taste. This time the excess crushes and kills us."

92 Janin, Jules. Review of *Les Grands Vassaux* by Victor Séjour. *Almanach de la littérature, théâtre et beaux-arts* (1860), p. 73.

The good friend of Victor Séjour, looking back on the year, recognizes "inventiveness, energy and talent" in *Les Grands Vassaux,* but, sadly, the sweep has been too vast; "the wider the reach, the weaker the grip."

93 Rodet, Alexis. Review of *Compère Guillery* by Victor Séjour. *La Presse théâtrale* (March 18, 1860), p. 1.

Another favorable critic, Rodet hails the play's second week as a "great success." He forecasts that the "excellent drama" will reach 200 stagings.

94 Rodet, Alexis. Review of *Les Aventuriers* by Victor Séjour. *La Presse théâtrale* (April 12, 1860), p. 1.

Rodet praises cast and scenery, but pans the play as "a drama ill concocted, poorly digested, made of bits and pieces, crumbs from the great masters, picked underneath all tables. From Act III on, you don't know where you are." Rodet, who liked to foretell how long a play would last, predicts with a pun that *Aventuriers* would not have a long stay (*séjour*) at the Gaîté.

95 Roux, Georges. Review of *Compère Guillery* by Victor Séjour. *Le Théâtre* (March 11, 1860), pp. 1-2.

The critic reports that the Guillery brothers had been bandits in a time of civil unrest, had indeed been pursued by the royal authorities, and had been executed at Saintes in 1608. "These lovable gentlemen," Roux goes on ironically, "certainly owe great gratitude to the author of *Fils de la nuit* for having rendered them, two centuries and a half after their death, the crowd's sympathies which during their lifetime, one must admit, they had hardly merited." Roux is severe in his review: "There is much killing in this play of M. Séjour, and [Guillery], for his part, is assassinated four or five times before receiving the five shots which send him definitively to taste the eternal repose where he can reflect on the displeasing aspects of firearms." Turning attention to the leading actor, Roux continues his critique: "This drama is written in that flowery prose which Mélingue [who plays Guillery] so loves to declaim, which M. Séjour so loves to write; it is a deluge of gallant comparisons, of brilliant images, of superabundant metaphors which carry us back to the good old days of Ronsard and of Desportes when the sun was but a being bewigged with rays. M. Séjour is no longer a dramatist; he is a rosebush full of blossoms."

96 Saint-Victor, Paul de. Review of *Compère Guillery* by Victor
Séjour. *La Presse* (March 11, 1860), p. 1-2.
Saint-Victor, after doing a tongue-in-cheek sketch of the
swashbuckling escapades and the incredible escape from the cistern
dungeon, has to admit: "The drama succeeded from start to finish; it
is lively, swift, interesting, picturesque, cleverly mixing passion and
fantasy."

97 Saint-Victor, Paul de. Review of *Les Aventuriers* by Victor
Séjour. *La Presse* (April 12, 1860), pp. 1-2.
The critic acknowledges that the fans went out to see the play and
were thrilled: "The play of M. Séjour is a nightmare, but it does not
put you to sleep. On the contrary. It interests, it moves, it amuses,
it smacks of the novel, phantasmagoria and mime."

98 Saint-Victor, Paul de. Review of *Les Massacres de Syrie* by
Jean-Michel Mocquard and Victor Séjour. *La Presse* (December 30
1860), p. 2.
Saint-Victor states : "Mix together the passion of drama, the color of
a panorama, the movement of a battlefield, the all-powerful interest
of a pathetic current event, and you will have an idea of this great
spectacle, one of the most magnificent the boulevard has ever given."
The audience, he notes in passing, broke into applause when Abd-el-
Kader appeared on stage to calm the riotous mob that was about to
tear up the French flag seized from the consulate. He recalls the
evening when Abd-el-Kader was actually honored at the Opera in
Paris.

99 Tiengou, J.-M. Review of *Compère Guillery* by Victor Séjour.
La Gazette de France (March 12, 1860), p. 1-2.
Tiengou believes that *Compère Guillery* has been written as a
medium for Mélingue, "the last of the cape-and-sword actors with a
cult of style." So the only question to be asked is whether it served
its purpose. From this point of view, Tiengou judges, "*Compère
Guillery* is, without fear of contradiction, one of the best plays that
M. Séjour has written." However, the problem is precisely that it
would be a success, "one of these great successes that make Victor
Séjour forget a little bit more each day, that before studying M.
Mélingue, he used to study his Shakespeare."

100 Tiengou, J.-M. Review of *La Tireuse de cartes.* by Victor
Séjour and Jean-François Mocquard. *La Gazette de France* (January
9, 1860), feuilleton, p. 2.
Government censorship had moderately controlled the newspapers in
reporting on the Mortara affair. "How could the censors allow to be
handed over to public passion a question which the government has
forbidden to the newspapers for eighteen months?" This is the
pointed but exaggerated question of J.-M. Tiengou. He does not like
the dénouement. Corneille, he says, would have had Gemea's eyes
opened to Christian faith; then Paula, from having no mother, would
have had two --one according to the flesh, one according to the
spirit-- to love, bless, and pray with her.

1861

101   Audrey-Deshorties, Eugène.   *A propos des* Massacres de
Syrie*: Réflexions sur les jeux scéniques de quelques hauts
personages, par une homme de rien.* Paris, 1861. 16 p.
Discussion of Mocquard's participation in writing the play and of the
Emperor's presence at the opening show. The risk in this sort of
situation is that the honest critic, when he blames the author, has, it
might be revealed, thereby criticized a member of the government.
Sycophantic critics would, on the other hand, applaud on signal.
This "little man" --as he calls himself-- goes on with irony: "I would
dare to tell M. Séjour, this Shakespeare of the boulevard, that his
new drama shocks me on more than one account. In a country
which has a press and a parliament, the theater seems a place ill
chosen for politicking. Is it the role of actors, on stage amid lightly
clad dancing girls and dazed camels, to pronounce the funeral oration
over Turkey and the panegyric of a great prince? But how can I
address these criticisms to M. Mocquard, especially when I hear all
around a concert of praise from the critics?" Neither art nor
government could profit from the interchange of roles, the observer
declares. The Société des auteurs et compositeurs dramatiques
should persuade high officials to terminate this odious competition
with working playwrights.

102 Belloy, André de. Review of *Les Massacres de Syrie* by Jean-
Michel Mocquard and Victor Séjour. *L'Illustration* (January 5,
1861), pp. 5-6.
De Belloy sees no problem in bringing to the stage "this humanitarian

issue," which France was "called upon to face." The drama was like a medieval mystery play, for each character seemed to personify a nation or an idea. "Opening-night outbursts of public feeling turned the play into a sort of demonstration, encouraged by the presence of the sovereign."

103   Gautier, Théophile.   Review of *Les Massacres de Syrie* by Jean-Michel Mocquard and Victor Séjour. *Le Moniteur universel* (January 7, 1861), feuilleton.
Gautier recognizes how stirring the play is, but he worries about drama getting ahead of history. "Is it not," he asks, "ambitiously premature to paint events still in the making?" For the sake of accurate understanding, Gautier urges that clearer distinction be shown between the Druses and mainstream Islam.

104   Gebauer, Ernest.   Review of *Les Massacres de Syrie* by Jean-Michel Mocquard and Victor Séjour.   *Le Monde dramatique* (January 3, 1861), p. 3.
It was common knowledge that Mocquard had contributed to the creation of the play.   "Séjour's mysterious collaborator," writes Gebauer "was a mystery to no one." Whatever gives pause to the critic (current events, foreign policy, or martyrs' blood hardly dry) he commends Séjour's craftmanship. He recognizes the complexity of the dramatist's task, and commends Séjour (and Mocquard). To sketch the historical background, to stage the cruel bloodshed of the Druses, to show the cynical complicity of the Turks, to introduce the compassionate role of the Algerian Abd-el-Kader --all the strands had to be woven together.   "I doubt," Gebauer acknowledges, "that any writer, even M. d'Ennery, could have acquitted himself of the task better than have M. Victor Séjour and his unknown collaborator ... whom everyone knows."

105   Hyenne, Robert.   Review of *Les Massacres de Syrie* by Jean-Michel Mocquard and Victor Séjour.   *La Presse théâtrale* (January 6, 1861), p. 2.
The critic discusses the supposition about Mocquard's yet undeclared co-authorship of the play and suggests: "we ought to bring him in on half of the congratulations which are rightfully coming to M. Victor Séjour." Indeed, according to Hyenne's tribute, "perhaps no other than Victor Séjour would have been so bold as to bring before the public's eye a tableau more or less realistic of the major Mid-East events in which France has taken a role so direct and so glorious."

Hyenne adds that Séjour has "a tendency to hide under the cloak of theater some ideas which are not ordinarily of the theater's domain. ... The action, so vast, so complex, is led along adroitly, and it would be perfect if, perhaps precisely because of the topic, our interest were not spread over too great a number of characters." He notes that plaudits went also to the original music of M. de Groot, to the dancers, to the scenery and costumes, yes, and to the camels brought in from Africa for the play. "All in all, this play is a success: success for the director, for the author."

106 Janin, Jules. Review of *Compère Guillery* by Victor Séjour. *Almanach de la littérature, théâtre et beaux-arts* (1861), p. 26.
Reviewing the year's plays, Janin judges *Guillery* implausible, and also oldish though it is new. Nor is the hero's flowing, flourishing eloquence to Janin's taste.

107 Janin, Jules. Review of *La Tireuse de cartes* by Victor Séjour and Jean-François Mocquard. *Almanach de la littérature, théâtre et beaux-arts* (1861), p. 20.
Looking back over the year, Janin estimates that 100,000 theater-goers have seen *La Tireuse de cartes*, the "unusual drama, in which one readily recognizes the raw energy and vigorous talent of Victor Séjour."

108 Saint-Victor, Paul de. Review of *Les Massacres de Syrie* by Jean-Michel Mocquard and Victor Séjour. *La Presse* (January 6, 1861), pp. 1-2.
In a favorable review of the play, Saint-Victor declares "Never was a drama more alive, --contemporaneous with its catastrophes... A brilliant success."

1862

109 Anon. Mention of *Les Volontaires de 1814* by Victor Séjour. *La Mode nouvelle*, (May 2, 1862). Clipping at Bibliothèque de l'Arsenal, Ref.48018 (14).
The problems and delays that preceded the staging of the play stimulated criticism directed against the Censorship Commission. Apparently the text of the play had first coasted by without causing difficulties. Then, while the cast was well into rehearsal, the Commission recalled the play. The inconvenience and the loss of time and money were underscored by other critics who lambasted the

Commission's awkward handling of this play. This author suggests, however, that "Dame Advertising" has calculatingly used the censorship to excite curiosity.

110 Baralle, Alphonse. Review of *Les Mystères du Temple* by Victor Séjour. *La Presse théâtrale* (August 31, 1862), pp. 1-2.
Baralle feels that Séjour has come down "from the high level of his *Richard III* and other truly literary works." The players are better than the play, the critic judges.

111 Belloy, A. de. Review of *Les Volontaires de 1814* by Victor Séjour. *L'Illustration* (April 26, 1862), pp. 262-263.
Séjour continued touching up the play while it was running. The critic jokes about how the number of acts and sets varied from one performance to another. These revisions seem to have nothing to do with the earlier ones made by the censors. In all of the rumors and the re-writes, Belloy suspects a coy contrivance on the part of the producers, for this atmosphere increases the audience --and the price of the tickets.

112 Bragelonne, A. de. Review of *Les Mystères du Temple* by Victor Séjour. *Le Figaro* (August 24, 1862), p. 2.
"A *ragout*", the melodrama is unworthy of M. Victor Séjour.

113 Cerfberr, Anatole. Review of *Les Mystères du Temple* by Victor Séjour. *Le Théâtre* (August 17, 1862), p. 3.
The reaction of the critic is casual: "M. Victor Séjour has done better than this. The historical drama is more his field." Cerfberr feels that Séjour is a capable artist, and does not want him to slip into grinding out plays for the trade.

114 Cerfberr, Anatole. Review of *Les Volontaires de 1814* by Victor Séjour. *Le Théâtre* (March 9, 1862), p. 1.
The entire editorial praises Séjour's play . The editor-in-chief of *Le Théâtre* writes here on censorship when the play was cleared but not yet presented. He exonerates Séjour of the charge by some that he tends to exploit mass feelings, as in the *Massacres de Syrie* and the *Tireuse de cartes*. A strange reproach, thinks Cerfberr, since it was precisely the artistic use of current, circumstantial material that won praise for Casimir Delavigne and Eugène Scribe. Cerfberr feels that stirring historical dramas need not be rejected as mere chauvinism. There is no reason why one could not mix instruction and recreation.

"The authorities share this view. They like such spectacles, and want the stage to shine for the *Volontaires de 1814*. The administration of the Porte Saint-Martin eagerly welcomes these plays; it appreciates boldness and novelty. The management has confidence in their author who has already, on its magnificent stage and under its direction, known how to get the people's attention with violence, with emotions, with Shakespearean grandeur, and who in the *Fils de la nuit* created a capital scene worthy of a rightful heir of Hugo, the great creator." See next entry.

115 Cerfberr, Anatole. Review of *Les Volontaires de 1814* by Victor Séjour. *Le Théâtre* (April 27, 1862), p. 3.
Cerfberr comes to the defense of Séjour's play. He feels that political considerations have influenced the reaction of the press and disagrees with those of his confreres who have harshly judged the censored play. It was not just theater-ology but rather theology, that appeared in Freemason Ulbach's complaint, when he apostrophized Séjour thusly: "In effect, you calumniate France, which, all bruised, all bleeding, rose up nonetheless proud and intrepid, and fought to the last man, without inspiration by miracles, by heavenly messengers, by apparitions. A Joan of Arc in 1814! What for? She would have followed the crowd, she would not have led it." Ulbach bowed to the historic Joan of Arc in acknowledging that she got her dauphin crowned--whereas Séjour's Jeanne la France gets her Napoleon to Waterloo. "Was it," he asks, "worth bringing her straight from heaven?" After reprinting his own entire editorial of March 9, 1862, with praise of Séjour, the editor of *Le Théâtre* goes on: "What we like....is the complete impartiality, full of dignity and grandeur, that prevails.... It is the delicate, hard-to-keep tact with which everything is handled. This enlightened *sang-froid* excludes neither patriotic warmth nor the poetry which is heroic, masculine, simple, true, generous."

116 Gautier, Théophile. Review of *Les Volontaires de 1814* by Victor Séjour. *Le Moniteur universel* (April 28, 1862), feuilleton.
Impressed by the beauty of the special effects, Gautier describes with relish the whole vision scene. (He was noted among critics for the exactitude of his reports.) In his general estimation of the play, although he feels that Jeanne's romance amid "the gigantic events" detracts from her epic grandeur, Gautier congratulates Séjour "on the sober, discreet, impartial way in which he brought to the stage this history still alive [and] almost contemporary" with the audience's

generation.

117 Gebauer, Ernest.   Review of *Les Mystères du Temple* by
Victor Séjour. *Le Monde dramatique* (September 4, 1862), p. 2.
Séjour is "a dramatist of exaggeration. He has to have violent and
implausible situations, strange characters the likes of which you
hardly ever meet in real life. As for his play, he builds it by
stacking, without measure, impossible effects on top of jolting
scenes, and by multiplying, with desperate abundance, sonorous
sentences, cries, and murders." Yet, the critic acknowledges, "a
large proportion of the public loves these mad dramas."

118 Gebauer, Ernest.   Review of *Les Volontaires de 1814* by
Victor Séjour. *Le Monde dramatique* (April 24, 1862), pp. 1-2.
Not only were political demonstrators quiet during the first
performance but also the audience. A glacial silence,met "this much
rehearsed, this much tossed about, this much chopped up drama.
We have just heard these five acts, badly sewn together, we have just
seen these fourteen tableaux, the last two of which were empty; we
remained patiently in our orchestra armchair for five and a half
hours, ever awaiting some new situation, and searching for the
reason why the *Volontaires de 1814* could have caused such upset to
the Censorship Commission." Gebauer found only a tedious play.
He would prefer rubbing out rather than playing up that period of
history, the invasion of France. "For all that, however overturned
the *Volontaires de 1814* may have been, we doubt that the play ever
resembled, even from afar, a masterpiece."

119 Goncourt, Edmond and Jules de. *Journal. Mémoires de la vie
littéraire.* Vol. 1. Paris (1851-1861), pp. 231-233.
Review of *La Tireuse de cartes* . The Goncourts attended the first
night, but their attention was drawn from the stage out into the
audience. The real "intrigue and drama [of the evening was] the
official declaration of the love of [Paul de] Saint Victor and the
actress on the stage [Lia Félix]." With clinical eye, the *Journal*
remembers the "marble face" of the critic and, up in the balcony, the
jilted ex-girlfriend. As for the play, the brothers Goncourt are
anything but complimentary: "A play like all those that rhetoricians
shove down the toilet. It is not even imitation Victor Hugo. And
[yet] in the audience one hears women murmur with that sort of
flutter 'Oh! It's so well written.'"

120 Goncourt, Edmond and Jules de. *Journal. Mémoires de la vie*

littéraire. Vol. 2. Paris (1852-1861), pp. 26-27.
Review of *Les Volontaires de 1814* by Victor Séjour. The Goncourts report: "This evening we went to the loge of [Paul de] Saint Victor for the first night of the *Volontaires*, a play which disturbs Europe, a play at whose finale Paris awaits a riot, a play where smart alecks are supposed to cry "*Bis*" when Napoleon I abdicates. Nothing like that happened. Boredom disarmed political passion. The play would put a revolution to sleep. Casanova once made a lion of butter, Séjour has made a Napoleon of marshmallow."

121 Saint-Victor, Paul de. Review of *Les Mystères du Temple* by Victor Séjour. *La Renaissance louisianaise* (September 21,1862).
Saint-Victor enters cooperatively into the spirit of the play, but he has plausibility questions for the author. The critic relishes the savory life of the Temple, "that picturesque neighborhood, [where] M. Victor Séjour set the vigorous drama." He finds forced elements in the play, but he respects Séjour's fabric of pathos and violence. In sum, "this drama, bizarre, tormented, jolted, uneven, but full of vigor and of scenic life, has perfectly succeeded."

122 Saint-Victor, Paul de. Review of *Les Volontaires de 1814* by Victor Séjour. *La Presse* (April 28, 1862), pp. 1-2.
The critic thinks rather highly of the play. "The honest and sincere drama" had stirring elements of national self-defense. "Beautiful scenes ... popular imagination ... impressive staging" would win victory --even though there has been no violent public battle at the premiere. Sweeping aside the unfulfilled forecast of violent outbursts, the critic terms the play "honest and sincere, contained in the idea of defense of the land and of the rallying together of factions when faced with the foreign invader. The play suffers from the mutilations censorship inflicted on it. But it has lovely scenes to sustain it." Shortly after first night, Séjour removed the sections of the play that had shown Jeanne la France as the natural daughter of a noble. Saint-Victor favors the cut as an improvement. "After all, Jeanne lost her name in finding her father. She was no longer la France; she was Mlle de Gouault." Allegories do not have fathers, the critic further observes, nor do they fall in love with young men. Saint-Victor pays tribute to the staging of what he calls the "apocalypse of the Old Guard": "The sepulchral cavalry pass at a gallop in a transparent fog. The heads and rumps of the horses rise and drop. The silhouette of the spectral [emperor] stands out in the

background of the plain. It is one of the most astonishing spectacles
that the art of stage designers and technicians has ever produced."

123 Tiengou , J.-M. Review of *Les Mystères du Temple* by Victor
Séjour. *La Gazette de France* (September 1, 1862), p. 3.
"An abominable melodrama" Tiengou calls it. "Improbabilities are
heaped upon improbabilities, horrors trample on horrors." Yet for
weeks to come his newspaper had to advertise the continuing success
of *Les Mystères du Temple*.

124 Ulbach, Louis. Review of *Les Mystères du Temple* by Victor
Séjour. *Le Temps* (August 18, 1862), pp. 1-2.
The theater columnist of *Le Temps* gives a lengthy, sarcastic
description of plot and characters. His conclusion is harsh: "Such is
this drama, thick and violent like a heavy southern wine. ... [Yet]
some scenes, strongly put together, [do] produce the illusion of an
emotion. ... All our reserves ... will not stop the crowd from going
to the play, and admiring all the old-time touches, all the faded worn-
out ways of the theater. The *Mystères du Temple* can become a sort
of theater rummage shop, where plays in tatters can garb themselves
in remnants of all periods and all colors."

125 Ulbach, Louis. Review of *Les Volontaires de 1814* by Victor
Séjour. *Le Temps* (April 28, 1862), pp. 1-2.
Ulbach acknowledges that Séjour can plead extenuating
circumstances as "his play suffered so many mutilations that it is no
longer recognizable." But he could reply "that a writer, preoccupied
with the dignity of his work, much more than with his royalties,
does not accept certain mutilations. He withdraws his play..." Not
knowing what the original had been, Ulbach judges only what
appeared on the stage. "What remains, alas!, is not of a nature to
serve as pretext for the troubles which seemingly were feared." And,
he feels, "it is strange that it is precisely under the Empire that it
becomes difficult to call forth memories of the Empire."   He
observes that Jeanne la France turns out to be the daughter, albeit
illegitimate and unknown, of a nobleman who had had an escapade
with a *paysanne*, and Jeanne marries a patriot nephew of that same
noble. In bringing together under the Empire this rallied nobleman
and this patriotic daughter of the people, "did M. Victor Séjour have
the intention of a philosophical and political idea in this marriage?"
Ulbach, in analyzing the scenery, finds a further political allusion.
In Napoleon I's dream on the Island of Elba, when Jeanne la France

and Jean Terrier come to call him back to the *patrie*, "we see the battle, or rather the precise moment of the victory of Solferino." It is on this "reality of our time" that the dream focuses and the curtain falls. The play ends, Ulbach concludes sarcastically, with the emperor's sleep; the entire audience yawned in sympathy.

1864

126 Anon. Review of *Les Fils de Charles-Quint* by Victor Séjour. *Le Théâtre* (February 21, 1864), p. 1.
Le Théâtre's critic is all praise. "If the everyday crowd finds its value, its meat in the dark, violent action imagined by M. Séjour, the literary spectator, the vigilant critic, all who demand of a play some thought and style, will consider themselves satisfied." Pleased with the prologue that he finds lively and robust, he is even more pleased with the finale of Philip II in tears: "An ending marked with grandeur -- which would suffice to class M. Victor Séjour's new play among works of powerful merit."

127 Anon. Review of *Le Marquis Caporal* by Victor Séjour. *Le Hanneton, Journal des toqués* (October 23, 1864), pp. 2-3.
The satirical periodical spoofs both Victorien Sardou and Victor Séjour. "Both playwrights swore to make us laugh, and they both succeeded." (Sardou's play on the boards was *Les Pommes du voisin [The Neighbor's Apples]*.) "The unfortunate thing is they both took their role seriously, and didn't see it was all a gag."

128 Aubryet, Xavier. Review of *Le Marquis Caporal* by Victor Séjour. [Unlocated publication] (October 14, 1864). Clipping at the Bibliothèque de l'Arsenal, Ref. 48018 (17).
Aubryet refrains from political considerations and judges the play with purely literary criteria. Implausibility is the main accusation he hurls against the play. Why did the marquis have to feign suicide instead of denouncing his brother-in-law? How could he not have been recognized sooner? To get out of the situation Valleroy gets into, he would, Aubryet jokes, have to be a Tolmacque [the mid-nineteenth-century French equivalent of Houdini]. But Aubryet is fair: "M. Victor Séjour has often been better inspired, and it would be unjust not to take into account his more literary endeavors."

129 Belloy, A. de. Review of *Les Fils de Charles-Quint* by Victor Séjour. *L'Illustration* (February 27, 1864), p. 135.

Séjour is so far away from historical reality that this critic declines to review the play. Had not scholars now proven the falsity of the charge that Philip poisoned Carlos? After a few words of praise for the actors, the critic cuts short his commentary --fortunately, he writes, for Séjour and for himself.

130 Belloy, A. de. Review of *Le Marquis Caporal* by Victor Séjour. *L'Illustration* (October 22, 1864), p. 263.
With a severe tone De Belloy declares that the *Marquis Caporal* merits burial with full military honors. Not yet dead, the Marquis is "not one of those wounded whom you can save by minor amputations. His wounds are in the head. The most charitable thing you can do for him is not poison his last moments with useless surgery and reproaches. His mistakes are those which succeed every day for our most famous generals. The Anicet-Bourgeois, the d'Ennerys won great victories with campaign plans as absurd as that of the *Marquis Caporal*. Perhaps, however, they understood better the weak side of the enemy, and by enemy I mean the public. ... Maybe it was just plain luck that favored them."

131 Fournier, Edouard. Review of *Les Fils de Charles-Quint* by Victor Séjour. *La Patrie* (February 23, 1864), feuilleton. Clipping at the Bibliothèque de l'Arsenal, Ref.48018 (16).
The judicious Fournier, although he regrets the minor roles that did too much upstaging, praises Séjour for his courageous independence of novels and his vigorous pursuit of history. The play has an "uncommon vigor." In Fournier's view "the plays of M. Séjour are never completely excellent, but in each one there is a noteworthy act, or at least some beautiful scenes. He is of those, quite rare today, who know how to hold a dramatic situation, develop it, mold it out of raw stuff, with great vigor, with fresh energy, contrast and color. If the whole does have some weaknesses and some parasitic elements, the excellence of the main lines suffices to pay the ransom a hundred times over."

132 Gautier, Théophile. Review of *Les Fils de Charles-Quint* by Victor Séjour. *Le Moniteur universel,* (February 15, 1864), feuilleton.
Gautier counsels Séjour to attend more to mainstream history in his writing than to episodic embellishments which do more hiding than revealing of historical reality.

133 Gautier, Théophile. Review of *Le Marquis Caporal* by Victor Séjour. *Le Moniteur universel* (October 24, 1864), feuilleton.
With a light touch Gautier sums up his critique in one sentence: "*The Marquis Caporal* is a sentimental, military drama, a mixture of domestic virtues, patriotic heroism, royalist prejudices, pure love, conjugal tenderness, gun shots, cannon and duels, from which we get a play more virtuous than interesting --in spite of the complicated plot."

134 Gebauer, Ernest. Review of *Les Fils de Charles-Quint* by Victor Séjour. *Le Monde dramatique* (February 18, 1864), p. 2.
Gebauer is, as usual, negative. "At least," he admits, "Victor Séjour seeks to step beyond the common paths of drama," and bring to life historical figures. This play, however, will not count among his successes. Philip II has too often been brought to the stage, and the fable Séjour places alongside of history is not that interesting. Gebauer foresees a short run.

135 Janin, Jules. Review of *Les Fils de Charles-Quint* by Victor Séjour. *Le Journal des débats* (March 15, 1864), p. 2.
Janin praises the "handsome, eloquent drama, well acted, full of surprises and passions."

136 Janin, Jules. Review of *Les Fils de Charles-Quint* by Victor Séjour. *Almanach de la littérature, théâtre et beaux-arts* (1866), p. 10.
Janin has second thoughts about the play. Séjour and Janin, despite their friendship, are far apart in taste. Janin respects "the talent of this terrifying inventor. But then! that's his failing: he frightens, and he goes too far in playing on pity."

137 Jouvin, B. Review of *Les Fils de Charles-Quint* by Victor Séjour. *Le Figaro,* (February 21, 1864), p. 2. Clipping at the Bibliothèque de l'Arsenal, Ref. 48018 (15).
Jouvin points out that Philip and Carlos were late in coming on the scene, too late to justify the title. "In theater it is always a serious fault to have a double plot ... that [approaches the dénouement] like a river dividing into two branches near its mouth." Walter Scott romanticized history, but when a real-life personage joined his fictional characters, the novelist was cautious. Not so Séjour, complains Jouvin, for he takes as much poetic license with historic figures as with his own creations; yet Scott is more captivating by

discretion. According to Jouvin's analysis, "the ambition of Victor Séjour is to do it up great and to grip the crowd by lively images." But the critic joshes the playwright on his flights of rhetorical questions. One character in the play, asked why he has acted as he has, responds: "Ask the lion why he chooses cave over desert, ask the eagle why he builds an eyrie upon the heights, ask the serpent why he slithers between the old wall's shaky rocks." Jouvin laughs: "The tirade is long, and, if need be, it could have gone on and on until the animal kingdom had been exhausted."

138 Listener, M. Review of *Les Fils de Charles-Quint* by Victor Séjour. *Revue et Gazette des théâtres* (February 18, 1864), p. 2.
The critic first tells how long the evening was: "The staging of this drama began Saturday about seven in the evening and did not end until Sunday about one in the morning. That, he complains, is "a lot, --not to say too much-- especially if you think of the space which that theater's small seats parsimoniously dispense to the playgoers. The audience is happily trained for this exercise of patience; it held well until the end, and did not withdraw until the dénouement, that is to say the death of Don Carlos." Complimenting Séjour for turning to major figures in history for his theater, Listener explains that Séjour "tried an undertaking whose boldness itself pleased us. We recall, --and this is one of the best titles of M. Victor Séjour,-- a certain *Richard III,* which lacked not in brilliance, nor in vigor." Séjour has again used history to advantage. "The play is a success, and, as a whole, in spite of length and of interruptions, is not without interest and feeling. The acting is good, almost always, and often remarkable." Particularly, "Beauvallet reproduces with that constructive talent we rightfully expect of him the severe portrait of Philip II." Listener also commends the setting and costumes. Nevertheless he observes: "Although there are impressive scenes in this play and cleverly presented dramatic situations, these are at times purchased at a price of languid, useless scenes that precede or follow. The multiplicity of episodic personages does not add more variety to the play, it just adds confusion." But that multiplicity probably pleases the public and is merit in their eyes. The play, he forecasts, will probably not have an extraordinarily long run.

139 Montret, Honoré de. Review of *Les Fils de Charles-Quint* by Victor Séjour. *La Presse théâtrale* (March 3, 1864), p. 1.
De Montret feels that Séjour had not rediscovered his earlier inspiration --abandoned when he joined with Mocquard to produce a

political work. Séjour was reputed to be "one of the most literary authors on the boulevard, and he merited that renown" until *Les Massacres de Syrie* weakened his strictly literary power. Montret damns with praise: "It is not that the new drama playing at the Ambigu is not succeeding. On the contrary, it is succeeding perfectly, but after the fashion of common melodramas." No heights, no depths are reached, according to the disappointed critic.

140 Saint-Victor, Paul de. Review of *Le Marquis Caporal* by Victor Séjour. *La Renaissance louisianaise* (November 27, 1864).
Soon after the closing of play, a review of it appeared in New Orleans. No reference to Séjour as a native son is included in the favorable critique: "Energy and vigor are not lacking in M. Séjour's drama; he knows how to tie situations up tight and how to get out of them theatrically. What is missing is clarity, plausibility, and balance both in characters and in dialogue. ... M. Séjour would be well advised to cut down on overdone metaphors and emphatic expressions. This heavy artillery of language is difficult to maneuver in the theater; and when it is not handled just so, it blows up in the hands of the cannoneer." Friend that he is of the playwright, Saint-Victor does not want to end on a negative note: "M. Victor Séjour gets back up as quickly as he falls; he will soon be winning again in this doubtful game."

141 Sarcey, Francisque. "Chronique théâtrale." Review of *Le Marquis Caporal* by Victor Séjour. *L'Opinion nationale* (October 17, 1864).
Sarcey calls attention to resemblances to Alarcón's *Weaver of Segovia,* but Séjour's play does not equal the Spanish masterpiece. Sarcey finds only uninteresting characters in unmoving scenes. For him, heavy drama in general is dying; only comedy and vaudeville are alive. "Drama is a prey of the Ennerys and the Séjours. ... The great era is over. ... I wonder," he writes, "if it would be better frankly to abandon a worn-out genre, and dive into vaudeville, until a genius puts drama back in style."

142 Ulbach, Louis. Review of *Les Fils de Charles-Quint* by Victor Séjour. *Le Temps*. (February 22, 1864), pp. 1-2.
Ulbach debates the characterization of Philip and of Don Carlos. Philip's tears in the finale, Ulbach jibes, seem more for the actor's display of talent than for historical fidelity. The sweet love affair of Don Carlos, rigid and unbalanced in real life, seems thrown in for

the boulevard's fans. Ulbach urges Séjour to live up to his promise: "M. Victor Séjour has the reputation of being an able dramatist. I beg him to be content with that glory, and not to have the ambition of being a facile phrasemaker"; the rhetoric in *Les Fils de Charles Quint* is overdone.

143 Ulbach, Louis. Review of *Le Fils de la nuit* by Victor Séjour. *Le Temps* (November 28, 1864), feuilleton.
On November 22, 1864, the Gaîté brought back *Le Fils de la nuit*. Ulbach renders hommage to "the liberal and revolutionary sentiments of the author" which he has just challenged in the *Marquis Caporal*. Yes, in this play, "authority is always wrong, insurrection always right. They arm themselves for the independence of the country."

144 Ulbach, Louis. Review of *Le Marquis Caporal* by Victor Séjour. *Le Temps* (October 17, 1864), feuilleton.
Ulbach is one of those who felt his "democratic principles" under attack in the play. There, commissioner Gourdier, the civil authority of the Revolution, was portrayed as a cruel hustler of the guillotine. A general of the army came to save the hero and the heroine, and to show up Gourdier as secretly spying for the Prussians. Ulbach is outraged: "The morality of this drama is doubtless this: Outside of the army there is no salvation. All parties have rascals for allies and leaders, with the exception of the military. Let's be soldiers then,--is that true happiness?" Monarchy and empire have their violent and corrupt agents, he argues, not just the revolutionary Convention. Sniffing out "insult to the nation's history," the reviewer expresses surprise that the censors "had not possessed that sense of shame which vanity took out of the writer." Ulbach continues : "For Victor Séjour to write a bad play in bad style, that's his right. For him to follow his passions, his prejudices, and to attack all delegates of the Convention... that's still a right I grant him. I want liberty for all, but I ask an equal right to respond." The régime of Emperor Napoleon III claims it has to be firm in order to maintain respect for authority in France. Addressing the "unforeseeing moralizers," Ulbach asks: "Do you think you rebuild that sentiment of respect, which authority needs, when you allow constant, unceasing, all-around humiliation of the civil official compared with the military officer,--the representative of the law compared with the representative of force?" Stunned by this political diatribe, Séjour had a letter published one week later in the columns of *Le Temps,* whose editor labeled it a "profession of faith."

145 Vignaud, Henri. Review of *Les Fils de Charles-Quint* by Victor Séjour. *La Renaissance louisianaise* (March 27, 1864), pp. 9-11.

Almost two weeks after the play closed, Union-occupied New Orleans was able to read about *Les Fils de Charles-Quint* when Vignaud's review appeared. A Confederate stranded in the French capital, Vignaud earned his living as a journalist. In his analysis, he sees the play as having two parallel plots juxtaposed, one with historical figures, the other with fictional characters, --two plots which almost never meet. The latter is weak, but the former, with Philip and Carlos, shows art and mastery. "There are beautiful scenes through which run a dramatic spirit hardly found except in plays of years gone by." Strangely, at no point does Vignaud speak of the playwright as a native son. After hammering at length on what Vignaud judges to be the scholarly history of Philip II, he admits that dramatists can freely enjoy poetic license. Once this liberty with the real history of the son of Charles V is granted, "you have to recognize that M. Séjour has sketched them with that talent of observation and that power of expression so amply proven in his *Diégarias,* his *Richard III* and his *Louis XI [Les Grands Vassaux].*" The white creole warmly wishes the play a successful long run at the Ambigu.

1865

146 Anon. Review of *Les Enfants de la louve* by Victor Séjour and Théodore Barrière. *La Vie parisienne* (April 22, 1865). Clipping at the Bibliothèque de l'Arsenal, Ref. 48018 (18).

Barrière was too contemporary, thinks the reviewer of *La Vie Parisienne*, and gave a tone of anachronism to the fifteenth-century setting. Séjour, he guesses, provided the self-conscious phrase-making. Nevertheless, to have attempted so daring a feat as to emulate Shakespeare in staging the rivalry of the Houses of York and Lancaster is in itself an achievement. To trip and fall in such a sport is not a disgrace. The final scenes are dramatic, he judges, but the opening acts are tedious.

147 Cerfberr, Anatole. Review of *Les Enfants de la louve* by Victor Séjour and Théodore Barrière. *Le Théâtre* (April 23, 1865), p. 1.

The critic regrets that he could not say "all the good we would have wished to say concerning this play. We counted a great deal on the authors; we wished well to the association of minds of merit. What is to blame for our disappointment? Does co-authorship resemble some marriages? Do they turn sour as a result of too great a difference of style between the partners? Or is it rather the fault of the subject matter?" Both causes, he answers. Barrière's quickness and Séjour's laboriousness could not mix. It would have been better if they had purely and simply *translated* the powerful Shakespeare. Reworking the subject matter, the co-authors have been unable to bring to life the War of the Roses.

148 Janin, Jules. Review of *Les Enfants de la louve* by Victor Séjour and Théodore Barrière. *Le Journal des débats* (April 24, 1865), p. 4.
The venerable Jules Janin gives, with reserves, a favorable judgment; however, he must have been disappointed to see that his long-time friend Séjour did not respond to his professional recommendations. "M. Victor Séjour, the terror, and his worthy associate, Theodore Barrière, --who can laugh and who brings humor amid the Two roses, both bloodstained,-- have a veritable success. I am quite pleased with it, but how much more we would praise them if they came round to less violent creations and more human sentiments!" The capture of Margaret, *la louve*, by Richard "is horrible, frightful, charming, and full of interest, of strangeness, of the unexpected," but with all the Shakespearean power Janin would have liked some Shakespearean gentleness --"a tear from Edward's little children."

149 Muro, François du. Review of *Les Enfants de la louve* by Victor Séjour and Théodore Barrière. *La Réforme théâtrale* (April 18, 1865), p. 2.
The critic reports that "this play, in spite of first-night slowdowns, was sufficiently well received." However, it is only the fourth act that he truly praises. In this scene Strickland-Wells, unable to decide which boy is his son and which is the prince he is to kill, identifies himself, confesses his mission and begs for his newly-found son's affection; all three then must fight together against Richard of Gloucester's band of kidnappers.

150 Ulbach, Louis. Review of *Les Enfants de la louve* by Victor Séjour and Théodore Barrière. *Le Temps* (April 24, 1865), pp. 1-2.
A drama of serious value, Ulbach judges, *Les Enfants de la louve* carries a deep moral message on kings and usurpers, on society and

politics, but the play does so with historical portrayals and without too-current pamphleteering. He theorizes that Séjour has contributed the violent struggle, and Barriere, the biting irony and comic relief.

151 Ulbach, Louis. Review of *Richard III* by Victor Séjour. *Le Temps* (May 11-12, 1865).
Ulbach, who never favored Séjour, is surprised to see *Richard III* come back, and wonders whether the box office will be rewarded; in spite of nightmares, exaggerations and an "impossible style," the critic is obliged to acknowledge the interest, the cleverness and the ingenious accumulation of detail.

1866

152 Anon. Comment on *La Tireuse de cartes* by Victor Séjour *Le Messager des théâtres et des arts* (1866) and Victor Séjour's letter to E. de Montrosier, editor of *Le Messager...*, August 30, 1866. Bibliothèque de l'Arsenal. Séjour, sans cote.
The emotions of the religious and political controversy about the Mortara case had calmed when a more cynical judgment was made on the playwright: Séjour was motivated, not by political or religious considerations but by money. "Knowing the advantages of the theater and the easy sweeping along of the public, he sniffed out a good business deal (in the misfortune of the Mortara family) and, catching the child on the bounce, used it as the foundation of a big hit and handsome royalties." Séjour protested: "Your assessment astounds me. I consider myself a soul little turned towards money, and more open toward great misfortunes. My sympathy for the Jewish race, as for all the persecuted, does not date from yesterday."

153 Ulbach, Louis. Review of *La Tireuse de cartes* by Victor Séjour. *Le Temps* (June 4, 1866), p. 1.
Ulbach is rather favorably disposed toward the revival of *La Tireuse de cartes*. The play ran for a full month, without the excited controversy of 1859.

1867

154 Goizet, J. *Histoire anecdotique de la collaboration au théâtre.* Paris, 1867. Pp. 109-110.
Séjour's royalties from *Le Fils de la nuit* ran high. But he had to share them, it seems, in accord with an out-of-court settlement. The

story was that playwrights Bernard Lopez and Gérard de Nerval had collaborated on a play entitled *Pirate*, which was looked over favorably at the Porte Saint-Martin. However, the management felt it needed some additions, and, with the authors' consent, turned the script over to Alexandre Dumas. After doing a little work on it, Dumas delegated his role and rights to Séjour --without consulting the originators and apparently without fully explaining the situation to him. Séjour rewrote the play in his fashion; the Porte Saint-Martin staged it under the title of *Fils de la nuit*. Lopez complained. Nerval had meanwhile died. The authors and the theater reached a satisfactory agreement: Séjour, while insisting on his ethical and artistic integrity, granted Lopez a half-share of the royalties.

1868

155 Anon. Review of *La Madonne des roses* by Victor Séjour. *La Chronique illustrée* (December 20, 1868), p. 21. Clipping at the Bibliothèque de l'Arsenal, Ref. 48018 (19)
The reviewer reports that the fiery spectacle was staged by using "limelight": a jet of gas-fed oxyhydrogen flame was shot on to a cylinder of lime; the cylinders were turned so that a fresh surface would be brought to incandescent glow. At the Gaîté, the stagehands wore costumes so as to be able to manipulate the equipment right on stage, and some fire-quenchers stood backstage with water buckets ready in case of any accident. No expense had been spared in the staging. Director Victor Koning, Séjour's good friend, wins praise for his casting, sets and special effects. The imaginative Eugène Godin, who had worked in England and in the U.S.A. was in charge of the theatrical machinery. Costumes and scenery had been executed by the finest in the craft.

156 Anon. Review of *La Madonne des roses* by Victor Séjour. *L'Eclipse* (December 27, 1868), p. 3.
Playfully, the *Eclipse* proclaims that the play after two weeks is still alive and flourishing, --not dead and buried in "the great dramatic cemetery of theater columns whose reviews crucify." The main danger is only that "it threatened the box office with an invasion of the Francs." In addition to all the brilliant stage effects, there is "an indefinable impetuosity in the play's pace and speech." In the midst of the French-language review comes an English sentence: "Shakespeare spoken here." But, since all eyes were hypnotized by the fiery demolition of the castle, the reviewer addresses the

playwright, saying: "William Séjour, let M. Eugène Godin's fire speak."

157   Gautier, Théophile.   Review of *La Madonne des roses* by Victor Séjour. *Le Moniteur universel* (December 14, 1868), feuilleton.
Veteran critic Gautier looks on "the burning of the palace [as] the most beautiful fire ever seen in theater." Stepping back from the fire, Gautier analyses Séjour's particular talent: "Behind this fresh and tender title, *La Madone des roses*, M. Victor Séjour hides one of the blackest, most complicated of dramas. With all his defects, [he] has a certain savage vigor that becomes ever rarer [in our time]. ...This violent playwright began as a poet, and to an extent he still is. ... [not] an ordinary playmaker."

158   Janin, Jules.   Review of *La Madonne des roses* by Victor Séjour. *Le Journal des débats* (December 14, 1868), pp. 1-2.
In *La Madone des roses,* Janin recognizes Séjour's force, fantasy and terror. "He has passion, life and courage along with force. He willingly mixes blasphemy and prayer, curses and sentiments most tender." Séjour had always employed poetic license to the fullest in handling historical personages, Janin recalls; no need, then, to challenge his revision of the known character of César d'Este. Janin singles out the scene in which Andrea, after being told of his illegitimacy, comes home to his mother: "The scene is touching... drawn with infinite artistry...written with a talent quite rare." What Séjour wants is to draw that tear, Janin notes; the fireworks later are for the crowd. The hurricane of flame that demolishes the castle leaves the audience pale with fright, Janin claims, but he prefers, as did Séjour, the stirring of deeper and tenderer emotions. All in all, a beautiful play, Janin concludes.

159   Sarcey, Francisque.   Review of *La Madonne des roses* by Victor Séjour. *Le Temps* (December 14, 1868), p. 1.
Sarcey is more impressed with the actors than with the play. He jokes about the physical danger of falling, flaming building material; and the risk has even been used as an advertisement! Yes, the *Madone des roses* is making money at the Gaîté. But the play, the author? "The play was long and obscure; M. Victor Séjour has written it in the flamboyant style that he has kept the secret of, and which is so displeasing to people nowadays." Yet all of Paris, he admits, will go see the crumbling, burning palace.

160 Wolff, Albert. Review of *La Madonne des roses* by Victor Séjour. *Le Figaro* (December 5, 1868), p. 3.
Séjour is complimented for being almost alone in those days in trying to do things on a big scale in theater. The imagery-filled language of his characters might bother the drab bourgeois tastes, the critics thinks, but he can not be discounted: "Just expect from him the historic hero, the passionate struggle, the velvet, the silk and the sword."

1870

161 Anon. Mention of *Henri de Lorraine* by Victor Séjour. *La Cloche* (March 21, 1870), p. 3.
Panning by the critics was so severe that Séjour wrote to his publisher: "All things considered, I ask you to countermand the printing order for *Henri de Lorraine*. Except for a few benevolent minds, Jules Janin, N. Roqueplan, Jules Claretie, Paul Foucher, etc., the play has not been judged; it has been crushed, assassinated. I will keep my dead to myself." In telling of this missive, *La Cloche* comments: "Not at all happy, this letter, but Victor Séjour is not a man to wilt in funeral orations; he will soon have his comeback."

162 Arago, Etienne. Review of *Henri de Lorraine* by Victor Séjour. *L'Avenir national* (March 21, 1870), pp. 2-3.
Arago is mild, giving most of his attention to the history of the real-life Henri de Lorraine. The play has some of the clever movement Séjour knows how to write, Arago concludes, but the cast has not much to be complimented for.

163 C., H. Review of *Henri de Lorraine* by Victor Séjour. *Le Figaro* (March 10, 1870), p. 3.
The critic is witty: "When you say that a play came apart at the seams, you understand that it was first sewed together. This one was only *basted*, and the pieces slipped apart of themselves." He gives the actors their licks: "Some did not know their lines, others played as if they were out in the boondocks." However, Séjour it was who made their job too hard. "Liberty, barricades, independence of the people, tyranny of the great, M. Séjour put everything into this historical-imagination stew, everything... except interest."

164 Gautier,Théophile. Review of *Henri de Lorraine* by Victor Séjour. *Le Journal officiel* (March 15, 1870), feuilleton.

Gautier is favorable. He is sorry that Henri de Lorraine had died before he could rally to the prince but he blames the lack of success of this historical drama on the banality of audience tastes. Unless the public sees some current political allusion, they are incapable of reliving past centuries. They cannot appreciate brave characters who do not speak the slang of the day, have never gambled on the stock market or gone to the theater with a "chick bedecked with huge opera glasses and an enormous bouquet." Gautier finds an artistry of style in the play; that, he writes with irony, is "always harmful when you want to succeed. Let the dramatist write a gag-filled vaudeville in vulgar language, and he'll have a run of a hundred nights." Thus does the venerable Gautier stand up for Séjour and "pour a drop of balm upon the wound." Summing up, he writes, Séjour "is not a manufacturer, like so many other playwrights; he is a poet forced by life's exigencies to put his dramas in the form of melodramas, and to write in prose what he could turn out quite well in verse."

165 Janin, Jules. Review of *Henri de Lorraine* by Victor Séjour. *Le Journal des débats* (March 14, 1870).
Janin's review is kind; perhaps friendship persuades his critical sense to go easy on the weary playwright's product. After a galloping, clinking-sword summary of the action, he gives his comments: Although the first three acts were slow, some portions were "lovely, calm, serene, eloquent and well spoken." (These were qualities Janin had long invited Séjour to adopt.) "Nothing is lacking for the new success in drama of M. Victor Séjour."

166 Sarcey, Francisque. Review of *Henri de Lorraine* by Victor Séjour. *L'Avenir national* (March 21, 1870), pp. 2-3.
Sarcey is slashing: "Let's finish off right now *Henri de Lorraine*. ... The play has this distinction --that it's impossible to understand. You don't know what any of the characters wants. The curtain falls on the denouement without our being able to guess why the action ends there rather than elsewhere,--nor indeed what action is ending... It was impossible for the cast to put anything into roles that don't exist."

167 "Théo". Review of *Henri de Lorraine* by Victor Séjour. *Le Théâtre illustré* (March 8, 1870). Clipping at the Bibliothèque de l'Arsenal, Ref. 48018 (22)
The reviewer is playful. The cast, he writes, can console itself with the thought that the drama will not have a long sojourn (*séjour*). "As

for a review, I'd gladly do it, but, having understood nothing, it would be difficult, and unless one of my colleagues is kind enough to take on the task in our next issue, our readers will be deprived of one.   In short, a fiasco for all --author, actors, directors, and therefore the cashier."

1872

168 Houzeau, Jean-Charles. "Le journal noir aux Etats-Unis, de 1865 à 1870." *La Revue de Belgique* (May-June 1872), pp. 5-27, 195-221.
Mostly retraces the story of Houzeau's own involvement with the editorship of the New Orleans *Tribune,* meanwhile providing valuable details on some of its literary collaborators, most of them local Creoles of color.

169 Sarcey, Francisque. Review of *Le Fils de la nuit* by Victor Séjour. *Le Temps* (August 12, 1872), p. 1.
The usually caustic Sarcey has a kind word to mix with the harsh: "*Le Fils de la nuit* is not an unimportant play. The style, which triggered some smiles a few years ago seems to us furiously out-of-date today. These lions, these serpents, these tigers, these hyenas, that whole menagerie of wild beasts which roar from every corner of Victor Séjour's prose have no more effect than to amuse the groundlings." But those roars are part of Séjour; he does not just stick them on. Sarcey allows that "Naiveté in art is so lovely a thing that it excuses all defects and renders all qualities more pleasant." The lively pace is there! "You feel the expert hand of the professional." In every Séjour drama there is a capital scene, towards which the whole work converges; in *Fils de la nuit* it is the confrontation of the two mothers. "It is superbly built, and the last line is an admirable *coup de théâtre.* This scene alone suffices to lift Séjour above his peers." Sarcey complains that the ship took twenty-five between-the-scenes minutes to put up and twenty-five minutes to take down. Costly delay for that toy, but that's what enraptures the people.

170 Vignaud, Henri. Review of *Le Fils de la nuit* by Victor Séjour.
Le Mémorial diplomatique (August 24, 1872), p. 558.
The ex-Confederate praises the revived play and chides the critics of its swirling language for not realizing that the vocabulary and style belong to the imaginative, heroic genre. Pirates should not talk like

Parisians. "*Le Fils de la nuit*, with its exaggeration of style and its airs of melodrama, unites the qualities which have in every age assured the fortune of theatrical works: dramatic action and poetic form." Vignaud commends Séjour for his weaving together of the strands of his characters' lives. He also admires the play's dramatic logic that moved artistically towards a culminating point of time. He is most explicit in praising Séjour's superior talent for dramatic construction: "No one knows better than he how to lead a vast array of personages through dramatic action, and inspire each of them with feelings that speak smartly to the imagination."

1874

171 Anon. On Victor Séjour. *Paris-Journal* cited in *La Gazette de France* (September 26, 1874).
A journalist who writes on Séjour looks back on his repartees and he unexpectedly surmises that the mulatto author was "distressed" by his "African blood" and was trying to cover up his Negro ancestry. In the light of Séjour's career, this conclusion seems unlikely as well as superficial.

172 Anon. Report on the death and burial of dramatist Victor Séjour. *Bulletin de la Société des auteurs et compositeurs dramatiques*, No. 13 (September-October 1874), in Vol. I (Paris, 1876), pp. 270-272.
On September 17, 1874, Auguste Maquet, the President of the Société called on the dying playwright. The two artists were deeply touched as their memories went back over the old days.   On September 20, Séjour breathed his last. The impoverished family had no funds, so L. Peragallo, agent general of the Société, took charge of arrangements.   Writers and actors turned out to honor their colleague. Playwrights, such as Jules Brésil, stage stars, Paul de Saint-Victor, led the long list of mourning theater folk. At the Père Lachaise Cemetery, Paul Féval, vice-president of the Société, gave the graveside eulogy. He dwelt on the sensitivity of the playwright. Critics' quips had wounded him; one *boutade* in particular had gnawed on him: "Séjour is not a talent, but rather a temperament." Séjour had talent, Féval insisted, but "an uneven talent, full of movement, of strong passion, with a gift of fecundity."

173 Caraguel, Clément. Mention of Victor Séjour. *Le Journal des débats* (September 28, 1874), feuilleton.

In the spring of 1874, Séjour thought his health was improving, he told theater critic Clément Caraguel in a voice so weak it could hardly be heard. He spoke of his hopes and of his current work. The 56-year-old playwright believed --and so did Caraguel-- that he still had within himself the power for a comeback. The critic states that Séjour is "much better than a common playmaker." Séjour "aimed high, doubtless much higher than he could reach. He had the aspiration of a man of letters, but, when wrestling with the ideas and passions of his characters, he drew inspiration less from himself than from the masters of romanticism."

1875

174 Clarétie, Jules. Review of Victor Séjour's *Cromwell*. *La Presse* (April 26, 1875), p. 2.
Clarétie points out the basic problem of the historical drama: how to keep unity in the episodes. And Séjour had simply not kept the play tight enough. Politician Cromwell, who suffers as he realizes that his work stands on himself alone, and will crumble because of a weak son, provides grandeur and energy. This portrayal and these scenes are the closest to Shakespeare Clarétie has ever seen.

175 Vitu, Auguste. Review of Victor Séjour's *Cromwell*. *Le Figaro* (April 26, 1875), p.3.
The Shakespearean touch is noted by Vitu in the scene where the shade of Charles I comes between Cromwell and the crown, and foreshadows the restoration of the Stuarts. Both the honor and the punishment given *Cromwell* exceed the drama's merits: "It's a play that is badly enough put together, loose, boring here and there, but which includes beautiful scenes, notably in the third act when Cromwell disarms his would-be assassin and pardons him. And in the fifth act, when Cromwell is dying."

176 Sarcey, Francisque. Review of Victor Séjour's *Cromwell*. *Le Temps* (May 10, 1875), feuilleton.
Sarcey, who maintained that each Séjour play had one masterful scene that other scenes led to and away from, finds that peak in the confrontation between Cromwell and the young royalist would-be-assassin who loves the Protector's daughter. Séjour's *Cromwell* is a pastel image of Hugo's, according to him; however, "the French, whether Catholics or skeptics, find it hard to get interested in Cromwell, sombre, puritan, bloodthirsty, fanatical, perhaps

hypocritical --a sort of soldier-preacher Robespierre-- whose faults as well as virtues wound at every point our ideal and our beliefs."

1876

177 Noël, Edouard and Edmond Stoulig. *Annales du théâtre et de la musique, 1875.* Paris, 1876, pp. 353-357.
Review of Victor Séjour's *Cromwell.* In a rather unfavorable review, the critics feel that one can hardly expect a French audience to join in the actors' thrill and joy over the English taking of Dunkerque from the Spaniards.

178 Sarcey, Francisque. Review of *La Tireuse de cartes* by Victor Séjour and Jean-François Mocquard. *Le Temps* (January 10, 1876), p. 1.
Sixteen years after the original production, a year-and-a-half after the death of Séjour, the Théâtre historique staged anew *La Tireuse de cartes.* Sarcey recalls how the press in 1859-60 had augured in the play the secret dispositions of Napoleon III toward papal temporal sovereignty and Italian unification. "We saw it again yesterday," he writes, "stripped of that newsy prestige, reduced to its force alone." The city and the theater were freezing cold but the play wound up winning out over the audience's discomfort. "In the fourth act is one of the most beautiful scenes I know of in theater." Since Sarcey was a new-generation critic, this is lofty praise. There is more: "Victor Séjour arrives at this magnificent scene only after many a twist and a turn. His exposition is slow and compact; his developments are brooding and towering; his style is labored and difficult. But he is a man of the theater, a writer through and through. When he sets his hand upon a situation, he does not let go, he turns it in and out, he chisels it, he imprints upon it a fascinating form which leaves a lingering remembrance in the imagination." Mme. Laurent, who had played the title role in 1859 and 1866, was still playing Gemea --with "marvelous brilliance."

179 Vitu, Auguste. Review of *La Tireuse de cartes* by Victor Séjour and Jean-François Mocquard, in *Les mille et une nuits du théâtre.* Paris, 1885, pp. 89-90. Clipping at the Bibliothèque de l'Arsenal, Ref. Séjour, sans cote.(January 7, 1876).
Attending the 1876 revival of the play, Vitu sees its power in its simplicity--spoiled, he feels, "by turgidity and melodramatic incidents." But the scene of the two mothers merits the comeback.

1883

180 Allain, Hélène. *Souvenirs d'Amérique et de France.* Paris, 1883.
Comments on black creole culture in Louisiana and reprints (p. 167) a creole song, "Lizette." [It had previously been quoted by Jean-Jacques Rousseau around 1740, recorded by Médéric Moreau de Saint-Méry in Saint-Domingue in the late eighteenth century, and again by Pierre Forest near Lake Pontchartrain in 1831.]

1885

181 Vitu, Auguste.   Review of *Le Fils de la nuit* by Victor Séjour. *Les mille et une nuits du théâtre.* (5 vols., Paris, 1885-1888), vol. I, pp. 247-249. Clipping at the Bibliothèque de l'Arsenal, Ref. Séjour, sans cote.
Séjour enjoyed the consolation of a revival of *Le Fils de la nuit* in August of 1872 at the Théâtre de la Gaîté. Vitu, too young to have seen the play in 1856, seems surprised at his own "interest and delight" in the drama, "wild as a comet, but, at bottom, simple as a nursery rhyme." The Shakespearean and Byronian elements are hardly as captivating for the crowd as is the famous ship. "It launched out proudly, sails filled, red flare lighting the stern, all hands on deck. It comes on stage, like a captured monster it greets the audience, it turns about. The audience clap to beat the band. It returns and dips again, to the extent of three protocol salutes. Audience enthusiasm knows no bounds. The mature and serious join in. A likeable diplomat, well versed in theater matters, took pains to assure me that, as for stagecraft ships, he had never seen a better." Vitu himself is fascinated with the water effects, especially the sparkling wave crests.

1901

182 Bentzon, Thérèse. Review of *Up from Slavery* by Booker T. Washington. *Revue des deux mondes* (October 15, 1901), pp. 774-95.
Enthusiastic review of the autobiography which will become "the Bible par excellence of a race, the star that will in fact guide it step by step, prudently and surely, ever higher." She finds Washington's European impressions the least interesting and least accurate portions of the book.

1902

183 Léger, Augustin. Review of *Up from Slavery* by Booker T. Washington. *Le Correspondant* (February 10, 1902), p. 449.
Favorable review quoting passages from the autobiography, noting Washington's success as an orator, educator and friend of presidents. "As a mulatto he seems to testify to the excellence of mixed bloods who even in the most favorable instances are subject to terrible atavistic tendencies." The book is the "perfect companion volume for that by Harriet Beecher Stowe."

1903

184 Gohier, Urbain. *Le Peuple du XXième Siècle aux Etats-Unis*. Paris: Charpentier, 1903.
Pp. 216-52 refer to *Up From Slavery* prior to its French publication, describing Booker T. Washington "whose character and work all America admires. He has told the story of his life in a language both simple and effective." A brief summary of the book follows.

185 Guerlac, Othon. Introduction to *L'Autobiographie d'un nègre*. de Booker T. Washington;   Paris: Plon-Nourrit, 1903. pp. i-iv.
A French resident in the U.S. and the translator of the book, Guerlac mentions favorable reviews of *Up from Slavery* in America, quotes William Dean Howells' praise for this "remarkable" book, and an article in French by Mrs. Bentzon together with the fact that the President of the United States invited B. T. Washington to the White House. The autobiography is told "with the élan and charm of a novel" and is a remarkably accurate picture of the black situation as well as a judicious discussion of the Negro problem, "more engrossing, more modern and truer than *Uncle Tom's Cabin*." The book was reprinted in 1961 by the same publisher

1904

186 Barthélemy, Edmond. Review of *Up from Slavery* by Booker T. Washington. *Mercure de France* (February 1904), p. 494.
Very laudatory review calling the autobiography "a new *Uncle Tom's Cabin*, equally captivating but more modern and truer."

187 Huret, Jules. *De New-York à la Nouvelle-Orléans*. Paris:

Fasquelle, 1904.
Mentions an interview with B.T. Washington. To Huret's questions and remarks, the black leader reacts as an American capitalist would do. "He inquires," Huret records, "whether there have been any original inventions in France... I sense in him as in all Americans an exaggerated national pride, which obviously stems from their utter ignorance of history. One of his complaints about Europe is the slowness of the people and lack of general activity. "It seems to me," he says, "that in Europe one is always on vacation. There are too many holidays." (p. 394)

188 Lichtenberger, André. Review of *Up from Slavery* by Booker T. Washington." *La Revue historique* (March-April 1904), p. 341.
The book is "the most vivid, the truest, and the most naive of autobiographies. Book lovers will enjoy these confessions in which one sees a personality singularly optimistic, active, and energetic, at once so 'Negroid,' if one may say so, and so American." Washington is characterized not only as the leading Black American, but "one of the most distinguished and popular citizens of the Republic."

1905

189 Finot, Jean. *Le Préjugé des races*. Paris: Félix Alcan, 1905.
"Does one wish to speak of the creative faculties of Negroes? One should mention their many poets, novelists.... such as Paul Laurence Dunbar (the Black Victor Hugo); mathematician Kelly Miller, Dr. Blyden, a linguist; Booker T. Washington, an educator of genius and a public figure of the first magnitude, Du Bois, a political writer and a historian, etc. " (p. 469) Finot insists on the odds which Dunbar had to overcome in order to make a career as a writer.

1906

190 Adam, Paul. *Vues d'Amérique*. Paris: Editions Ollendorf, 1906.
On the career of B.T. Washington as mirrored in his autobiography, the French visitor remarks: "The example of his life would support all the claims of the enthusiastic negrophiles if it were not an exception. In Haiti and in Liberia, republics founded long ago by former slaves, a deplorable state of barbarism persists." (p. 158)

1911

191 Desdunes, Rodolphe Louis. *Nos hommes et notre histoire*; *Notices biographiques accompagnées de réflexions et de souvenirs personnels*. Montréal: Arbour & Dupont, Imprimeurs-Editeurs, 1911.
Includes detailed first-hand biographical information about, and an laudatory evaluation of the Louisiana Creole poets represented in *Les Cenelles,* and also of Victor Rillieux and Hippolyte Castra.

192 Huret, Jules. "A Tuskegee." In his *L'Amérique moderne*. Paris: Lafitte, 1911, pp. 185-201.
Mentions *Up From Slavery*, "an admirable book," and the rise of Booker T. Washington. Huret quotes Washington at length on his gospel of work and wealth as expressed in an interview with him.

1915

193 Fortier, Edouard J. *Les Lettres françaises en Louisiane*. Québec: L'Action sociale, 1915. 25 p.
Briefly mentions *Les Cenelles*, an anthology of verse compiled by Armand Lanusse.

1921

194 Dekobra, Maurice. "Le Monde noir américain: Marcus Garvey, prophète." *L'Illustration* No. 473 (March 26, 1921), pp. 486-87.
Garvey is described as "a new Booker T. Washington, an extraordinary man." A biographical note stresses the opposition of Dr. Robert Russa Moton and the black clergy to Garvey; it describes the black crowd at a Liberty Hall meeting where Garvey proved to be "a great rhetorician and speaker." Quotes Garvey's claim that "the black man was indispensable to victory over the Germans, but that he has learnt to kill and should be granted freedom." Dekobra admires Garvey's talent but smiles at his "gentle chiding of French colonial policies." Illustrations and photograph.

195 Joanides, A. *La Comédie française de 1680 à 1920. Tableau des représentations par auteurs et par pièces*. Paris, 1921.
Lists Victor Séjour's *Diégarias*.

1924

196 Locke, Alain Leroy. "La jeune poésie africo-américaine." *Les Continents* (September 1, 1924), p. 3.
A brief, general presentation of new Afro-American poetry, insisting on its positive offerings as exemplified by Countee Cullen's "The Dance of Love (After reading René Maran's *Batouala*)" which is printed here in English.

1925

197 Maran, René. "Le mouvement négro-littéraire aux Etats-Unis." *Vient de paraître* No. 49 (December 1925), pp. 645-46.
By the pioneering black Goncourt prize-winner, this article mentions several Afro-American periodicals as well as the work of Charles S. Johnson and Alain Locke. Many writers are mentioned: Jessie Fausett (sic), Paul Lawrence (sic) Dunbar, Countee Culler (sic), Hughes, J.W. Johnson, J.A. Rogers, Georgia D. Johnson.   A detailed review of Walter White's *Fire in the Flint* concludes that this "truthful, well-balanced, human, and exceedingly moving" novel deserves to be translated into French.

198 Schoell, Frank Louis. "L'agonie du français en Louisiane." *La Revue de Paris* (January-February 1925), pp. 883-96.
Alludes to the black creole use of French, notably in popular literature.

1926

199 Anon. Review of J.W. Johnson's *The Book of American Spirituals. Mercure de France* No. 666 (March 15, 1926), p. 733.
Brief but very favorable review of Johnson's collection of spirituals published in New York City by the Viking Press.

1927

200 Catel, Jean. "Lettres anglo-américaines." *Mercure de France* No. 707 (December 1, 1927), pp. 488-93.
Brief presentation of *God's Trombones* by J.W. Johnson as "an original work," followed by extracts (in English) from "The Creation" sermon. Mentions that "Mr. Johnson claims that he only

had to transcribe what he was hearing in Negro churches."

201 Salemson, Harold. "Quelques livres sur la question nègre aux Etats-Unis." *Le Monde* (October [?], 1927), p. 6.
  Mentions James Weldon Johnson's *The Autobiography of an Ex-Colored Man* most favorably.

1928

202 Anon. "Bilan de l'année littéraire." *Mercure de France* No. 731 (December 1, 1928), p. 474.
Mentions the publication of James Weldon Johnson's *The Autobiography of an Ex-Colored Man* in the United States. Claims it is "the best book ever written by a colored American."

203 Jolas, Eugene. "Claude McKay - 1889." In his *Anthologie de la nouvelle poésie américaine*. Paris: Editions Kra, 1928. P. 155.
Brief biographical notice listing McKay's Jamaican origins, his diverse jobs, his work at *The Liberator* in 1920. "A full-blooded Negro, McKay brought a new violent accent to the poetry of his race." "Black Spiritual" follows.

204 Jolas, Eugene. "Countee Cullen - 1903." In his *Anthologie de la nouvelle poésie américaine*. Paris: Editions Kra, 1928. P. 48.
Brief biographical notice: the son of a protestant pastor, Cullen graduated from New York University and became famous with "The Shroud of Color" (1924). He is the "youngest of Black American poets." "Simon the Cyrenian" is translated.

205 Jolas, Eugène. Introduction to his *Le Nègre qui chante*. Paris: Editions des Cahiers libres, 1928. Pp. 9-28.
One must distinguish between the pure primitivism of Blacks below the Mason-Dixon line and the imitation of it by whites. Blacks' songs of all kinds (blues, spirituals, work songs, ballads) express the yearnings of the oppressed black people. Their African origins are no longer questioned. The major themes and the language of these songs are discussed. A selection of some thirty folk songs follows.

206 Jolas, Eugène. "Jean Toomer." In his *Anthologie de la nouvelle poésie américaine*. Paris: Editions Kra, 1928. P. 332

Brief notice: Toomer was born in the South and he is "probably the most gifted poet of his race." The publication of *Cane*, a collection of stories or prose poems revealed his great originality and imagination. He lives in utter solitude from literary circles. "Harvest Song" follows.

207 Jolas, Eugène. "Langston Hughes - 1902." In his *Anthologie de la nouvelle poésie américaine*. Paris: Editions Kra, 1928. p. 108.
A brief bio-bibliographical notice, mentioning Hughes' origins, studies, work as a ticket collector and sailor. "He is a Negro poet who makes use of the rhythms of jazz and Negro songs in his poetry." "Po' Boy Blues" follows.

208 Maurois, André. "La poésie nègre aux Etats-Unis." *Candide* No. 203 (March 15, 1928), p. 3.
In the brief article, the well-known novelist praises the lyrical achievements of Countee Cullen, Langston Hughes, Claude McKay, and Angelina Grimke, providing quotations from their poems. He concentrates, however, on a favorable review of *Porgy*, the translation of DuBose Heyward's play *Porgy and Bess*, to be published the following year.

209 Michaud, Régis. *Littérature américaine*. Paris: Editions Kra, 1928.
America is the home of the blues, jazz, and the spirituals, characterized as "the revenge of the blacks in poetry and art." At the dawn of the American poetic renaissance, Negro poetry brims over with rhythm and color: Paul Laurence Dunbar, W.E.B. Du Bois, William S. Braithwaite, James Weldon Johnson make up the established generation. Countee Cullen, Langston Hughes, the "errant bard" Claude McKay, Jean Toomer, Joseph Cotter, Jessie Fausett, Gwendolyn Bennett, Jeffrey Hays, and Lewis Alexander, among others, "tell the regrets, rancors, and aspirations of their race." They adore the "Black Venus" with "a strange fragrance of paganism" in their "luxuriant imagery" and "lively rhythms." (pp. 206-08).

210 Schoell, Franck Louis. "Un romancier noir américain: Jean Toomer." *Les Nouvelles littéraires* No. 290 (May 5, 1928), p. 6.
In this favorable, largely descriptive review of *Cane*, Schoell extols Toomer's artistry and delicate handling of language by contrasting him with other black writers (probably McKay) who are

characterized by "primitive impetuosity" and exaggeration. Only in Toomer's case is "the novelist the true essence, and the black man the accident."

1929

211 Lévinson, André. "Aframérique." *Les Nouvelles littéraires* 7 (August 31, 1929), p.6.
Expressing surprise at the "perfect balance" of DuBose Heyward, whom he thinks to be black, Lévinson denies the Negro any great intelligence: "The art of the primitive is intense, colorful, direct; it is also superficial, monotonous and short-winded." Jean Toomer, Eric Walrond, and Countee Cullen are mentioned but most of the piece is devoted to a biography of McKay and an evocation of *Home to Harlem* which, paternalistically, insists on the "debauchery of Harlem life." Jessie Fauset's *There Is Confusion* is mentioned as dealing with "quasi-whiteness."

212 Lévinson, André. "De Harlem à la Canebière." *Les Nouvelles littéraires* 7 (September 14, 1929), p. 7.
A rather unfavorable review of McKay's *Banjo*. To its tone of revolt and "primitive racial vainglory," Lévinson opposes Toomer's *Cane* as a literary model representing the "victory of spirit over instinct." *Banjo* is anti-French and an apology for the abdication of the intellect. Eric Walrond's *Tropic Death* is analyzed sympathetically, and praised.

213 Lévinson, André. *Figures américaines: dix-huit études sur des écrivains de ce temps.* Paris: Victor Attinger, 1929. Pp. 177-95.
The two chapters "Aframérique" and "De Harlem à la Canebière" deal mostly with Claude McKay and reprint Lévinson's articles published in *Les Nouvelles littéraires* in August and September 1929.

214 Piérard, Louis. "Poètes de l'Aframérique." *Les Nouvelles littéraires* No. 372 (November 30, 1929), p. 9.
This short historical retrospect mentions Phillis Wheatley and several nineteenth-century black poets, but centers on the Negro Renaissance. Translations of poems by Hughes ("Je suis noir" and "Le noir parle des rivières") and by Cullen ("Les presque blancs" and "Les dieux") are printed. J.W. Johnson's *God's Trombones* is reviewed favorably and sympathetically.

215 Schoell, Franck L. "La Renaissance nègre aux USA." *La Revue de Paris* No. 1 (January 1, 1929), pp. 124-65.
This long and important study examines the situation of Afro-Americans after World War I, their urbanization and the growth of a middle class, the development of the black press and the vogue of Negro art. The first section deals with the fashion of Negro art and jazz. The second focuses on literature about the Negro (by Sherwood Anderson, Carl Van Vechten, Eugene O'Neill, and Paul Green), as well as by the Negro. "Our Land" and "I Too" by Hughes, "Tropics in New York" by Claude McKay, and poems by Countee Cullen are quoted. *Cane* by Jean Toomer is called "a most curious. . . collection of tales." *Fire in the Flint* by Walter White and *There is Confusion* by Jessie Fauset are mentioned, together with *Tropic Death* by Eric Walrond, and "a very fine book by James Weldon Johnson, *The Autobiography of an Ex-Colored Man*, for long out of print." Black dramatists are few, by reason of their "lack of detachment and objectivity," but excellent actors abound, "brimming with vitality." Schoell cites "Shuffle Along," out of which came "this beautiful jumping animal, Josephine Baker." Poetry, according to Gobineau, is more attuned to the Negro's sensual gifts: it blossomed in the twenties, with "such a high class poet" as Langston Hughes. McKay vibrantly celebrates Harlem, and Cullen sings exquisitely of dancing girls. "The African theme probably remains most characteristic in this poetry, which is endowed with fresh sensitivity and originality." James Weldon Johnson is also mentioned as a poet. In the section entitled "The Negro horizon broadens preoccupations with Africa," Du Bois and Garvey are mentioned alongside the travels of black writers like McKay, Hughes, etc. An attempt is made to relate U.S.Blacks to their African origins and to examine the future of the New Negro movement.

216 Schoell, Franck L.[ouis] *U.S.A.: Du côté des Blancs et du côté des Noirs*. Paris: Honoré Champion, 1929.
This collection of essays, most of them previously printed in *La Revue de Paris* includes "La Renaissance nègre aux Etats-Unis" under the heading "A Harlem (New York), la Renaissance nègre" (Chapter V). In his foreword, the author, who taught at Tulane University and lectured extensively in the US, mentions his personal acquaintances with Du Bois and Walter White.

217 Schoell, Franck Louis. "Un poète nègre: Langston Hughes."

Revue politique et littéraire No. 14 (June 20, 1929), p. 436-438.
An often erroneous biographical retrospect precedes the translations of six poems: "Cabaret," "Jeune Danseuse," "Lamentation pour les hommes au teint foncé," "La peur," "Moi aussi," and "Une mère à son fils." It is hoped that Hughes will not confine himself to racial themes, "the source of which would soon become dry."

1930

218 Anon. Review of *Anthology of American Negro Literature*. *Mercure de France* No. 772 (August 15, 1930), p. 226.
A brief mention of V. F. Calverton's anthology, judging it "a necessary but far from perfect volume."

219 F., L. "Langston Hughes." *Les Cahiers libres* N.S. Vol. 1, No. 6 (October 15, 1930), pp. 353-54.
This mostly biographical study emphasizes the original, powerful talent of the young poet, and his role as a representative of his race. "Spiritual power and the power to dream" are said to be "magnificently imprinted on the face and the poetry of Langston Hughes."

220 Hirsch, C.H. "Un sermon nègre issu du folklore: la Création du monde." *Mercure de France* No. 779 (December 1, 1930), pp. 420-22.
This brief note on an article by Roux-Delimal in *Cahiers du Sud* (October 1930) emphasizes the genius of the spirituals in the American South and quotes Delimal's parallel between that genre and the medieval French *chanson de geste*. A two-page extract from "The Creation" by James Weldon Johnson follows in translation.

221 Nardal, Paulette. "Une noire parle à Cambridge et à Genève." *La Revue du monde noir* No. 1 (1930), pp. 36-37.
Review of a reading by Grace Walker, mentioning that she "recited certain poems by Countee Cullen, Claude McKay, Langston Hughes, and Jean Toomer, chosen in such a way as to touch on the highlights of the artistic temperament of these different Negro poets, distinctive in inspiration and style."
It should be noted that many Afro-Americans were represented in the bilingual publication: Countee Cullen; Claude McKay by an excerpt from *Banjo*, "Spring in New Hampshire," and "To America;" Hughes by "I Too Sing America;" John F. Matheus by "Fog;"

Walter White by the lynching scene in *The Fire in the Flint*. Jessie Fauset, Margaret Rose Martin, and Clara Shepard also contributed.

222   Roux-Delimal, Olga et Jean.   "Nègres d'Amérique."   *Les Cahiers du Sud* No. 125 (October 1930), pp. 561-566.
Before presenting a panorama of the Negro race in the United States, the study introduces J.W. Johnson's *God's Trombones* to the reader, insisting on the creativity of the American Negro dialect.

1931

223   Friedmann, Georges. Preface to Claude McKay's *Banjo*. Paris: Rieder, 1931. Pp. 7-24.
Contrasting with the Booker T. Washington generation, the New Negro writers deal with popular themes and criticize Western civilization.   Such is the case with Jamaican-born McKay, whose career is retraced.   Several poems by McKay are quoted and Friedmann evokes his personal contacts with the novelist in Antibes. *Banjo* unites deep and colorful sensitivity with a meditation on black life in a white racist environment.   The more picturesque scenes in the novel are evoked.   The novel is said to go beyond entertainment, towards an intelligent, acute analysis of racial relations, not only in Marseilles and not only within groups of the black diaspora, but in a global context of economic oppression that cuts across color lines. Personal impressions of McKay are also evoked: "One could have said of him, in order to recommend him, not: 'I am sending McKay, a young Negro writer to you,' but 'You'll love to hear McKay's laughter.'   The entire personality of this robust youngster expressed the radiant life I have loved from the start, but mostly his surprisingly young face where the liveliest mirth turned at once into earnestness; his straightforward eyes, wide open on the world and people, his strong forehead which, I suppose, was inhabited by all the cares of the mind."

224   Anon. Note on Alain Locke.   *Europe*, No. 102 (June 15, 1931), p. 288.
A brief preface to Locke's introduction to the 1924 "New Negro" number of the *Survey Graphic*, translated by Louis and Renée Guilloux (pp. 289-300).

225   Louis, Léone.   "Langston Hughes.   *Nouvel Age* No. 12 (December 1931), pp. 1060-61.

This biographical and critical essay quotes Hughes' manifesto, "The Negro Artist and the Racial Mountain," and his desire to express his black self without shame or fear. Hughes dedicates his art to the defense of his race. His major themes are Africa, the hope of obtaining victory, and a great confidence in the beauty of his race. He also points to instances of racial discrimination in the U.S. *The Weary Blues*, *Not Without Laughter*, and other works are analyzed and quoted.

226 Nardal, Paulette. "Eveil de la conscience de race." *La Revue du monde noir* No. 6 [1931], pp. 25-31.
This early, seminal essay deals with Afro-American literature: slave narratives; the dialect poetry of Paul Laurence Dunbar; the influence of W.S. Braithwaite; the "new attitude" embodied in the poetry of Claude McKay and Langston Hughes, who reject any inferiority complex; the theories of Marcus Garvey; the "revolt of [our] American brothers," and the latest phase in their intellectual evolution. Nardal parallels its blossoming in the United States and in France. In France, where the atmosphere was more liberal and open, black consciousness had taken more moderate forms, while black American revolt was more explicit, as exemplified by the New Negro movement: "Quite different was the situation among the American Negroes. Though they are not of pure African origin either, the deliberate scorn with which they have always been treated by white Americans, incited them to seek for social and cultural pride in their African past" (p. 30). Literature has forsaken the romantic, imitative poetics of *Les Cenelles* and become the vehicle of debate and protest; the impact of Garveyism, the first Pan-African Conference in Paris, the launching of René Maran's *Les Continents* and of Maurice Satineau's newspaper, *La Dépêche africaine*, were so many steps towards a new awareness patent in the Antillean and African students' desire to complete Sorbonne M.A.'s on Negro topics. Louis Achille was writing on Dunbar, Léopold Senghor on Baudelaire's black mistress, and Nardal herself on Harriet Beecher Stowe.

1932

227 Bertin, Gabriel. " Claude MacKay: *Banjo*." *Les Cahiers du Sud* No. 141 (June 1932), pp. 397-400.
This very favorable review emphasizes several aspects of life on the Marseilles waterfront which McKay seems to know extremely well.

The author even claims to have met the actual person upon whom McKay based his character of Banjo.

228 Guilloux, Louis. "Banjo." *Europe* No. 110 (February 15, 1932), p. 270.
A biographical sketch of McKay and a summary of the novel precede a very positive evaluation of *Banjo* by the left-wing novelist. He emphasizes the "serene humaneness of the characters" and declares McKay "a genuine artist ... without doubt one of the most gifted" Negro writers.

229 Léro, Etienne. "Misère d'une poésie." *Légitime Défense*, 1 [June 1932], pp. 11-12.
The Martiniquan iconoclast mentions very favorably the poetry of the Harlem Renaissance. He claims that "The wind that blows from black America will soon manage, let us hope, to cleanse our Antilles of the aborted fruit of an obsolete culture. Langston Hughes and Claude McKay, two revolutionary black poets, have brought us, marinated in red alcohol, the African love of life, the African joy of love, the African dream of death."(p. 12) An excerpt from *Banjo* is used to criticize assimilated French West Indians: it deals with a Martiniquan student who refuses to enter the café kept by a Senegalese because he is afraid of demeaning himself by associating with Africans.

230 Tinker, Edward Laroque. *Les Ecrits de langue française en Louisiane au 19eme siècle. Essai biographique et bibliographique.* Paris: Honoré Champion, 1932. 502 p.
Partly based on Desdunes's book (q.v.), this is a basis for the study of the literary production of many Creoles of color. Besides a historical panorama, focusing on the white creole production and detailed notices on them, it contains basic notices on a score of colored creole writers. (Repr. Kraus, 1970)

1933

231 Anon. [Mathilde Camhi] Note on Eric Walrond. *Lectures du soir* (February 4, 1933).
Brief biographical note. Mme Camhi was supposed to translate *Tropic Death*, but the book never saw publication in France. She only translated "Sur les chantiers de Panama" and "Harlem," a colorful reportage on how the smart set had invaded the Harlem

cabarets and how a few Strivers' Row entrepreneurs like Jasbo Brown had capitalized on that fashion. "Harlem" appears in this issue. A similar piece, "Harlem, la perle noire de New York," came out in *Voilà* on May 27, 1933.

232 Lebar, Jacques. "Avec Eric Walrond." Brussels *Lectures du soir* (January 14, 1933), p. 4.
Walrond is introduced as "one of the most characteristic and colorful representatives of Negro literature together with Claude McKay." He considers Flaubert a major novelist, having read *Madame Bovary* repeatedly, likes Blaise Cendrars best among contemporary French writers for his "unique understanding of the world, the psychology and the art of the Negro" He utterly dismisses Paul Morand's depictions of the Negro. Walrond contrasts the black Frenchman's and the black American's psychological choices. The U.S. is a paradoxical country, and Blacks a creative race drawn to mysticism, the arts, and music. [The January 7, 1933, issue of *Lectures du soir* carried Walrond's story "Sur les chantiers de Panama." Its theme was racial conflict among the canal workers when a Spanish shopkeeper shot a couple of Negroes as a threatening mob drew near.]

233 Lorson, Pierre. "*Quartier noir.*" *Etudes* No. 215 (April 5, 1933), p. 118.
Descriptive review concluding unfavorably: "the composition of the book is so disordered that, if Mr. McKay is a Negro, he certainly provides M. Lévy-Brühl with arguments for his theory on the pre-logical mind of primitive peoples." *Home to Harlem* is judged to be "weak, foul, and demeaning."

1934

234 Cestre, Charles. "*Banana Bottom*, roman de Claude McKay." *Revue anglo-américaine* No. 5 (June 1934), pp. 471-72.
Emphasizes the value of the novel as a social document: the lack of ideological and racial bias, either concerning tyrants or in favor of the victims, makes the novel of indisputable interest, "a living book" and "a crucial document in the itinerary of a race."

235 Joseph-Henri, Georges. "*Banjo*, par Claude Mac Kay." *Revue de la Martinique* 2, No. 20 (July 1934), pp. 54-59.
A detailed and favorable review, focusing on McKay's denunciation

of so-called "civilization" and the Negro's attempt to whiten himself psychologically and culturally. Black nationalism is extolled and McKay's declarations in the novel quoted at length.   The myth of black hypersexuality is deflated. Like Aldous Huxley, D.H. Lawrence and Katherine Mansfield, McKay does not spare the deleterious influence of Christianity. The book deserves close reading: "maybe, some of those who are asleep will awaken and listen to its important message about the adverse effects of racial exclusion."

236 Lorson, Pierre. *"Banana Bottom." Etudes* No. 220 (August 20, 1934), pp. 511-12.
The author mentions that McKay is a Jamaican Negro. The review focuses on the plot: a black girl, Bita, comes back home to Jamaica after having enjoyed a refined education in Great Britain.   She gradually scrubs the white education off her black skin and can only find happiness when marrying a male of her race, one hundred per cent black.

237 Lorson, Pierre. *"Sandy." Etudes* No. 221 (November 5, 1934), p. 416.
Brief review of the translation of Langston Hughes' *Not without Laughter* published by Editions Rieder. "Yet another American Negro novel..." It is found "less brutal than others in the same series" [McKay's *Banjo* and *Home to Harlem*], and "moving because of the depth of feeling expressed." Because of these qualities, it would "bring honor to any white-skinned novelist."

1935

238 Flavia-Léopold, Emmanuel. *"Negro.* Anthologie préparée par Nancy Cunard." *Europe* No. 140 (February 15, 1935), pp. 301-304.
The French West Indian poet examines the ideological perspectives of the anthology, emphasizing its comprehensiveness, the "indisputable link" between racial and social oppression, and how the former stems from economic exploitation. He denounces disguised job discrimination in France. Rayford Logan, Walter White, Countee Cullen, Alain Locke, Arthur Schomburg, W.E.B. Du Bois, and Zora Neale Hurston are mentioned as distinguished black

U.S. contributors to the volume.

1937

239 Catel, Jean. *"Black Man's Verse." Mercure de France* No. 927 (February 1, 1937), p. 637.
A short review of the collection of poems by Frank Marshall Davis with appreciative aesthetic comments and some twenty lines in translation.

240 Miller, Ezechiel-Henri. *L'Education des noirs aux Etats-Unis.* Dijon: Bergniaud et Privat, 1937.
This doctoral dissertation accepted at the University of Dijon includes a veritable eulogy of the work of Booker T. Washington. Not seen, information derived from Mercer Cook, "Booker T. Washington and the French," *Journal of Negro History*, 40 (1955), pp. 318-340.

1938

241 Anon. Notice on Richard Wright. *Littérature internationale*, 10 (1938), p. 46.
Introducing his "Big Boy s'en va," translated by A. Lichnevskaia, (pp. 48-78), a brief summary of the young proletarian writer's career precedes the very first appearance of Wright's work in French, a translation of "Big Boy Leaves Home."

242 Schneider, Isidor. "Un livre sur la nouvelle génération nègre." *Littérature internationale*, 10 (1938), p. 98-101.
An article by Isidor Schneider, apparently never before published in English, celebrates Richard Wright: the title of his book, "Uncle Tom's Children," is explained at length; his stories portray the militant, rebellious Black and it is significant that he should be a Communist himself. His poetry reverberates with the spirituals and also with the manly accents of black workers. "The Negroes in America have finally found in him an authentic writer of the people, *their* own writer."

1939

243 Senghor, Léopold Sédar. "Ce que l'homme noir apporte." In his *L'Homme de couleur*, Paris: Librairie Plon, 1939.

The Negro "negrifies God, and he makes man (whom he does not deify) partake of the supernatural world. Cullen is quoted as "making black Gods" and the African American poet is said to "speak to Christ preferably, i.e. man in God." (p. 27).   Further, Senghor states that black workers in the North of the United-States look nostalgically at the Southern countryside where their brothers toil like serfs. He quotes McKay as an instance and cites that Aimé Césaire was able to write a M.A. on "the theme of the South in Afro-American literature." (p. 31).   He later quotes Lewis Alexander to show that "to those who have destroyed their culture, to the slave trader and the lyncher, Afro-American poets only reply with words of peace. (p. 33).
Reprinted in Senghor's *Liberté I: Négritude et Humanisme*. Paris: Editions du Seuil, 1964.

1941

244   Césaire, Aimé.   "Introduction à la poésie négre américaine." *Tropiques* No. 2 (July 1941), pp. 37-42.
Black American poetry speaks in the name of millions of the "most pitiful humanity," which explains its closeness to original man, its ability to sympathize;   it boasts no beautiful images but deep, self-conscious drives towards art: frenzy, ancestral paganism reach for a form of mysticism but also for "poetry as the escape of wounded for centuries."   "Black lyricism remains short of grandeur;" it flows tempestuously like a torrent and remains devoid of artifice;   but its grandeur lies in its ability to remain alive, "to open onto the whole of man."   Translations of poems by Jean Toomer and James Weldon Johnson follow. [Césaire elsewhere claims those poets have rehabilitated "the everyday and commonplace Negro, whose grotesque appearance and exoticism an entire literary tradition is entrusted with pursuing."   They "depict him earnestly, passionately suggesting even the deep forces that command his destiny."]

245   Piquion, René. *Un Chant nouveau*. Port-au-Prince: Imprimerie de l'Etat, [1941].   139 p.
The first book-length study of Langston Hughes's works and career is an enthusiastic and laudatory but rather superficial treatment which enjoyed remarkable success in Port-au-Prince where Piquion was teaching in a lycée. A lengthy but unevenly documented biographical sketch is followed by a thematic study of Hughes' poetry, focusing on his commitment to the social and racial struggle.

1943

246 Cabrières, Jean-François. *Booker T. Washington, éducateur de sa race*. Genève, Paris: Editions "Je sers." n.d. [1943?]
This study, mostly dedicated to the political and educational career of the black leader, makes heavy use of his autobiography, always considered as documentary proof of the author's declarations.

1945

247 Anon. "Richard Wright, écrivain américain." *Archives internationales* (March 1945), Sec. A, p. 6.
A biographical-critical sketch of Richard Wright approached as an American novelist.

248 Ozanne, Jean-Louis. "Aspects de la littérature américaine: Témoin du peuple noir, écrivain de combat, Richard Wright dénonce l'oppression raciale." Rouen *Paris-Normandie* (July 4, 1945).
Mainly a review of *Black Boy* with extensive summary and quotations. Ozanne also sketches Wright's later career, emphasizing his theme of the psychological effects of white supremacy on blacks.

249 Picon, Gaëtan. "Les romans." *Confluences* (April 1945), pp. 314-21.
Contains a favorable mention of the publication of "Big Boy Leaves Home" by Richard Wright whose translation appeared in the underground magazine *L'Arbalète* .

250 Roy, Claude. "Air d'Amérique." *Les Lettres françaises* No. 27 (March 17, 1945), p. 3.
No mention is made of black literature as such but a note states that "Richard Wright... must henceforth be taken into account."

251 Senghor, Léopold Sédar. Introduction to "Trois poètes négro-américains: Countee Cullen, Jean Toomer, Langston Hughes." *Poésie 45* No. 23 (February 1945), p. 32-33.
Senghor made a point of translating poems by African Americans for a French-speaking audience. In his introduction to this selection, he stresses the energy and sense of rhythm of that poetry.   Song and poetry are said to be the same for the black man, rooted as they are in folk expression. Jupiter Hammond is mentioned as the first Negro

poet in the United States and Paul L. Dunbar as "the first poet of any stature." Among the New Negro poets are J.W. Johnson, Hughes, McKay, Cullen, F.M. Davis, and Richard Wright. Characterized by "fecund differences," this poetry is unsophisticated, full of rhythm and images, "the poetry of peasants who have not lost contact with telluric forces ..., the most human face of America."

252 Villard, Léonie. *La poésie américaine; trois siècles de poésie lyrique et de poèmes narratifs.* Paris: Bordas, 1945.
Chapter IV deals with "Emily Dickinson," "Humorous Poetry," and "Negro Spirituals." P.L. Dunbar and Cullen appear under the second heading after Oliver Wendell Holmes and Bret Harte. Dunbar renders "in exquisite and simple pieces the authentic voice of his people." He is best when writing in dialect (p. 82). Cullen sings in "language of impeccable and musical purity" the bitterness of the cultured man isolated by his color from other Americans (p. 89). Yet such poets are but a small portion of the immense contribution represented by the blues and spirituals.

253 Zizine, Pierre. *La vie prodigieuse de Booker T. Washington.* Paris: Imprimerie Pourtout, n.d. [1945 ?]
A 16-page sketch of "a slave, college teacher, and the founder of the most important black university in the world" written by a French West Indian.

1946

254 Astre, Georges-Albert. "Un grand romancier noir: Richard Wright." *Fraternité* (October 10, 1946), p. 3.
Examines *Native Son* in the context of Wright's career and thought. Wright is an important spokesman but he is also a brilliant literary artist at the height of his career.

255 Balthazar, Albert. "L'évolution de l'âme nègre. Un grand romancier: Richard Wright." *L'Occident* (August 10-11, 1946).
Places Wright in the American literary tradition as a major writer and analyzes *Native Son*. Wright is a great artist, comparable to Dostoevsky, Tolstoy and Albrecht Dürer.

256 Beaufils, Marcel. Introduction to his *Christ noir*. Lausanne, Abbaye du Livre, 1946.

A one-page introduction characterizes much of black poetry as an attempt to "sing one's pain in orphic chants, deep like the very stuff of the world is made of" (p. 7). It digs up gold from the Harlem underworld and testifies to "a fateful and messianic loneliness exorcized by the jazz rhythms of Duke Ellington." Beaufils' poems are free adaptations of spirituals, blues and poetry by Joseph Cotter, Countee Cullen, Georgia Douglas Johnson, Otto Leland Bohannan, Langston Hughes, Claude McKay, Jean Toomer, and Waring Cuney.

257 Coindreau, Maurice-Edgar. *Aperçus de littérature américaine.* Paris: Gallimard, 1946.

In the chapter on "Alcoholic Novels," Wright's *Native Son* is analyzed (along with novels by Hemingway and John O'Hara) as a plea against the capitalist system and in favor of the disinherited. The author of *Native Son* has been compared to Dreiser and Dostoevsky, but "time will reduce such dithyrambs to more accurate proportions." Less clever than Erskine Caldwell in *Trouble in July*, Wright ascribes Bigger's murder to fear. His books belong to the great family of social and sentimental tracts; the propaganda is naive and primary.

258 Delpech, Jeanine. "Un romancier noir à Paris." *Les Nouvelles littéraires* 24 (May 23, 1946), p. 6.

Interview with Wright centering on the melodramatic but not exaggerated realism of his books, the reactions of the American audience, his racial and social commitment, his favorite forms of recreation and jive trends in jazz.

259 Escoube, Lucienne. " 'Aucun film n'a jamais dépeint la vie des noirs dans les villes américaines', nous dit le romancier Richard Wright." *L'Ecran français* (November 19, 1946), p. 12.

Interview with Wright who talks about censorship in America, pointing out that it is to be felt in the movies more than on Broadway or in print. He describes Americans as the unhappiest people on earth because easy material life does not compensate for lack of balance and spiritual zest. Americans know what to do in a time of crisis, but they are depressed after victory.

260 Fleurent, Maurice. "Richard Wright à Paris." *Paru* No. 25 (December 1946), pp. 7-8.

Interview with Wright who comments on his early career, the French publication of his short stories, and the coming translation of *Black Boy*.   Wright mentions Cullen, McKay and Hughes, and lists Gide and Malraux among his favorite French authors.

261 Gautier, Madeleine. "Blues." *Poésie 46* No. 31 (April, 1946), p. 53.
An introduction to a selection of five blues songs. These anonymous poems are assuredly poetic "due to the light-heartedness, the creative heedlessness which led the words to alight here and there on the page without any attention to the form."

262 Gordey, Michel. "L'écrivain Richard Wright nous parle des nègres d'Amérique." *Les Etoiles* (October 22, 1946).
Interview with Wright dealing mostly with his experiences and his opinions on the racial question in the United States, as treated in his own fiction and as a current issue.

263 Guerre, Pierre. "Le Sang noir." *Les Cahiers du Sud* No. 279 (2nd semester 1946), pp. 179-82.
An introduction to poems and songs from Africa and the Americas and African folk tales. Considers the American part of "the black body" through which the blood of the black diaspora flows. Translations of Negro spirituals, extracts from Zora Neale Hurston's *Jonah's Gourd Vine*, popular songs, blues by Josh White, poems by Hughes, Waring Cuney, Paul L. Dunbar, F.M. Davis and Sterling Brown are printed.

264 Guth, Paul. "L'interview de Paul Guth: Richard Wright." *La Gazette des lettres* No. 20 (September 14, 1946), pp. 1-2.
Wright speaks mainly of his childhood and youth, with some comments on his work habits in Paris. Guth emphasizes Wright's difficulties in speaking French.

265 Merceron, Jacques. "Richard Wright rencontre à Paris le premier metteur en scène qui s'intérese à son oeuvre." *Libération* (December 18, 1946), p. 2.
Interview with Wright, whom Merceron considers both one of the best American writers and a spokesman for his race. Wright speaks of his literary beginnings, his influence in America, the warm reception given him by French writers, and Roberto Rossellini's intention of making a film of *Native Son*.

266 Nadeau, Maurice. " 'Pas de problème noir aux U.S.A., mais un problème blanc', nous dit l'écrivain Richard Wright à son arrivée à Paris." *Combat* (May 11, 1946), p. 1.
Interview with Wright surveying his life and commitment and giving his early impressions of France.

267 Oulmont, Charles. "La vie étrangère en France: un Américain découvre l'Ancien Monde." *Le Spectateur* (July 2, 1946).
Interview with Wright who calls Europe, which represents culture, the New World, and America, which represents material civilization, the Old World.

268 Papo, Alfredo. "Jazz et littérature." *Jazz hot* 12, 4 (April 1946), p.9.
Starting with examples drawn from popular blues songs, the reviewer moves on to the spirituals and, "quite naturally" to black poetry. Langston Hughes is said to be the greatest poet while Claude McKay and Richard Wright vie for first rank as novelists. White writers have misunderstood the Negro, including even Carl Van Vechten and Sherwood Anderson who were afraid to go to the heart of "black laughter." McKay's best books are *Home to Harlem* and *Gingertown*. The former, a series of hardly related sketches, is deprived of tenderness for the black man who wants to escape ghetto life. The short stories in the latter evoke the Southern atmosphere with the ever-preent shadow of white oppression, and the difficulties arising from mixed ancestry in "Near White" or "Brownskin Blues." Such writing is "not philosophical but simple, fresh, unpretentious and full of life." Wright's *Native Son* is a bitter, desperately somber book. It should be known that "jazz and poetry properly constitute the message of the American Negro."

269 R., S. "Quelques livres: *Les Grandes Profondeurs; Histoires de blancs*." *Poésie 46* No. 39 (December 1946), pp. 142-44.
This review of *The Big Sea* and *Not without Laughter* by Langston Hughes stresses their value as testimonies to the depths of Negro life and the stereotypes about it. It is written after the fashion of Jacques Prévert's poem "Inventory" and the reviewer puns on that notion, contrasting discordant aspects of American society from ghettoes to jazz, brass spitoons to lynchings in order to celebrate the variety of black resilience.

270 Ruspoli, Mario. "Avant-propos." In his *Blues, poésie de*

l'Amérique noire. Paris: Les Publications techniques et artistiques, 1946. Pp. 9-23.

Analysis of the blues as "the epic of black America" originating in Africa but dealing with specific themes of oppression and suffering. Mentions Erskine Caldwell and the New Orleans Setting, and scores of blues singers; praises the "poetry of a simple-hearted race, close to nature and to God." Fifty blues follow in translation.

271 Stane, Frédéric. "Avec Richard Wright, romancier noir de la terreur 'sous-jacente'." *Gavroche* (June 20, 1946), p. 5.

Interview with Wright who conveys his negative reactions to postwar developments in race relations in the United States. Wright also discusses the state of French culture, particularly as it parallels his own existential position. He names André Gide's *Voyage to the Congo* as his favorite French book. He also speaks about *Native Son*.

272 Tardon, Raphaël. "Richard Wright nous dit le problème blanc aux U.S.A." *Action* (October 1946), pp. 10-11.

Lengthy interview ranging over Wright's opinions on the political, psychological, economic, religious and social consequences of white racism directed against Blacks in America. Wright also touches on racism in Europe.

1947

273 A., J. "Le Livre du jour: *Un Enfant du pays* par Richard Wright." *Ce Matin* (August 1, 1947).

Favorable review of *Native Son*. It is not only a crime story, but "an anguished drama, a psychological novel, an essay on the black soul, and an anti- racist document."

274 Adam, Georges. "Les livres du mois." *La Petite Illustration* (May 1947), p. 2.

Briefly reviews Faulkner's *Light in August*, mentions Erskine Caldwell and the forthcoming publication in France of Wright's *Black Boy* and *Uncle Tom's Children*, which will place him among "writers of international scope." Hughes's *The Ways of White Folks* is admirable and makes him a heir to Maupassant and Tchekhov; the translation is not on par with Hughes's "pure, direct, and sober style."

275 Altman, Georges. "A travers tous les barreaux." *Franc-Tireur* (August 9, 1947), p. 2.
Contains a favorable review with plot summary of *Native Son*. If Wright seems hopeless and merciless in his assessment of the racist situation, the fault lies with those whites responsible for creating the problem.

276 Anon. "Les Livres: Richard Wright, *Un Enfant du pays.*" *L'Echo de Normandie* (November 18, 1947).
Contains a favorable notice of *Native Son* summarizing the plot and emphasizing the realism and the militancy of its heroes.

277 Anon. "Livres: *Un Enfant du pays* par Richard Wright." *Mercure de France* Vol. 301(October 1, 1947), p. 346.
Favorable notice of *Native Son* summarizing the plot and hailing the novel as a remarkable achievement on all counts.

278 Anon. "*Les Enfants de l'oncle Tom,* par Richard Wright." Bourges *Le Berri républicain* (November 18, 1947).
Favorable notice of *Uncle Tom's Children* emphasizing the theme of black resistance and citing the examples of Reverend Taylor and Silas.

279 Anon. "Les Livres." Rouen *L'Écho de Normandie* (November 18, 1947).
Contains a favorable notice of *Uncle Tom's Children* emphasizing its realism and the courage of its protagonists.

280 Anon. "Livres: *Un Enfant du pays*, par R. Wright." *Mercure de France* (October 1, 1947), p. 346.
Favorable notice of *Native Son* summarizing the plot and hailing the novel as a remarkable achievement on all counts.

281 Anon. "Mais ne lisez pas: *Un Enfant du pays*, par Richard Wright." *La Vache enragée* (August 20, 1947).
Unfavorable notice of *Native Son* calling it pro-Communist propaganda, not a novel.

282 Anon. "Noirs et blancs aux Etats-Unis." *La Terre* (September

4, 1947).
Favorable review, with a plot summary, of the translation of
Wright's *Native Son*. The third part is too propagandistic, but the
novel nevertheless has great value both as a social document and an
artistic creation.

283 Anon. "On publie *Un Enfant du pays*." *La Presse* (August 12,
1947).
Favorable notice of the translation of Wright's *Native Son*, a
"powerful and passionate" novel.

284 Anon. "Richard Wright: *Les Enfants de l'oncle Tom*." *La
Gazette de Lausanne* (December 5, 1947), p. 3.
Favorable review of *Uncle Tom's Children* placing it in the great
tradition of the American short story. The heroes of Wright's stories
are in the militant vein of Nat Turner, Sojourner Truth, Denmark
Vesey, and Frederick Douglass.

285 Anon. "Tout Paris le dit. *Une Semaine dans le monde*
(January 4, 1947).
Notes that Richard Wright and Langston Hughes are the two writers
most responsible for the increasing importance of black literature.
They both concentrate on "satirizing" white attitudes and protesting
abuses. Wright is more tragic in his approach.

286 Anon. "*Un Enfant du pays* par Richard Wright." Bourges *Le
Berri républicain*; (July 25, 1947).
Favorable review of *Native Son* by "a European puzzled by
American racism." Notes the novel's cinematic narrative technique
and its power of analysis.

287 Anon. "*Un Enfant du pays* par Richard Wright." *L'Avenir de
Cannes et du Sud-Est* (June 22-23, 1947).
Favorable review of the translation of *Native Son* that stresses the
novel's power and violence. It is both an exciting crime story and a
penetrating analysis of racial psychology. As no other book has
done, it reveals the racial situation in the cities of the United States.

288 Astre, Georges-Albert "Sur le roman américain." *Critique* No.2
(March 1947), p. 278-280.
Mostly a survey of the career of Langston Hughes, who remains the

"greatest Negro poet," but is also the author of *Sandy*; his sense of rhythm and use of jazz go along with humor and an informed perspective on the plight of black people in the capitalistic United States. Mentions Wright as a recently recognized black novelist.

289   Bauër, Gérard. "Auteurs noirs: Richard Wright et René Maran." *Paris-Presse* (August 10-11, 1947).
Comments on Wright's fame and stature in American literature. Called a "black Dostoevsky," he ranks with Hemingway and Faulkner.

290   Bauër, Gérard. "Une littérature noire: Richard Wright et René Maran." Brussels *La Lanterne* (August 19, 1947).
Nearly duplicates his August 10, 1947 review in *Paris-Presse*. General article on black literature, mainly in America. Wright is foremost, a genuinely talented writer though not quite a Dostoevsky. He has great power and intensity.

291   Blanzat, Jean. "Les romans de la semaine: *Un Enfant du pays* de Richard Wright." *Le Figaro littéraire* (July 5, 1947), p. 5.
Somewhat favorable review of *Native Son*. Plot summary and comments on racial problems in the United States. Blanzat finds a number of scenes in the novel unnecessarily melodramatic and lurid. He objects to the melodramatic quality of certain episodes.

292   Bokanowski, Héléne. "Carson MacCullers et le roman métaphysique." *L'Arche* (May 27, 1947), pp. 155-58.
This friend and translator of Wright discusses *Native Son* in her essay on McCullers, claiming that the novel in fact has some comic elements indeed (p. 155).

293   Brodin, Pierre. *Ecrivains américains du vingtième siècle*. Paris: Horizons de France, 1947.
Includes a chapter on Richard Wright (pp. 165-72) sketching his life and discussing his early works in the American tradition of brutal realism. His style is direct and powerful. His message is an indictment of racism.

294   C., J. "Wright (Richard): *Les Enfants de l'oncle Tom*." *J'ai lu* No. 11 (November 1947), pp. 50-51.
Favorable notice of *Uncle Tom's Children* commenting on Wright's

ability to dramatize racial injustice in varied and striking images and plots.

295 D.[ebidour], V.[ictor]-H.[enri]. "Richard Wright: *Les Enfants de l'oncle Tom.*" Lyon *Le Bulletin des lettres* 9 (December 15, 1947), pp. 285-286.
Favorable review of *Uncle Tom's Children* focusing on "Big Boy Leaves Home" but also exploring briefly other stories. The review emphasizes Wright's style--forceful, searching, but too lurid at times. The stories are seen in a more general context of growing into manhood and initiation.

296 D.[ebidour], V.[ictor]-H.[enri]. "Richard Wright - *Un Enfant du pays.*" Lyon *Le Bulletin des lettres* 9 (July 15, 1947), p. 139.
Favorable review of *Native Son* comparing it to *Crime and Punishment*. It is remarkable for its psychological and social analysis. If it is as true as it seems, America should be ashamed and afraid. Debidour finds Wright's style somewhat faulty --wooden at times, too extreme, and occasionally repetitious.

297 D.[umay], R.[aymond]. "Wright (Richard): *Un Enfant du pays.*" *La Gazette des lettres*, 3 (August 23, 1947), p. 10.
Favorable review of *Native Son* stressing the psychological reaction of Bigger to the fear instilled in him by the white power structure. Quotes from the novel at random, including a long extract from the death scene of Mary Dalton.

298 Doyelle, Henri. "La condition noire." Lille *Nord-Eclair* (October 4, 1947).
Favorable review of *Native Son* with references to *Uncle Tom's Children* and *Black Boy*. Wright's subject is of great topical interest, but his literary merit is evident.

299 Du Passage, Henri. "Richard Wright -- *Un Enfant du pays.*" *Etudes* No. 255 (October 1947), p. 140.
Review of *Native Son* with a plot summary. Praises Wright's approach to the racial problem, but notes several flaws in technique and style: Bigger seems too articulate at the end; detail is sometimes excessive; the violence is overdone. Nevertheless, "the problem remains fully posed, with all its complex data whose cruel actuality and permanence are felt throughout the novel."

300 Fauchery, Pierre. "Comment peut-on être nègre?" *L'Action* (July 25, 1947), p. 11.
Favorable review of *Native Son* comparing Wright to Dostoevsky in his ability to penetrate the consciousness of a killer. Fauchery considers Boris Max too theoretical and awkward in developing Wright's message.

301 G., R. "Wright (Richard): *Un Enfant du pays.*" *J'ai lu* Nos. 8-9 (August-September 1947), p. 71-72.
Favorable review of *Native Son* noting that Bigger's plight is symbolic of his people's. Perhaps the third book is too explicit and systematic, but the earlier narrative is gripping in its intensely realized violence.

302 Gallois, Auguste. "Les hommes et les livres." *Le Peuple* (October 18, 1947), p. 5.
A joint review of the French translations of *Uncle Tom's Children* and *Tobacco Road*, finding them very similar in deriving a certain poetry from Southern degradation and social injustice. Wright is a better artist than Caldwell.

303 Gautier, Madeleine. "Un romancier de la race noire: Richard Wright." *Présence africaine* No. 1 (October-November 1947), pp. 163-65.
Favorable review of *Native Son*. As a racial spokesman, Wright goes to the heart of the social problem of racism. He projects Bigger as a racial symbol in order to punish the whites. Whites in the novel are dehumanized and mechanized in contrast to the vital blacks. The scene in Mary Dalton's bedroom is crucial. Throughout, Wright's analysis of the frightening psychological dimension of the racial problem is a remarkable achievement. Gautier wonders how such a country as the United States is going to achieve unity.

304 Gével, Claude. "Romans: *Les Enfants de l'oncle Tom.*" *Les Nouvelles littéraires* 25 (October 23, 1947), p. 3.
Favorable review of *Uncle Tom's Children* considering the work as a novel rather than as a collection of disparate tales. Wright's stories all treat racial injustice and sexual taboo. Gével prefers "Long Black Song" to the other stories for its balance and treatment.

305 Gordey, Michel. "Une Interview de l'écrivain Richard Wright: L'Amérique n'est pas le nouveau monde." *Les Lettres françaises*

(January 10, 1947), pp. 1, 7.
Interview with Wright in his Paris apartment shortly before his return to the United States. He comments on his favorable reception in France, compares the humanism of French life with the materialism of American life, expresses admiration for Sartre's *The Respectful Prostitute*, and discusses postwar life in France and French colonial problems. Gordey ranks Wright among the five or six greatest living American writers.

306 Guérard, Albert-J. Introduction, in his *Prosateurs américains du XXe siécle*. Paris: Robert Laffont, 1947. Pp. 7-34.
Mentions Wright as a radical writer and a naturalist (p. 19-30), and lists him along with nine others in a group of important American novelists in their thirties (p. 26).

307 Guilleminault, Gilbert. "Au pays de Jim le Corbeau." Paris *La Bataille* (December 31, 1947), p. 4.
Contains a favorable review of *Black Boy* praising Wright's artistic achievement and his honest presentation of racial suffering in the South. Credits Martha Foley with discovering Wright.

308 Guyot, Charly. "Un problème irritant: Noirs d'Amérique." *La Tribune de Genève* (February 7, 1947).
A discussion on the racial question in the U.S. enters into cultural considerations: the film "Hallelujah" is mentioned among a spate of novels by white Americans; the author concludes on Wright's *Black Boy* and *Native Son*, books "full of persuasion and authenticity," and ends with a review of *Black Metropolis* by St. Clair Drake and Horace Cayton.

309 Hesse, Jean-Albert. "Les livres et les hommes: L'oncle Tom n'existe plus." *Franc-Tireur* (November 25, 1947).
Favorable review of *Uncle Tom's Children* stressing the racial and social problems raised. Wright is acclaimed for the power and representativeness of his writing.

310 Howlett, Jacques. "Les Revues." *Présence africaine* No. 2 (December 1947), p. 353-55.
Among other things, the reviewer responds to the attacks directed against Wright, as the representative of "a certain type of black American literature" by Communist critics in *Poésie 47*, No. 41. Also discusses the U.S. Communist magazine *Mainstream* and its

attacks on Wright. Notes that the CPUSA prefers the characters Johnny Boy and Sue to Bigger as representative black heroes.

311 Jamati, P.[ierre] "Les Revues." *Europe*, 15 (March 1947), p. 117.
Cites a brief excerpt from "Early Days in Chicago" by Richard Wright, published in *Les Temps modernes*.

312 Kanapa, Jean. "Petite anthologies des revues americaines." *Poésie 47* No. 41 (November 1947), p. 115-133.
Examines Wright's relation to *Les Temps modernes*, concluding that the magazine approves him because he is a despondent mystifier. Despite his talent, Wright no longer serves the cause of black people. Quotes frequently from an article by Theodore Ward in *Mainstream*.

313 Lalou, René. "Le Livre de la semaine: *Un Enfant du Pays*, par Richard Wright." *Les Nouvelles littéraires* 25 (July 17, 1947), p. 3.
Favorable review of *Native Son* with a detailed analysis stressing the work's exemplarity.

314 Le Breton, Maurice. "Une jeune génération de romanciers américains." *France-Amérique* Nos. 25-30 (1947-1949), pp. 571-74.
Mentions Caldwell, Farrell and Wright as using realistic settings.

315 Le Hardouin, Maria. "Richard Wright parmi les siens." *Combat* (July 11, 1947), p. 2.
Interview with Wright in New York discussing existentialism and the American character. Wright looks forward to returning to France.

316 Loewel, P.[ierre] "La vie des lettres: Du côté de chez l'oncle Sam." Paris *L'Aurore* (August 1, 1947), p. 2.
Mixed review of *Native Son* with a plot summary. Loewel praises the novel for its power, but notes its lurid exaggeration. He admits the psychological effects of racism depicted by Wright, but resents their depiction.

317 Loisy, Jean. "Un homme, un écrivain: Richard Wright." *Ici France* (October 17, 1947), p. 10.
Favorable review of *Native Son* with a long description of the salient episodes and characters. Wright's achievement in this novel is

remarkable.

318 M., L. *"Blues, poésies de l'Amérique noire."* *Les Lettres françaises* No. 156 (May 16, 1947), p. 4.
Brief, descriptive and favorable review of *Blues*, a collection of blues songs in translation published in 1946. The genre accurately reflects and most powerfully expresses the yearnings and joys of the African American soul.

319 Magny, Claude-Edmonde. "Richard Wright ou l'univers n'est pas noir." *Une Semaine dans le monde* (August 30, 1947), p. 8.
This major review discusses Wright's work, especially *Uncle Tom's Children, Native Son,* and *Black Boy.* More than documentaries on the racial problem, they are depictions of the condition of modern man as an innocent murderer. In Wright's fiction, violence and crime, however sensational they seem, assume a metaphoric value. The complex impartiality of Wright's vision leads him to see Bigger as an anti-hero, a distorted product of white society, but *Native Son* can be read as a palimpsest, with a black perspective under the white perspective. Magny compares *Native Son* to Kafka's *The Castle* and Graham Greene's *Brighton Rock*, other novels with innocent criminals as protagonists. Wright may be read in either a racial or universal context. His power stems from his control of the "concrete universal."

320 Magny, Claude-Edmonde. "Témoignages américains." *Une Semaine dans le monde* (May 17, 1947), p. 11.
Quotes from "Early Days in Chicago" and comments on Wright's racial testimony.

321 Molbert, Suzanne. "Noirs et blancs." *L'Arche* No. 23 (February 1947), pp. 146-47.
Review of *The Ways of White Folks*. Hughes's short stories provides a deep insight into the psychological conditioning of black Americans and white attitudes toward them. American racism is condemned --"it is in Paris that a young Black can discover an atmosphere of freedom."

322 Morel, Henriette. "'Ce qui m'a amené à tuer, c'est ça que je suis." Paris *Ce Matin* (August 2, 1947).
Favorable review of *Native Son* comparing it to Greek tragedy. Morel analyzes at length the liberating effect of Bigger's killing of

Mary in existential terms.

323 Nadeau, Maurice. "Un Enfant d'Amérique." *Combat* (July 11, 1947), p. 2.
Highly favorable review of *Native Son*. Wright treats the American racial situation, but his powerful genius transcends national and ethnic categories. He uses the effects of shock and horror to force the reader to confront truth, especially the truth of murder as a regenerative force for a social victim. Nadeau compares Wright to Kafka, Tolstoy, and, especially, Racine.

324 P., J. "Les Livres: *Un Enfant du pays.*" *Libération* (September 7-8, 1947), p. 2.
A rather unfavorable review of *Native Son*. Wright brings little that is new to the racial issue. The form of the novel often tends to the lurid and melodramatic.

325 P., J. "*Un Enfant du pays* par Richard Wright." *Le Courrier de Bayonne* (November 22-23, 1947).
Highly favorable review of *Native Son* praising the novel for its important racial and social message and for its high literary art. It has the excitement of a crime story, the power of great art, and a deep knowledge of the human heart.

326 P., O. "Richard Wright: *Un Enfant du pays.*" *Réforme* (December 13, 1947), p. 4.
Favorable notice of *Native Son* with a brief plot summary. Praises Wright's honesty and literary gifts.

327 P., P-M. "Au hasard des lettres: *Un Enfant du pays* de Richard Wright." *Lyon libre* (August 12, 1947).
Review of *Native Son* consisting mostly of plot summary.

328 Paz, Magdeleine. "*Un Enfant du pays* par Richard Wright." *Paru* No. 34 (September, 1947), pp. 44-47.
Favorable review of *Native Son*. Paz, a militant anti-racist, focuses on the racial issue, but also considers the motives and fears of the protagonist, stresses the importance of Wright's indictment of American capitalism, and concludes with attention to technical and formal aspects of the novel.

329 Rabaud, Jean. "Un grand écrivain noir: Richard Wright." *Le Populaire de Paris* (July 16, 1947), p. 2.
Favorable review of the translation of *Native Son* with biographical background. Although he has a tendency to explain too much, Wright demonstrates a narrative talent that makes this thesis novel an artistic success. Wright deserves his renown. Rabaud compares him to James M. Cain and Faulkner.

330 Rousseaux, André. "Les Livres." *France-Illustration* Nos. 104-106 (October 11, 1947), p. 321.
Generally favorable review of the translation of *Native Son*. The scope of the novel is impressive, but the thesis is pressed too insistently.   Rousseaux admires the depiction of fear and the rendering of the inferiority complex in Bigger, as well as the fundamental truth and rigorous accuracy in Wright's delineation of the interracial attitudes in which fear prevails.

331 Saint-Hély, Marc. "Littérature étrangère: Peaux noires." *Rolet* (October 30, 1947).
Favorable review of *Native Son*. Viewing it mainly as a statement against racism, the author considers the last book of the three the most important. A work of exceptional power and wide distribution, it may, Saint-Hély hopes, help to ameliorate the racial situation.

332 Sartre, Jean-Paul. "Qu'est-ce que la littérature?" *Les Temps modernes* No. 2 (March 1947), pp. 961-88.
Using *Black Boy* as his primary example, Sartre argues that Wright addresses two audiences and employs two strategies simultaneously. For blacks he provides an emotional focus, for whites an intellectual argument (pp. 968-69). Repr. in his volume *Qu'est-ce que la littérature?*

333 Sorel, Jean-Jacques. "Richard Wright: *Un Enfant du pays*." *La Nef* No. 33 (August 1947), pp. 148-49.
Highly favorable and detailed review of *Native Son* praising the book as a social testament and as a literary masterpiece. Recognizing the centrality of violence in human life, Wright places American society on trial. Bigger is presented with completely authentic realism. Sorel compares Wright to Dostoevsky. He adds "Albert Camus' *The Plague* is nearly indecent when compared with such a book. On one side, abjection is ignored, which allows one to make a pact with it; on the other, one tries obstinately to become conscious

of reality, which entails revolt. On one side, an ethical perspective, on the other, life itself. The abyss which separates seeing from understanding." This is a "literary event of the magnitude of surrealism and Jean Genet." The rhythm is breathtaking yet the climaxes in the book are moments of meditation.

334 Stephen, S. "*Les Enfants de l'oncle Tom*, par Richard Wright." *Noir et blanc* (circa November 12, 1947).
Favorable review of the translation of *Uncle Tom's Children* emphasizing the themes of flight and revolt.

335 Stephen, S. "*Un Enfant du pays*, par Richard Wright." *Noir et blanc* No. 3 (August 6, 1947), p. 510.
Favorable review of the translation of *Native Son* praising the novel for its literary skill and its social message. Few writers can excel Wright in depicting horror. Includes a plot summary.

336 T., C. "Romans." *Les Lettres françaises* (August 8, 1947), p. 5.
Favorable review of the translation of *Native Son* stressing its social relevance. Bigger is essentially an antipathetic character, perhaps excessively so, but the novel has both poignance and grandeur.

337 Theis, Edouard. "Un grand écrivain noir américain, Richard Wright." *Christianisme social* No. 55 (January-February 1947), pp. 57-63.
General estimate of Wright's work, particularly *Black Boy* and *Native Son*. Notes Wright's rejection of the religion of the churches, both in his books and in remarks to Theis because it does not help blacks. Kierkegaardian religion is more appealing, however. As a man as a writer, Wright is characterized by his sincerity and commitment to truth and justice.

338 Thiébaut, Marcel. "Parmi les livres." *La Revue de Paris* No. 54 (October 1947), pp. 162-63.
Unfavorable review of the translation of *Native Son*, seen as a clumsy apology for crime and communism. Thiébaut strongly criticizes Wright for attempting to present Bigger, who is a "downright bad boy" as "a kind of black Christ." Bigger's crimes can be explained neither by his psychological complexes nor by white oppression. The novel has some value as a detective story, however.

339 Thomas, Edith. "Un Enfant d'Amérique." *La Marseillaise* (July 23-29, 1947).
Review of the translation of *Native Son* analyzing Bigger's plight and stressing its representative value.

340 Trédant, Paul. "Vie sociale et littéraire en Amerique." *Les Nouvelles littéraires* No. 1016 (January 23, 1947), pp. 1- 6.
The author emphasizes current fraternity among Black writers and their white colleagues, who all own Richard Wright's and Langston Hughes's works.

1948

341 Algren, Nelson. "Du rire en bocaux: Reportage de Chicago." *Les Temps modernes* 3 (January 1948), pp. 1301-07.
Contains a comparison of *Native Son* and Willard Motley's *Knock on Any Door*. Wright's book is profound and creative; Motley's is superficial and journalistic (pp. 1303-04).

342 Altman, Georges. "Nostalgie d'un monde plus libre." *Franc-Tireur* (October 27, 1948).
Brief comparison of Ann Petry's *The Street* to Wright's works.

343 Anon. "Une conférence de Richard Wright." *Le Figaro littéraire* No. 98 (March 6, 1948), p. 5.
Announcement for Wright's lecture on Black poetry in the United States, sponsored by the Club Maintenant in Paris, on March 11, 1948.

344 Anon. "*Black Boy* par Richard Wright." *Libération* (February 25, 1948), p. 2.
Very favorable notice of the autobiography in translation.

345 Anon. "*Les Enfants de l'oncle Tom* par R. Wright." *Mercure de France* (January 1, 1948), pp. 151-52.
Notice of *Uncle Tom's Children* emphasizing the theme of black revolt. The book is powerful, and well-written, but less important than *Native Son*.

346 Anon. "*Les Enfants de l'oncle Tom* par Richard Wright, traduit de l'américain par Marcel Duhamel." *L'Afrique* (January 1948), pp.

31-32.
Favorable review of *Uncle Tom's Children* taking up some crucial episodes in the stories, especially in "Big Boy Leaves Home," and praising Wright's role of spokesman for oppressed blacks and his ability as a creator of vivid, swift-moving fiction.

347 Anon. "Les Livres étrangers: Noir sur noir." *Carrefour* (April 28, 1948), p. 8.
Favorable review of *Black Boy*, which analyzes American racism, and *Native Son*, which provides an example. In *Black Boy*, the protagonist achieves heroic status in rejecting his racial role. In *Native Son*, Wright excels in depicting instinctive man.

348 Anon. "Quelques idées, quelques livres. Noirs et blancs: Richard Wright: *Black Boy*." Lille *La Voix du Nord* (May 29, 1948).
Favorable review noting the relation between *Black Boy* and *Native Son*. Wright's psychological insight in depicting black anxiety in a world dominated by whites is worthy of Kafka.

349 Anon. "Richard Wright, *Un Enfant du pays*." *Les Fiches littéraires* No. 2, fiche 22 (March 1948), p. 2.
After noting French interest in Wright and summarizing the plot of *Native Son*, this article reviews criticism of the novel by G.-A. Astre, Jean-Jacques Sorel, André Rousseaux, Marcel Thiebaut, and Henri du Passage. The major categories concern the racial theme, the question of realism vs. propaganda, and style.

350 Anon. "Trois livres de Richard Wright." *Aux Ecoutes* (January 30, 1948).
Mentions the three works of Richard Wright available in French [*Native Son, Black Boy* and *Uncle Tom's Children*], citing their relevance to the racial problem and their Faulknerian and Kafkaesque qualities.

351 Anon. "Wright (Richard)." In *Nouveau Larousse universel*. Paris: Librairie Larousse, 1948. Vol 2, p. 1074.
Biographical notice.

352 Baufrère, Marcel. "Un fils de l'oncle Tom juge Richard Wright." *Confrontation internationale* No. 2 (May-June 1948), pp.

54-55.
Interview with an unnamed young African who praises Wright but
considers him to belong to a transitional generation between *Uncle
Tom Cabin* and *Uncle Tom's Children*. *Native Son* is an excellent
analysis of black-white relations, applicable to Africa as well as
America.

353 Beauvoir, Simone de. *L'Amérique au jour le jour*. Paris:
Gallimard, 1948 .
Mentions a few literary events she shared with Richard Wright in
New York and his acting as a host to show her aspects of Harlem
life.

354 Bercher, Marie-Louise. "Le moi est haïssable." Mulhouse
L'Alsace (November 21, 1948).
Refers to Simone de Beauvoir's analogy between the position of
French women and that of Bigger Thomas.

355 Berys, José de. "La vie littéraire - Le problème noir: *Bagarre de
Juillet*." Marseilles *Midi-Soir* (March 24, 1948).
Contrasting the treatment of lynching by Steinbeck, Caldwell, and
Wright, de Berys points out the latter's emotion and poignant horror
in "Big Boy Leaves Home."

356 Blanzat, Jean. "Les romans de la semaine: *De Sang royal* de
Sinclair Lewis et *La Rue* d'Ann Petry." *Le Figaro littéraire* (October
16, 1948), p. 4.
After reviewing *Kingsblood Royal*, the author analyzes the plot of
The Street, which sounds autobiographical but not new: it is the
rather banal story of a forsaken woman which happens to take place
in Harlem rather than in Belleville. The naturalistic style is if
somewhat clumsy; a well-meaning attempt to sing rebellion against a
sordid world.

357 Bouvier, Emile. "A l'Ouest, rien de nouveau." *Midi Libre*
(December 1, 1948), p. 6.
This essay on United States novels includes a review of *The Street*
by Ann Petry. It is "a creditable novel in the naturalistic style," not
without brutality. From the ideological angle, it constitutes an
eloquent plea for the disinherited of Harlem, "half-way between the
style of Dashiell Hammett or James M. Cain and that of Theodore
Dreiser."

358 Buenzod, Emmanuel. "Vues sur l'âme noire." *La Gazette de Lausanne* (February 7, 1948).
Reviews Erskine Caldwell's *Trouble in July* and *Black Boy*, giving more space and praise to Wright's novel. Like Gorky's autobiography, *Black Boy* compels the reader's confidence in its authenticity. Wright has literary gifts, intellectual insight, and great humanity.

359 Cestre, Charles. *Les Poètes américains*. Paris: Presses Universitaires de France, 1948.
Only in his conclusion does the professor at the Sorbonne, mention the names of a few black poets: "One would have to stop at the work of Negro poets, Paul Dunbar, James Weldon (sic), Fenton Johnson, Langston Hughes, Countée Cullen, Jean Toomer and Miss Weeden." (p. 223) The reader is referred to the frequent anthologies of poets of color, Catholic poets, student poets, etc.

360 Chabot, Solange. "Aux USA, la poésie est devenue une activité anti-américaine." *Les Lettres françaises* No. 227 (September 30, 1948), p. 3.
A propos of the publication of *Anthologie de la poésie américaine contemporaine* by Maurice Le Breton, the reviewer notes "The most original and authentic part in his uneven collection is the voice of a few Negro poets." Langston Hughes is well represented.

361 Chonez, Claudine. "De l'enfant noir à la libération de l'homme." *Présence africaine* No. 3 (March-April 1948), pp. 515-18.
Discusses *Black Boy, Uncle Tom's Children,* and *Native Son.* By analyzing in detail a number of episodes from Wright's youth, Chonez places his suffering in a perspective wider than race, concluding that his experience has universal value.

362 Fontaine, Pierre. "Nous avons lu *Black Boy* (Jeunesse noire) de Richard Wright." *L'Action sociale* (March 13, 1948), p. 4.
Favorable notice summarizing some of the important episodes and praising the authenticity of the work.

363 Howlett, J.[acques] "Richard Wright, romancier de la liberté." Dakar *L'A.O.F.* (May 16, 1948).
Favorable review of *Native Son.* Howlett considers the novel in international perspective and focuses on its depiction of the effects of

racism and repression on Bigger's personality.   Praises Wright's powerful writing and racial commitment.

364 Howlett, Jacques. "Notes sur Chester B. Himes et l'aliénation noire." *Présence africaine* No. 4 (2nd trimester 1948), pp. 697-704.
A laudatory review of Himes's *If He Hollers Let Him Go*, with emphasis on its social message: "Millions of alienated human beings bear witness to a world whose economic structures are outdated but still powerful, in which supposedly dead myths are still very much alive." Includes a comparison of *If He Hollers* and Wright's *Native Son*.

365 Humeau, Edmond.   "Le Courrier des lettres: Un Kanapiste découvre la double Amérique." *Arts et Spectacles* (February 13, 1948).
The author protests against Communist critic Jean Kanapa's "stupid" denigration of such American novelists such as Faulkner, Henry Miller, and Richard Wright in his *Lettres françaises* article. (q.v.) Wright was for a long time the leader of proletarian literature in the U.S. and neither Sandburg not Langston Hughes would brand *Black Boy* as the "work of a renegade."

366 Kanapa, Jean. "Il y a deux littératures américaines." *Les Lettres françaises* (February 5, 1948), p. 3.
Contains a paragraph of very adverse criticism of Wright as a saboteur of the struggle against racism. He promotes racial hatred. Langston Hughes is classified among the progressives.

367 Las Vergnas, Raymond. "Lettres Étrangéres: Variations sur un théme en noir et blanc." *Hommes et Monde* (December, 1948), pp. 692-96.
In a discussion of the racial problems in the U.S. as a literary theme, the reviewer contrasts *Kingsblood Royal* by Sinclair Lewis and *The Street* by Ann Petry. The story of Lutie Johnson, who attempts to shelter her son from the brutal, attractive streets of Harlem, shows that the novelist never questions the psychological equality of the Black American. "The merit of Ann Petry consists precisely in neglecting symbolism in order to reach humanity. The sobriety, density and life of her characters are extraordinary."

368 Le Breton, Maurice. Introduction to his *Anthologie de la poésie américaine contemporaine*. Paris: Denoël, 1948.

Among the "jazz age" poets, the blacks have adapted to the contemporary scene the poetry to be found in black folklore anthologies dealing with the South. Langston Hughes is the greatest American Negro poet and his directness renders the language and particular sensibilities of his race. Countee Cullen is too impregnated with white culture to be able to go back to the naivety and spontaneity of Hughes even in his self-conscious search for African ancestry. Cullen's "Heritage" and Hughes' "Brass Spittoons" and "Homesick Blues" are the only pieces by Negro poets included in the anthology (pp. 55-57).

369 Le Majeur [pseud.]. "*S'il braille, lache-le*, par Chester Himes." *Les Lettres françaises* (December 18, 1948).
The love-hate relationship between a black man and a white woman and the subsequent symbolic lynching of the protagonist in *If He Hollers* are of less interest than its depiction of the racial complexities of American labor. He is amused by the ironic humor of the character Bob Jones and that some of the action of the story takes place against the strange backdrop of an armored warship.

370 Lesdain, Pierre. "Richard Wright, *Black Boy*." *Volonté* (April 10, 1948).
Highly favorable Belgian review with many quotations from the autobiography. *Black Boy* is "a beautiful book, a great book, and ... a necessary book." Its chief themes are fear and hunger.

371 Lesdain, Pierre. "Richard Wright, *Un Enfant du pays*." *Volonté* (April 17, 1948).
Highly favorable Belgian review of *Native Son,* explaining how Wright's reading helped to elevate him from the circumstances of his youth, Lesdain compares Wright to Steinbeck and comments extensively on Native Son, giving a detailed plot summary. He notes the symbolic significance of the killing of the rat and of Mrs. Dalton's haunting presence.

372 Maynard, René. "Les Lettres et les arts: *Un Enfant de son* [sic] *pays* de Richard Wright. " Casablanca *Le Petit Marocain* (April 14, 1948).
Favorable review of *Native Son* focusing on its statement against racism. Maynard notes that Communists as well as Blacks suffer persecution from exploiters who resist efforts to create a humane society.

373 Mégret, Christian. "Les Livres: *Black Boy*, par Richard Wright." *Radio 47* (February 29-March 6, 1948).
After discussing the existence of racism in France, Mégret reviews *Black Boy* favorably as a statement against racism.

374 Mégret, Christian. "Les livres étrangers: Noir sur noir." *Carrefour* (April 28, 1948), p. 8.
Favorable assessment of *Black Boy*, which analyses American racism, and of *Native Son*, which provides an example of it. In the former book the protagonist achieves heroic status in rejecting his racial role. In the latter, Wright excels in depicting instinctive man.

375 Minne, Pierre. "Langston Hughes ou 'Le train de la liberté'." *Présence africaine* No. 2 (January 1948), pp. 340-42.
Minne believes that *"The Big Sea* retraces, after Claude McKay and before Richard Wright, a quest for freedom which is being pursued from country to country, from continent to continent..." Hughes's writings are the expression of mass conflicts as well as racial problems and these will only be solved when economic justice is established.

376 Morel, Henriette. "Un témoignage sur la haine: *Black Boy*." Paris *Ce Matin* (February 26, 1948).
Favorable review of the French translation. Morel praises Wright's effort to recreate not only the stages of his early growth, but the conditions of black life in the South as well.

377 Nadeau, Maurice. "La Chronique littéraire de *Gavroche*: La jeunesse d'un homme: *Black Boy*." *Gavroche* (February 4, 1948).
Highly favorable review with extensive summary. Transcending racial and national categories, *Black Boy* is a world masterpiece. Nadeau admires Wright's only apparently simple style and his artistic restraint.

378 Nadeau, Maurice. "Richard Wright, *Black Boy*." *Sélection du livre français* No. 3 (1948).
Favorable review praising Wright's ability to engage the reader, to make him feel the suffering of the protagonist and desire to struggle against the forces of oppression.

379 Orgeville, Gérard d'. "Noirs et nègres blancs." *La Voix du*

Nord (February 4, 1948), p. 2.
The review of *Les deux messieurs des Carolines*, a novel by Edouard Lavergne discusses "passing" and the racial problem in the United States . Wright is mentioned as a reference and quoted, claiming that "the gropings of blacks are those of mankind in general...since the Negro from the South to whom the North has given a helping hand can see that the whole world is prisoner to a deadly terror."

380 Palante, Alain. "Les Lettres: Richard Wright, *Les Enfants de l'oncle Tom; Un Enfant du pays*." *La France catholique* (February 13, 1948).
Favorable review of the French translations of *Uncle Tom's Children* and *Native Son* noting how Wright has clarified the American racial situation for Frenchmen. He has the talents of a storyteller and a philosopher. Palante observes, somewhat disapprovingly, an existential element in *Native Son*.. He thinks that, contrary to Wright's opinion, only the theological virtue of charity, not revolt, will ameliorate racial problems.

381 Panassié, Hughes. "Richard Wright, écrivain de race noire." *Les Cahiers du Sud* No. 289 (lst series, 1948), pp. 252-54.
The noted jazz critic provides a very favorable description of *Native Son* and *Black Boy* in his column, generally well-disposed toward Wright.

382 Paz, Magdeleine. "Romans: *La Caravane noire*." *Présence africaine* No. 4 (2nd trimester 1948), pp. 714-18.
Favorable review of the English version of *The Negro Caravan*, edited by Sterling Brown, Arthur Davis, and Ulysses Lee. This "admirable and invaluable anthology" makes clear the position of Afro-American writers: they are American writers and "the works by Negro writers should not be set under a special heading." The left-wing reviewer rejoices at such a perspective, requiring that "black" works be judged "according to the same human and artistic criteria as other works of art."

383 Rabaud, Jean. "*Présence africaine* et la montée des noirs d'Amerique et de l'Union française." *Le Populaire de Paris* (January 6, 1948), p. 2.
Article on *Présence africaine* discussing Wright and *Black Boy*. Compares him to Hemingway, Dos Passos, and Steinbeck; with

respect to style and the use of violence. Wright is more American than African.

384 Radine, Serge. "Roman américain: *Un Enfant du pays*." *Le Journal de Genève* (January 17-18, 1948), pp. 3-4.
Favorable review of the translation of *Native Son* placing it in the context of *La Putain respectueuse* by Sartre, *Strange Fruit* by Lilian Smith, and *Kingsblood Royal* by Sinclair Lewis. Wright indicts a racist society that produces criminals, but he also creates a novel with "a deep, durable, and universal significance."

385 Rougerie, R.J. "*Les Enfants de l'oncle Tom* par Richard Wright." *Présence africaine* No. 3 (March-April 1948), pp. 518-19.
Very favorable review of the translation of *Uncle Tom's Children*. Rougerie somewhat objects to Wright's use of black dialect, but otherwise his praise is high, especially for Wright's representation of black attitudes. The work is "more than a testimony--a prophetic cry."

386 Rousseaux, André. "Richard Wright et la terreur noire." *Le Figaro littéraire* (January 17, 1948), p. 2.
Analyzes Wright's works in terms of white-inspired fear and black anxiety. Rousseaux focuses on *Black Boy*, placing it in the context of the American literature of the period.

387 Rousselot, Jean. "Amérique-Russie-tradition." *L'Echo d'Oran* (November 13, 1948).
Briefly compares Wright's novels to Ann Petry's *The Street*.

388 Rousselot, Jean. Review of *Black Boy* by Richard Wright. *Le Libre Poitou* (January 21, 1948).
Favorable notice of the translation of *Black Boy* calling it effective both as a racial protest and as "a great and beautiful book, full of humanity and faith."

389 Roy, Claude. "La Poésie des blues." *Action* (March 24, 1948), p. 4.
In an essay analyzing the major themes and formal components of the blues, Ralph Ellison's definition of the blues is quoted from his "Richard Wright Blues" (*Antioch Review*, 1945). Blues and romance are both considered as living expressions of folklore,

"enriched and furthered by major writers," and Hughes,W.H. Auden and Carl Sandburg in the USA are equated with Federico Garcia Lorca and Manoel Altolaguirre in Spain.

390 Roy, Claude. "Pourquoi me tuez-vous?" *Europe* (July 31, 1948), p. 99-105.
Contains a short review of the translation of *Black Boy* critical of Rousseaux's opinion in *Le Figaro littéraire* that Wright's works overstep the limits of the racial problem.

391 Schmidt, Albert-Marie. "Rentrée des noirs dans la littérature française." *Réforme* (March 20, 1948), p. 7.
Contains a favorable review of *Black Boy* praising its universal appeal and calling it "one of the most important works of our time."

392 Tavernier, René. "Livres." *Le Progrés de Lyon* (June 7, 1948).
Contains a favorable review of the translation of *Uncle Tom's Children*. Wright denounces the plight of his race and calls for human dignity.

393 Thérive, André. "La vie des livres." *Paroles françaises* (January 16, 1948).
Contains a mixed review of the translation of Wright's *Black Boy* expressing interest in the subject but objecting to a few tediously pedantic passages.

394 Trédant, Paul. "De Brooklyn à Harlem--Lettre de New York." *Les Nouvelles littéraires* No. 1072 (March 18, 1948), p. 1-2.
This essay contains long allusions to Lorca's "Poeta en Nueva York" and of the poetry and personalities of Langston Hughes and Countee Cullen in relation to their Harlem setting.

395 Villemagne, François. "Qui est responsable du crime 'noir' en Amérique?" *Syndicalisme* (October 28, 1948).
Favorable review of *Native Son* along with a general account of the American racial situation. Villemagne emphasizes Wright's explanation that black fear induced by white racism leads to crime.

396 Watteau, Maurice. "Situations raciales et condition de l'homme dans l'oeuvre de J.-P. Sartre." *Présence africaine* No. 3 (1st

trimester 1948), pp. 405-17.
A study based upon the analysis of the works by Richard Wright in relationship with Sartre's own theories about racism and his views of Wright's position regarding the racial situation.

397 Zana, Jean. " 'Esthétique' et 'politique', ou quand Kanapa juge la littérature américaine". Tunis *Le Petit Matin* (February 29, 1948), p. 3.
The author disapproves of Kanapa's attacks against Henry Miller and Richard Wright as traitors to the proletariat in *Les Lettres françaises* (q.v.). They, as well as Dos Passos, Steinbeck, and others write out of "a common love for man."

1949

398 Anon. "Ann Petry, *La Rue*." *Mercure de France* No. 1026 (November 1, 1949), p. 354.
Brief mention of Ann Petry's *The Street*, considered to be "a fine novel which did not obtain the success it deserved."

399 Anon. "Les Livres." *Midi libre* (March 17, 1949), p. 8.
The author briefly mentions *If He Hollers...*, which he describes as a "pro-black and satirical novel of the most violent kind." He finds Himes's book reminiscent of the realism of Erskine Caldwell, full of erotic frenzy dramatically expressing the irreducibility of racial conflicts in America.

400 Anon. Notice on Langston Hughes. *Europe*, No. 38 (February 1949), p. 7.
A brief introduction to "the greatest black American poet," followed by his poem "La charrue de la liberté" ("Freedom's Plow"), pp. 7-12.

401 B., J.-C. "Chester Himes: *S'il braille, lache-le*." *La Nef* No. 50 (January 1949), p. 130.
The reviewer notes that, since the advent of Richard Wright, there has been a tendency among French writers to exploit the popularity of the protest novel. Himes' *If He Hollers* seems to be a way of exploiting the reader's interest in Wright. His art is mediocre although the plot is lively enough to make a good reading. However, there is some difference between the "black" novels of Frenchmen Yves Malartic [*Au pays du bon dieu*] and Boris Vian

[*J'irai cracher sur vos tombes*] on the one hand and Chester Himes on the other. The difference is Himes' authenticity, due to his personal experience as a black man. Although the experiences of the character Bob Jones do not seem very original or the writing particularly distinguished to the reviewer, the story is exciting.

402   De Jouvenel, Renaud.   "D'une bibliothéque américaine." *Europe* No. 39 (March 1949), pp. 108-15.
This essay on American literature is very adverse to the works of ex-Communist Richard Wright, who is dubbed a reactionary, while the reviewer praises two volumes by Langston Hughes, his novel *Not without Laughter* and *The Big Sea*.

403   Danoën, Emile.   "A bord d'un navire en construction, une blanche provoque un nègre dans l'espoir de le faire lyncher" (*S'il braille, lache-le*, roman de Chester Himes)." Brussels *Le Soir* (February 5, 1949).
Danoën provides a lengthy description of the climax of *If He Hollers* in order to explain how Himes uses his story to denounce racism. Himes' picture of organized labor enthralled the reviewer, and his description of the bustling navy yard lingered long after Danoën had finished reading the book.

404   Kanapa, Jean. "Deux romans sur la condition des Noirs aux USA." *La Nouvelle Critique* No. 3 (February 1949), pp. 74-77.
Rather negative review of *The Street* by Ann Petry and adverse review of Chester Himes's *If He Hollers* by a French C.P. "Kommissar." Petry has an undeniable and powerful talent but no political perspective; Himes's novel is unauthentic. In both novels, "the Richard Wright operation' is pursued, showing the Negro in an iron cage, emphasizing their despair and inability to revolt. Himes's protagonist is too close to Bigger Thomas; by forsaking realism, both novelists play into the hands of those who divide the working class.

405   Lauras, André.   "*La Rue* d'Ann Petry et *De Sang royal* de Sinclair Lewis." *Etudes* No. 260 (March 1949), p. 429.
Petry's *The Street* is found "hard and heart-breaking... with a cruel and authentic accent." Because of its sometimes unwieldy writing, it remains a testimony more than a novel. Sinclair Lewis's novel of miscegenation is said to be "a great novel, probably his best."

406 Lauras André. "Richard Wright--*Black Boy*." *Etudes* No. 260 (January 1949), p. 157.
Favorable review analyzing Wright's perspectives and literary art. Lauras finds the book to be "an authentic biography" and an "irrefutable piece of evidence" delivered "without passion but straightforwardly."

407 Lauras, André. "*S'il braille, lache-le*, par Chester Himes." *Etudes* No. 261 (April 1949), p. 142.
Mixed review of *If He Hollers*: is the novel really authentic and a true testimony? One hesitates to believe it "because of the tone of the writing, a cry of anger and hatred which does not appear always to come out spontaneously." The protagonist's sexual obsession seems sickly. The style is direct, lively, rich in slang --is this the result of Himes' writing or of the translation by Marcel Duhamel?

408 M., J. "Chez le libraire..." Brussels *Contacts* (February 1949), pp. 97-98.
The critic favorably compares Himes' use of racial themes with that of Richard Wright, finding that Himes is the more original. In summarizing the plot of *If He Hollers*, he says that Himes describes intense brutality without straining credibility. The reader will be caught up in the unraveling of Bob Jones' fate.

409 Maran, René. "Le Professeur Alain Leroy Locke." *Présence africaine* No. 6 (1st trimester 1949), p. 135-38.
This essay by Maran, who first knew Locke in 1924, is a kind of homage to "one of the highest and noblest illustrations of black American university life." The general scope of Locke's work and his attempt at promoting the "New Negro" are emphasized, as well as his frequent trips to Europe.

410 Mohrt, Michel. "Le plus grand romancier américain, William Faulkner, a écrit un livre pour dire aux Yankees du Nord et aux Européens..." *Carrefour* (September 15, 1949), p. 8.
Review of *Intruder in the Dust* crediting Wright with creating "the new European image" of race relations in the United States in *Black Boy*.

411 Olivier, Daria. "Chronique des livres: Les noirs jouent et perdent." *Réforme* No. 222 (June 18, 1949), p. 7.
Review of *If He Hollers* by Chester Himes, *The Street* by Ann

Petry, *Kingsblood Royal* by Sinclair Lewis, and *Manassas* by Upton Sinclair. *If He Hollers* is a "beautiful and violent book." In summarizing the plot, she stresses the black man/white woman relationship to explain Bob Jones' predicament. She compares his fate to that of Lutie Johnson in Petry's *The Street*: although Lutie is the stronger character, she is as unable as Bob Jones to escape her fate. Petry's ability to convey a few positive features of black life through her heroine is praised although the general atmosphere of her novel is bleak.

412 Paz, Magdeleine. "Derrière la 'ligne de couleur': Deux tableaux de la vie des noirs aux Etats-Unis." *Présence africaine* No. 6 (1st trimester 1949), pp. 155-158.
In talking about racial problems in the United States, Paz compares Sinclair Lewis's *Kingsblood Royal* and Himes' *If He Hollers* and finds that both provide compelling pictures of the topic. Himes' book provides an interesting and insightful example of the emotional plight of the black American male.

413 Paz, Magdeleine. "Littérature américaine: *S'il braille, lache-le,* par Chester Himes." *Paru* No.54 (October 1949), pp. 31-32.
Paz compares Himes' novel to those of Wright. She finds them of comparable quality and caliber and thinks that Himes' work is a fine exploration of the social plight of the Negro.

414 Radine, Serge. "Ecrivains américains non conformistes." *La Suisse contemporaine* No. 9 (June 1949), pp. 287-95.
Contains a paragraph on *Native Son* (pp. 288-89) praising Wright's objectivity, characterization, and sense of fatality.

1950

415 Anon. "Auteur-acteur." *Le Figaro Littèraire* (September 9, 1950), p. 2.
Reports Wright's return to Paris after the filming of *Native Son*. He expresses satisfaction at working in the film medium.

416 Anon. "Richard Wright, interprète de Richard Wright dans 'Un Enfant du pays' de Pierre Chenal". *Libération*; (November 30, 1950).

Interview with Wright on the circumstances behind the project to film *Native Son*.

417   Anon. "Richard Wright: *Un Enfant du pays*." *Liens* No.38 (July 1950), p. 8.
Notice of *Native Son*, a selection of the Club français du livre. Wright's achievement in creating a profound and representative character in Bigger is stressed. The plot is summarized concisely, showing that the protagonist only becomes a criminal because of an oppressive society. "No black writer has ever known the worldwide fame of Richard Wright; none has ever reached such a large audience." The problems of the black man are those of Man himself and concern everyone. The "hallucinatory narrative" has the nerve-raking tempo of a detective novel. *Native Son* is "one of the great books of our time," fit for those who are passionately interested in justice."

418   Anon. "Six écrivains avouent qu'ils ont cessé d'adorer le dieu des ténèbres." *Paris-Presse* (June 11, 1950), p. 5.
Review of the translation of *The God That Failed* containing a drawing and a biographical sketch of Wright, as well as a quotation from the episode concerning Ross.

419   Anon. "Six témoignages sur les autocrates moscoutaires." *Le Montagnard du Cantal* (February 17, 1950).
Review of the translation of *The God That Failed* commenting on Wright's experience with communism.

420   Anon. "Tourisme et vacances: *Le Dieu des ténèbres* (Calmann-Lévy)." *France-Illustration* 6 (July 8, 1950), p. 49.
Favorable review of *The God That Failed* with special praise for Wright's contribution.

421   Anon. "Trois livres bouleversants á propos de l'attribution du Prix Nobel de la paix à Ralph Bunche." *Bibliographie de la France* 139 (October 13, 1950), p. 3285.
Brief notes on, and advertisement for the French translations of Wright's *Native Son, Uncle Tom's Children*, and Alan Paton's *Cry, the Beloved Country*.

422   Aron, Raymond. "Fidélité des apostats." *La Table ronde* No.

30 (June 1950), pp. 52-65.
Notes that Wright, disillusioned with the Communist Party, continues to denounce the injustices of American society.

423 Boutang, Pierre. "Six renégats du communisme." *Aspects de la France* (June 15, 1950).
Favorable review of *The God That Failed*. Although a "foolish Negro," Wright "has a real poetic sense." His story could have been better written by Faulkner, however.

424 Cary, E. "Trois cent trente ans d'esclavage." *Europe* No. 50 (February 1950), pp. 6-7.
A historical and sociological introduction to the poetry of Langston Hughes, considered largely from an ideological perspective and represented by eight poems: "Le noir", "Le nègre parle des fleuves", "Le matelot", "Rues qui vont vers le port", "Entrée de vieillesse", "Simplement pour cela", "Quand Suzanna s'habille de rouge" et "Ceux qui marchent avec l'aube."

425 H., Ed. "*Le Dieu des ténèbres.*" *Arts, Lettres et Spectacles* (September 22, 1950), p. 2.
Review of *The God That Failed* noting that Wright's testimony is the most moving in the book.

426 Heuzé, Geneviève. "Connaissance des Etats-Unis: Notre problème essentiel est aujourd'hui d'éclairer l'homme sur lui-même". *France-USA* (November 1950), p. 2.
Brief interview with Richard Wright. The main topic is a comparison of American and French culture, highlighting American concerns with industrial production and French conceptions of education.

427 Loewel, P.[ierre] "De l'engagement." Paris *L'Aurore* (June 27, 1950), p. 9.
Review of *The God That Failed* mentioning Wright.

428 Maulnier, Thierry. "Les écrivains devant le communisme." *Hommes et Mondes* No. 12 (August 1950), pp. 592-96.
Review of *The God That Failed*. Comments at length on Wright's personal motivations, activities, and tragedy when he had to leave the Party because they indicate, more clearly than those of other

contributors, the existential dilemma people in his position had to face.

429 Montas, Lucien. "L'Histoire déchirante d'un nègre: Richard Wright." Port-au-Prince *Le Nouvelliste* (August 2, 1950), p. 1, 6; August 8,1950), p. 1, 4; (August 12, 1950), p. 1, 4.
Biographical-critical study with analyses of *Black Boy* and *Native Son*. Essentially a realist, Wright also has a slight romantic streak. His main subject is race, but his approach is psychological and intensely individualistic. His literary power places him among the greatest of contemporary writers. Montas hopes that his influence on young Haitian writers will be as great as that of Langston Hughes.

430 Musard, François. *"Le Dieu des ténèbres."* Algiers *Dernière Heure* (July 19, 1950).
Review of the translation of *The God That Failed* mentioning Wright.

431 Nadeau, Maurice. Introduction to *Un Enfant du pays* by Richard Wright. Paris: Club français du livre, 1950.
Based in part on Nadeau's previous articles on Wright, this introduction to the French translation of *Native Son* stresses Bigger's social, economic, and psychological condition and the way in which murder could be affirmative for him. Nadeau also links his case with that of victims of racism elsewhere.

432 Nadeau, Maurice. "Koestler, Silone, Wright, Gide, Fischer, Spender: *Le Dieu des ténèbres."* *Cahiers du monde nouveau*; No. 6 (June 1950), pp. 123-25.
Review of the translation of *The God That Failed* alluding to Wright's grandiose vision of human freedom and his subsequent moral suffering when he left the Communist Party.

433 Pagosse, R. "Koestler (Arthur), Silone (Ignazio), Wright (Richard), Gide (André), Fischer (Louis), Spender (Stephen) -- *Le Dieu des ténèbres."* *La Revue socialiste* No.42 (December, 1950), pp. 587-88.
Review of the translation of *The God That Failed* emphasizing Wright's contribution.

434 Petitjean, A. "Jadis communistes, Gide, Koestler, Silone,

Richard Wright confessent leurs espérances et leurs déceptions."
Carrefour (June 27, 1950), p. 9.
Review of *The God That Failed* mentioning Wright, whose
testimony is poignant in its account of his confrontation with
American racism and Stalinist imperialism.

435 Piquion, René. "Tonnerre dans la littérature." *Haiti-Journal*
(August 3, 1950).
The author of this article announces Wright's presence in Haiti,
recalls meeting him at a party in Harlem in 1944, and sketches his
life and literary career, ranking him with Langston Hughes as a
leading black writer.

436 Riou, Gaston. "La Situation internationale." *Hommes et
Monde* No. 13 (September 1950), pp. 129-34.
Includes a review of the translation of *The God That Failed*
mentioning Wright.

437 Schmidt, Albert-Marie. "Littérature engageante et littérature
engagée." *Réforme* (June 24, 1950), p. 7.
Includes a review of *The God That Failed* mentioning that Wright
and Silone can move the reader as well as interest him because their
proletarian origins made a tragedy of their break with the Party.

438 Simon, Jean. *Le Roman américain au XXe siècle*. Paris:
Boivin, 1950.
"The terms of 'social realism' suits better the black writer Richard
Wright who, born on a Mississippi plantation and confronted from
childhood with hard suffering, has undertaken to fight for his
oppressed race in his truthful, moving and indignant works."
Wright's *Native Son* is the study of a court case: the blame for
Bigger's murder lies in the social conditions which victimized him
(p. 174).

439 T., G. "*Le Dieu des ténèbres*, R. Crossman, Koestler, R.
Wright, L. Fischer, S. Spender, Silone, A. Gide." *Contacts
littéraires et sociaux* (September 1950).
Review of the translation of *The God That Failed* mentioning
Wright.

440 Theis, Edouard. "Personnalités noires: Un écrivain, Richard

Wright." *Présence africaine* Nos. 8-9 [Special issue on "Le monde noir"] (March 1950), pp. 141-48.
Retraces Wright's career up to his exile in France. Discusses his books and remarks that "in writing this book [*Native Son*] in a mood close to prayer Wright was guided by this principle: 'The degree of morality in my work depends upon the degree of true experience that I succeed in expressing.' "

441 Thérive, André. *"Le Dieu des ténèbres." Paroles françaises* (July 3, 1950).
Review of the translation of *The God That Failed* comparing Wright's honesty to Jean-Jacques Rousseau's.

442 Wolfe, Bernard. "Extase en noir: le noir comme danseur et chanteur." *Les Temps modernes* No. 59 (September 1950), pp. 389-401.
The essay focuses on stereotypes of the Negro and explores their causes and basis. Mention is made of the Brer' Rabbit stories of Uncle Remus. Even the white American admirers of Katherine Dunham, the readers of Lillian Smith and the "disciples of Richard Wright" are readily carried away by their own "enthusiasm for the immediate."

443 Zobel, Joseph. "Richard Wright, témoin de la tragédie de 13 millions d'êtres." *Liens* No. 38 (July 1950), p. 4.
Tribute to Wright as a witness to racial injustice and an advocate in the struggle for black liberation by a prize-winning novelist from Martinique. Comments mostly on Wright's forceful, realistic style of writing

1951

444 Achille, L.[ouis] T. "Negro Spirituals." *Esprit*, No. 179 (May 1951), pp. 707-09.
This article analyzes the conditions of creation and performance of the spirituals, focusing upon their role as an "instrument of spiritual liberation" and their function in the preservation of values of forbearance as well as resistance within the black community.

445 Anon. "A Venise, Richard Wright a été consacré vedette de cinéma." *Paris-Presse* (September 1, 1951), p. 4.

Favorable notice of the film "Native Son." According to the Italian critics Wright is a good actor, but he does lack some credibility in the role of Bigger. Bigger becomes a black Raskolnikov.

446 Anon. "Je choisis mes auteurs: *Le Dieu des ténèbres.*" Brussels *La Cité* (February 13, 1951).
Review of *The God That Failed* praising Wright's chapter as moving and informative.

447 Anon. "*Le Dieu des ténèbres* par Arthur Koestler, Ignazio Silone, Richard Wright, André Gide, Louis Fischer, Stephen Spender." *La Croix* (January 21-22, 1951), p. 4.
Favorable review of *The God That Failed* noting that Wright still believes in a socialist revolution.

448 Anon. "Richard Wright: *Un Enfant du pays.*" Rabat *Le Journal du Maroc* (February 10, 1951).
Favorable review of Marcel Duhamel's translation of *Native Son.* The violent novel is not a pleasant book to read, but it is very moving.

449 Fréminville, Claude de. "De la part du feu à celle du lion à venir: Wright?" *Le Populaire de Paris* (March 13, 1951), p. 4.
Review of Claude McKay's *Banjo* anticipating a future treatment of the same material by Wright.

450 Jacno, Simone. "Déception américaine, plaisir anglais." *L'Observateur* No. 69 (September 6, 1951), p. 23.
Includes a brief review of Wright's film based on *Native Son.* For the reviewer, the film is a failure.

451 Lalou, René. "Le Cru de 1950." In *L'Almanach des lettres,* Edited by André Billy. Paris: Les Editions de Flore et La Gazette des lettres, 1951, pp. 9-16.
 Mentions Wright favorably as a contributor to *The God That Failed* .

452 Lucas-Debreton, J. "Le Moïse Noir." *Les Oeuvres libres* No. 50 (January 1951), pp. 81-116.
A long, detailed and rather favorable evaluation of the political career of Marcus Garvey in London in 1928 and Prince Kojo-Touvalou. Booker T. Washington is called "Hamilton" but his actions and

ideology are assessed correctly.

453 Nadeau, Maurice. "A. Koestler, I. Silone, R. Wright, A. Gide, L. Fischer, S. Spender: *Le Dieu des ténèbres.*" *Cahiers critiques du communisme* No. 1 (January 1951), pp. 47-50.
Review of the translation of *The God That Failed* mentioning the grandiose perspective of the class struggle which Wright presents and his psychological depression when he is rejected by the Communist Party. "A real ex-Communist cannot find the integrity of his personality again," the reviewer remarks.

1952

454 Brissaud, André. "Il y a bien des manières de tuer un négre." *Arts , Lettres et Spectacles* No. 361 (May 29, 1952), p. 8.
In a very favorable review of *Lonely Crusade*, Brissaud praises Himes' accurate descriptions of the moral and social dilemmas of the Negro protagonist, his problems with American labor unions, and his inability to overcome stereotyped reflections of himself.

455 Delpech, Jeanine. "Avec l'enfant du pays." *Les Nouvelles littéraires* 30 (September 14, 1952), p. 1.
Wright comments on the film version of *Native Son* and future screen ventures. The interviewer comments on the film, especially Wright's acting ability and production plans. Translated as "An Interview with Native Son." *Crisis* 57 (November, 1952).

456 Domenach, Jean-Marie. "Louis Fischer *et al., Le Dieu des ténèbres.*" *Esprit* No. 18 (November 1952), pp. 713-14.
Review of the translation of *The God That Failed* comparing Wright's unhappy experience with the Party following a miserable childhood with Silone's similar personal history. Joining the Party to combat fear and injustice in society, they discovered their existence among Communists as well.

457 Dupuy, Henri-Jacques. "Poésie des blues." *Les Lettres françaises* No. 429 (September 4, 1952), p. 6.
Short, mostly descriptive article on the meaning of the blues,

considered largely as a poetical voicing of Afro-American protest.

458   Gautier, Madeleine. "Le blues." *Le Point* No. 40 (January 1952), pp. 16-17.
The essay in this issue devoted to jazz deals more with the music than with the words of the blues, and is followed by a translation of Big Bill Broonzy's "Lowland Blues."

459   Howlett, Jacques. "Le problème noir en Amérique." *Présence africaine* No. 13 (2nd trimester 1952), pp. 420-423.
Howlett gives a rebuttal to Baldwin's attempts to speak on the racial problem in the United States. Baldwin "minimizes the evil" of this serious American problem. Baldwin's article would never have been written by a man politically aware. Unlike Baldwin, Howlett does not see America as the best of all possible worlds. He regrets that Baldwin will continue to write.

460   Marceau, Félicien. "Etrange Amérique." *La Table ronde* (1952), p. 152-56.
A review of several American titles includes a look at Ethel Waters' *La Vie en blues [His Eye Is on the Sparrow]* and Himes' *Lonely Crusade*. Marceau compares and contrasts these two different visions of American racial problems.

461   Wright, Richard. "Introduction." In Chester Himes. *La Croisade de Lee Gordon*. Paris: Corréa, 1952.
Wright places Himes' *Lonely Crusade* on par with Myrdal's *An American Dilemma*, but advises that the novel "is much, much more than a contrast between America's preaching and practice. It is a scathing criticism of the Negro, the Communist Party, trade unionism, and the anti-Negro feelings of white American workers." He notes that "in these pages we have for the first time a truthful and realistic picture of the American Negro's relationship to Communism and the American trade union movement." Although the anti-Negro feelings of the trade union characters may shock French audiences, the American worker is only human and shares the faults of a "young, crude, violent, confused nation which as yet does not fully know itself and which, in many respects, can hardly be called a nation at all," because of its social, racial, and geographical divisions. Wright commends the book to readers "who want to know the truth of a phase of American life." [Original English version in Michel Fabre, *Richard Wright: Books and Writers*

[(Jackson: University Press of Mississippi, 1990), pp. 208-10]

1953

462 Arnavon, Cyrille. *Histoire littéraire des Etats-Unis*.   Paris
Hachette, 1953. 462 p.
Pages 16-17 are devoted to Negro poetry: the Negro spirituals result
from a fusion between atavistic African chants and the Protestant
hymnal. "These child-like, wounded souls" have thus come to
represent oppression all over the world. Dunbar is mentioned, with
Countee Cullen, J. W. Johnson and Langston Hughes. "Poetry
written by people of color has not produced any masterpieces yet."
Richard Wright is mentioned on p. 340: the simplification of his
protest novels is often fatal to their aesthetic scope.

463 Brissaud, André. "W.G. Smith sera le Louis Armstrong des
lettres noires américaines." *Arts, Lettres et Spectacles* No. 425
(August 21, 1953), p. 5.
An interview of the Afro-American novelist about his move to Paris
and the themes and racial perspectives of *Anger at Innocence* and
Last of the Conquerors.

464 Fanon, Frantz. *Peau noire, masques blancs*. Paris: Le Seuil,
1953.
Wright's works influenced Frantz Fanon's analysis of the
psychological and social plight of the Negro in the New World. In
Black Skin, White Masks, he repeatedly refers to, and draws upon
examples in Wright's *Black Boy* and *Native Son* as well as Chester
Himes' *If He Hollers Let Him Go.*

465 Parot, Jeanine. *"Malheur aux justes."* *Les Lettres françaises*
No. 484 (October 1, 1953), p. 3.
Review of William Gardner Smith's *Anger at Innocence* summing up
the plot briefly and praising the psychological analysis of a situation
that goes beyond black and white.

466 Terrex, Jean-Luc. "William Gardner Smith: *Malheur aux
Justes." La Table ronde* No. 69 (September 1953), pp. 147-48.
A rather unfavorable review of W.G. Smith's *Anger at Innocence*
published in translation by a prestigious French Book Club. A

summary of the novel's major themes is followed by a few comments- "at any rate, this is not very 'American', not very 'Negro'. It is grey, sad and dull..."

1954

467 Anon.[?] *"Pietro, chevalier d'Amour." Dernières nouvelles d'Alsace* (July 5, 1954).
This review of *The Saracen Blade* by Frank Yerby characterizes the novel as "fiction after the style of Alexandre Dumas...with its qualities and its drawbacks."

468 Anon.[?] *"Pietro, chevalier d'amour* de Frank Yerby." *Le Hérisson* (June 3, 1954), p. 8.
The review of *The Saracen Blade* mostly discusses details of the plot- such as "battles, splendid love scenes, a rose-perfumed atmosphere."

469 Anon.[?] *"Pietro, chevalier d'amour* de Frank Yerby." *Le Progrés de Lyon* (June 25, 1954), p. 6.
Review of *The Saracen Blade*, praising the pace of this novel "full of blood, voluptuousness, and death." The protagonist acts against a historical setting recreated with liveliness and splendor.

470 Anon.[?] *"Pietro, chevalier d'amour* de Frank Yerby." Lille *Nord-Matin* (May 29, 1954).
Review of *The Saracen Blade*. Pietro Di Donati and Frederick II "linked by their sign of the zodiac and their temperament... take us around 13th century Europe." The novel is rich in deeds of valor but also in emotion and sensitiveness.

471 Anon.[?] *"Pietro, chevalier d'amour* de Frank Yerby." *Pour vous, madame* (July-August, 1954).
The Saracen Blade announces the confirmed reputation of "a new Alexandre Dumas." The review focuses on the adventures of the protagonist.

472 Anon.[?] *"Pietro, chevalier d'amour* fera pâmer les dames et rêver les messieurs." *La Presse* (September 15, 1954).
This review of Frank Yerby's *The Saracen Blade* hails the novel as

"the future best-seller of the season." Yerby is called "a modern Dumas...for he is a Negro and he has the ability to make historical events live again." An analysis of the major protagonist follows, concluding that "he is the synthesis of an impressive number of heroes of all ages."

473 Anon.[?] *"Pietro, chevalier d'amour." L'Echo de la Côte d'Azur* (July 2, 1954).
The Saracen Blade by Frank Yerby is compared with the works by Alexandre Dumas as "a successful historical novel." The hero unites all the qualities of chivalry and daring, and as far as lovemaking is concerned, Yerby is more daring himself than the Romantic novelists. His imagination is splendid and his gift for telling tales remarkable.

474 Anon.[?] "Treizième siècle garanti: *Pietro, chevalier d'amour." Le Parisien libéré* (June 15, 1954).
This review of *The Saracen Blade* by Frank Yerby praises its recreation of the world of tournaments and crusades. "Pietro, a commoner more wealthy than a duke, is the hero of this novel rich in heroines."

475 Brièrre, Annie. "Entretien avec Chester Himes." *France-U.S.A.* (1954 [?]), pp. 8-12.
An essay based upon an interview in which Himes recalls the beginnings of his life leading up to the publication of *The Third Generation.* Himes comments on a number of writers and at one point suggests the possible influence of Stephen Crane and Conrad on Hemingway. He considers Zola's *Nana* to be a masterpiece, both as an exploration of the protagonist's character and as a portrayal of French society. He discusses the rise of the black bourgeoisie in America and attempts to explain the psychological conflicts that such people suffer. He goes on to recall his work for the WPA and at Malabar Farm. Speaking about religion, Himes for some reason describes himself as "a very bad Catholic, but one who cannot stop believing in God."

476 Brown, John. *Panorama de la littérature contemporaine aux Etats-Unis.* Paris: Gallimard, 1954.
Pages 174-178 are devoted to Richard Wright and a few contemporary black novelists. Wright's career is evoked up to his settling in France, "he no longer is a Negro novelist," he insists, and

has opened up to existentialist theories; his evolution brings him closer to Kafka and Dostoevsky and away from his naturalist masters. *The Outsider*, however, is too consciously philosophical for Brown. Other names are mentioned: Zora Neale Hurston, Arna Bontemps, Countee Cullen, Claude McKay, Rudolph Fischer, George Lee, W.E. Turpin, and also Richard Gibson, Willard Motley, James Baldwin and Ralph Ellison. The latter's *Invisible Man*, which received the American Book Award, poses the problem of the individual as an invisible man, whatever his color, in modern society.

477 Elm, Robert. "Chronique littéraire." *Maroc-Presse* (September 23, 1954).
A review of Frank Yerby's *The Saracen Blade*. The novelist is hailed as a "new Alexandre Dumas." A brief summary of the plot follows, extolling the impressive qualities of the protagonist. The novel beautifully and apparently accurately evokes Europe in the 13th century.

478 Moussy, Marcel. "Notes de lecture: *Au-delà du regard.*" *Les Lettres nouvelles* No. 16 (June 1954), pp. 917-19.
Invisible Man by Ralph Ellison is "both an introspective and demonstrative work. The Negro must always fight alienating stereotypes." Ellison had already denounced the role of the stereotype ("maybe to console the white man more than to crush the Negro") in an essay on American literature. The novel's preoccupation with racism is stressed and Ellison's writing placed within the context of an aesthetic protest, a post-war, anti-Hemingway rebellion in American letters.

479 Venaissin, Gabriel. "Le roman du faux-témoignage: à propos de Chester Himes, *La Croisade de Lee Gordon.*" *Esprit* No. 212 (March 1954), pp. 465-67.
Venaissin deals mainly with French novels that pretend to bear witness to historical events, such as the massacre of Oradour villagers by the Nazis, or to a social condition, such as that of the "worker priests," by writers who have no real knowledge of their subjects. He goes on to say that Himes' *Lonely Crusade* is a far more genuine work because the author has been a victim of both blacks and whites in the American labor system.

480 Viatte, Auguste. *Histoire littéraire de l'Amérique française des*

origines à 1950.   Paris: Presses Universitaires de France, 1954.
Mentions the production of the free people of color, mostly *Les Cenelles,* an anthology compiled by Armand Lanusse and the works of Thierry and Victor Séjour (pp. 260-61, 265-66).

1955

481 Anon. "James Baldwin: *Go Tell It on the Mountain.*" *Mercure de France* No. 1097 (January 1, 1955), p. 150.
Mentions the original publication in English.

482 Anon. "Je maudis le jour où pour la première fois j'ai entendu le mot 'politique.'" *L'Express* (October 18, 1955), p. 8.
Interviewer's questionnaire with Wright's responses on the novelist's motives, influences, favorite writers, relation of the writer to society and politics, and other topics.

483 Delpech, Jeanine. "*Puissance noire* par Richard Wright." *Les Nouvelles littéraires* 33 (November 3, 1955), p. 3.
Favorable review of *Black Power.* Noteworthy for his intellectual honesty, Wright is estranged from black Africans but he depicts their problems compassionately.

484 Dodat, François. "La poésie de Langston Hughes." Introduction to *Poèmes/Poems* by Langston Hughes. Paris: Seghers, 1955.
The translator and editor of this bilingual edition of 36 poems by Hughes compares his poetry to that of Carl Sandburg but emphasizes his debt to Wordsworth and Shakespeare. His race accounts for his themes and militancy; the "black poet laureate" has introduced the blues and spirituals into American poetry and his work is no more "folkloristic" than Chopin's music.

485 F.[ranklin], A.[lbert]. "*Puissance noire* par Richard Wright." *Présence africaine* NS No. 5 (December 1955-January 1956), pp. 115-17.
Unfavorable review of *Black Power* by an African. He stresses Wright's "lack of understanding which is still more evident in Chapter 3" on the Ashanti world view. He notes self-contradictions. Discusses Wright's political perspective. "In its deepest sense, the African world remained inaccessible to Wright."

486   Mohrt, Michel. *Le Nouveau Roman américain*. Paris:
Gallimard, 1955.
The author merely mentions *Native Son* and *Black Boy* by Richard
Wright as "naturalistic testimonies" in the same breath as the fiction
of Erskine Caldwell. Such militant literature is now out of favor (p.
264).

487   Piel, Jean. "Richard Wright, *Puissance noire*." *Critique* No.
103 (December 1955), pp. 1110-12.
Short review of *Black Power*. Wright describes the birth of a
nationalist movement in its raw state --a personal, emotional, quasi-
religious phenomenon-- and discusses the coming independence of
the Gold Coast.

488   Rousseaux, André. "Tragédies raciales." *Le Figaro littéraire*
No. 496 (October 22, 1955), p. 2.
Review of *Black Power*. Like all of Wright's books, it contributes
to the liberation of blacks but its most important theme is the
confrontation of westernized blacks with Africa. Wright himself is
unable to communicate with or relate to the African people.
Rousseaux agrees with most of Wright's conclusions but finds his
"attempt at explaining everything through psychology... perfectly
monstrous."

489   Schmidt, Albert-Marie. "Sombres Histoires." *Réforme* No.
554 (October 29, 1955), p. 7.
Contains a review of *Black Power*. In relating the problems of
emerging Africa, Wright retains his skill as a storyteller, but his basic
attitude is ambivalent.

1956

490   Achille, Louis T. "Les Negro-Spirituals et l'expansion de la
culture noire." *Présence africaine* N.S. Nos. 8-10 (June-November
1956), pp. 227-37.
Deals mostly with the influence of the Negro spirituals on the
Western world and Christianity following on the impact of Negro
music, namely jazz, and African arts on Western sensibilities. "This
constitutes one of the most elevated forms of the dialogue which
black culture must initiate with other cultures."

491 Anon. Biographical note. In Chester Himes. *La Fin d'un primitif.* (Paris: Gallimard, 1956), pp. 7-9.
A brief bio-bibliographical note about Himes [probably by himself] is followed by extensive quotes from Himes concerning the theme of *The Primitve* and his intentions in writing it.

492 Anon. *"Les Elus du Seigneur,* James Baldwin." *Mercure de France* No. 1119 (November 1, 1956).
In a brief mention of the translation of *Go Tell It on the Mountain,* the reviewer stresses its original, dense style, and its sincerity.

493 Anon. *"Le Transfuge* par R. Wright, trad. de Guy de Montlaur." *Mercure de France* No.1111 (March 1, 1956), p. 593.
Favorable review of *The Outsider* as a tragic and revealing existentialist story. "A man of his time, Wright has written a novel of isolation."

494 Anon. "Noirs et blancs." *L'Express* No. 270 (August 21, 1956), p. 16.
A mixed review of *The Primitive* by Chester Himes that comments upon the possible intent of a writer who would want to depict a relationship between a white woman and a black man "whose motivations represent the stupidity typical of the twentieth century."

495 Anon. "Richard Wright: *Bandoeng, 1.500.000.000 d'hommes." Bulletin critique du livre français* No. 53 (March 1956).
Favorable review of *The Color Curtain.* Praises Wright's clarity, precision and magnanimity in presenting an excellent account of one of the world's major problems.

496 Anon. "Richard Wright, *Bandoeng, 1.500.000.000 d'hommes." Christianisme social* (March 1956),pp. 297-80.
Favorable review of *The Color Curtain* recapitulating Wright's argument and endorsing it. Wright's analysis of Bandung will help French readers understand the Algerian situation. In the Third World communists will win if Christians default.

497 Anon. "Richard Wright: *Bandoeng, 1.500.000.000 d'hommes." Revue française de science politique* No. 6 (January-March 1956), p. 249.

Notice of *The Color Curtain* briefly describing the contents.

498 Anon. "Traductions: Sous le signe de la solitude." *L'Express* No. 246 (March 9, 1956) pp. 18-19.
Review of the translation of *Savage Holiday* praising Wright's theme of existential solitude but complaining that the translation is weak.

499 Anon. "Wright, Richard. *Le Transfuge*." *Profils* No. 15 (Spring 1956), p. 258.
Waylaid by the central episode in which the hero mixes with New York Communist circles, a superficial reader might conclude *The Outsider* is a political study. But Wright's design is wider and he is "looking for the meaning of life itself." The result of this tragic experience is summed up by Cross Damon when he is about to die: "Man is nothing by himself," Cross Damon is an American Negro but his experience is by no means limited to his racial condition.

500 Bosquet, Alain. Introduction to his *Anthologie de la poésie américaine des origines à nos jours*. Paris: Stock, 1956. Pp. 7-37.
Although no black poets appear other than Langston, Hughes, Countee Cullen and P.L. Dunbar, black folk poetry is well represented in this anthology. The author mentions Phillis Wheatley, but Dunbar's pieces in black dialect are the "first true achievement." Adequate biographical notices are provided: Dunbar is, "with James Weldon Johnson, the first important Negro poet but his work will last longer" than Johnson's (p. 288). Hughes has "done more than anyone to bring jazz and poetry, folklore and language closer together" (p. 302). Cullen is an "admirable craftsman in verse, influenced by Baudelaire..." a most accomplished black poet, greatly underrated (p. 302).

501 Bosquet, Alain. "Jeune poésie américaine." *Les Cahiers du Sud*, No. 336 (August 1956), pp. 163-167.
Includes a brief evaluation of the poetry of Cullen and Hughes and alludes to the music of Louis Armstrong.

502 Brièrre, Annie. "Sur quelques romans américains." *La Table ronde* No. 106 (October 1956), pp. 175-76.
Comments on *The Color Curtain* and on *Black Power*, finding Wright's Marxist " a propos prepossessions" not quite convincing. *Savage Holiday* is a psychological study with no mention at all of the racial situation. *The Outsider* discusses the problem of the individual

vis-à-vis Communism as well as the isolation of Blacks in society. Both novels are very worthwhile.

503 C., J. "Un 'Bandoeng' culturel noir à la Sorbonne." *Paris demain* (September 27, 1956), p. 15.
Article on the Congress of Black Writers and Artists mentioning the French translation of *Black Power* and quoting Wright: "I am black but I am also a man of the West."

504 Chapsal, Madeleine. "Le livre de la semaine: *Le Transfuge.*" *L'Express* (January 20, 1956), p. 11.
Rather unfavorable review of *The Outsider*. Wright's narrative skill is apparent in this novel, but his philosophical ideas are imposed on the action rather than emerging from it. As a man divested of myth and devoid of fear, Cross Damon is not a credible character.

505 Delpech, Jeanine. "Un Noir chez les blancs." *Les Nouvelles littéraires* 34 (March 8, 1956) pp. 1, 6.
Interview with Wright, who comments on his work in progress [*Pagan Spain*)] as part of a non-fiction trilogy including *Black Power* and *The Color Curtain*, as well as on African religions, on himself as an ordinary American who looks to the future, on male-female relations, and on the writer in exile. Delpech refers to Wright as "the black Dostoevsky."

506 Depestre, René. "Deux poètes d'aujourd'hui." *Présence africaine* N.S. No.6 (February-March 1956), pp. 165-67.
Includes a review of *Poèmes* by Langston Hughes, a Seghers bilingual edition of a selection made by François Dodat whose "excellent translation of some thirty poems reveals the realism in Hughes' gifts." More space should have been devoted to his revolutionary poetry, however, and to the celebration of Africa and Harlem. "Unity is basic to Hughes' inspiration... the authenticity of his lyricism, the emotional efficacy of his song" characterize his poetry, whether it makes use of the blues, the spirituals or the Whitman-like stanza.

507 F., P.-L. "Aux midis de la poésie: Léopold Sédar Senghor parle de la poésie négro-américaine." Brussels *Le Journal des poètes* No. 26 (January 1956), p. 1.
Senghor's lecture begins with P.L. Dunbar and Langston Hughes, the latter seen as the embodiment of the Harlem Renaissance. This

movement comprised two schools --the dialect poets with J.W. Johnson represented the epic and mystical trend, and Sterling Brown and Hughes himself represent the elegiac and secular perspective. Both trends are close to the blues and spirituals. McKay, Arna Bontemps and Countee Cullen all sing their blackness with pride, but Jean Toomer vindicates the South and the land as well as a return to the African sources. Anti-racist racism sustains black American poetry, according to Senghor. On p. 18 of the same journal, the French publication of Hughes' poems is hailed by Louis Guillaume.

508 Fernandot, R. "Langston Hughes." *Le Figaro littéraire* No. 547 (October 13, 1956), p. 10.
Brief review of François Dodat's *Langston Hughes*. Much appreciation is shown for Hughes' *The Weary Blues*; he is called "the most authentic black American poet, an author of well-appreciated blues and spirituals."

509 Glissant, Edouard. "Notes sur le premier congrés des écrivains et artistes noirs." *Les Lettres nouvelles* No. 43 (November 1956), pp. 677-81.
Includes a summary of the views expressed by Wright at the congress and commentary on the dual identity of the Afro-American.

510 Granet, Marie. "Wright (Richard): *Bandoeng, 1.500.000.000 d'hommes*." *La Revue socialiste* No. 101 (November 1956), pp. 438-40.
Unfavorable review of *The Color Curtain*. Although Granet concurs with Wright's assessment of the importance of the issues at the Bandung Conference and with a number of his observations, she questions his objectivity in denouncing Western colonialism while ignoring religious and colonial wars initiated by others, including China. She also disagrees with his characterization of the American Revolution as a anti-colonialist war. Wright seems to leave the Third World no choice other than anarchy or dictatorship. The book closes on an expression of anguish which may not be justified by political realities.

511 Guérin, Daniel. "Richard Wright à Bandoeng." *France-Observateur* No. 7 (February 23, 1956), p. 13.
Favorable review of *The Color Curtain* stressing Wright's analysis of colonialism and his skillful and balanced coverage of the Bandung Conference.

512 Guérin, Daniel. "Richard Wright en Afrique." *Les Lettres nouvelles* No. 34 (January 1956), pp. 128-34.
Favorable review of *Black Power* by a Trotskyite friend of Wright. Guérin admires the vigorous denunciation of colonialism in Africa. The major problem raised by the book is that of the Afro-American's relationship to the ancestral continent --the questions of cultural retentions and "negritude." Wright sincerely tries to analyze the causes of his misunderstandings with Africans; but there is some contradiction between his regret that the West has destroyed traditional African culture and his own rationalistic dislike of superstition.   On the other hand, Wright proves to be a good anthropologist in observing the status of women in the struggle for national liberation, as well as sexual customs and old taboos. Wright's political analysis of the emergent Nkrumah regime partly fails because his justified suspicion of Stalinists prevents him from integrating the liberation of the God Coast into a world revolutionary movement.

513 Ki Zerbo, J.[oseph]. *"Bandoeng: 1,500,000,000 d'hommes* par R. Wright." *Présence africaine* N.S. No. 6 (February-March 1956), pp. 168-69.
Mixed review of *The Color Curtain*.   Ki Zerbo praises the perception, accuracy and finesse of Wright's report as well as his sympathy for the Third World. But Wright oversimplifies --putting excessive emphasis on religious and racial feelings in the East. His use of psychoanalysis is vague. All things considered, he offers no real solution to the problems of the Third World, for his advocacy of Western help outside the framework of Western capitalism is unrealistic.

514 Lalain, Odile de. "De tout un peu; Richard Wright: *Puissance Noire.*" *La Nouvelle Revue française* 38 (February 1956), p. 352.
Paradoxically, our first discovery when reading *Black Power* is "how much more American than black" Wright is.

515 Lalou, René. "Le Livre de la semaine: *Le Transfuge* par Richard Wright". *Les Nouvelles littéraires* No. 1482 (January 26, 1956), p. 3.
Review of *The Outsider* summarizing the plot and analyzing some of the themes. Lalou finds the style a bit heavy, with theoretical speeches at times impeding the flow of an otherwise exciting narrative.

516 Lauras, André. "Richard Wright - *Le Transfuge*." *Etudes* No. 291 (November 1956), p. 316.
Mostly unfavorable review of *The Outsider* which finds fault with the writing but praises several "moments of terrible lucidity." Includes a plot summary.

517 Messiaen, Pierre. "Lettres américaines: Richard Wright, romancier noir." *La Croix* (February 12-13, 1956), p. 3.
Review of the French translations of *The Outsider* and *Black Power*. Less successful than *Native Son* or *Black Boy*, *The Outsider* is too sensationalistic in a cinematic way and contains objectionable language. *Black Power* is unjustified in its criticism of Christian missionaries in Africa.

518 Parot, Jeanine. "Lumiéres et camouflage." *Les Lettres françaises* (February 1, 1956), p. 3.
Contains a review of *The Color Curtain* finding Wright's report brisk and full of revealing details. Although the book is accurate on the whole in its description of the general fight against colonialism, its angry anti-communist mood is a defect. In spite of his "bad faith," Wright is forced to conclude that the lack of a Western solution to the problems of industrialization in the new nations will turn them to communism for economic freedom.

519 Rétif, André. "Arthur Campbell - *L'Ecole de la jungle*; Richard Wright - *Bandoeng: 1.500.000.000 d'hommes*; Lion Chao-Tchi - *Pour être un bon communiste*; Luce-Claude Maitre - *Introduction à la pensée d'Iqbal*; Michel Leiris - *Contacts de civilisation en Martinique et en Guadeloupe*." *Etudes* No. 290 (September 1956), pp. 306-07.
Contains a notice of *The Color Curtain* pointing out the important role of race and religion. The article mentions the Bandung conference, and agrees with Wright about the urgent need for help in the Third World from the West. With "somewhat longish interviews" the book goes farther than good reporting.

520 Rousseaux, André. "Les Livres: l'Espagne impériale." *Le Figaro littéraire* No. 507 (January 7, 1956), p. 2.
Contains a short generally favorable review of the translation of *The Color Curtain*. Rousseaux criticizes Wright for his "narrow rationalism too closed to the mysterious reserves of religious spirit of the Asian and African people."

521   Roussel, Jean.   *"Bandoeng*, par Richard Wright." *Les Nouvelles littéraires* 24 (April 12, 1956), p. 3.
Review of *The Color Curtain* noting Wright's sociological and psychological approach.   His optimism may be premature, but Wright is both a good reporter and a thoughtful analyst.

522   Sohier, A.   "A la rencontre des hommes." *Eglise vivante* No. 8 (November 28, 1956), pp. 75-76.
Review of the translation of *The Color Curtain* objecting to Wright's anti-religious rationalism.   He particularly fails to understand Catholics.   His analysis of Chinese Communist tactics at Bandung is perceptive, however.

523   Vallette, J.[acques].   *"Puissance noire*, par R. Wright." *Mercure de France* No. 1109 (January 1, 1956), p. 199.
Favorable mention of *Black Power*, "an honest and generous book which all Europeans who care about the future should heed."

1957

524   Anon.   "Avez-vous lu?" *Les Débats de ce temps* (April 30, 1957), p. 3.
Transcending the issues of the times, *Go Tell It on the Mountain* deals with themes prevalent in Western civilization.   Elements of *L'Homme de Dieu* by Gabriel Marcel and *La Femme pauvre* by Léon Bloy, both of them Catholic authors, come to mind when reading Baldwin's novel.   A plot summary is included.

525   Anon.   "Chrétien, noir et américain: Auteur du roman *Les Elus du Seigneur*, James Baldwin répond à nos questions." *Réforme* (June 22, 1957), pp. 4-5.
Baldwin's serene manner of treating racism and his noble presentation of human suffering in *Go Tell It on the Mountain* are a lesson for all.   The interview comprises eight questions which primarily probe the Christian influence on Baldwin's work and his racial views, and racism in America.

526   Anon.   *"La Troisième Génération."* *Mercure de France* No. 1116 (August 1957), p. 535.
A brief, favorable mention of *The Third Generation*, commenting on the beautiful translation by Chester Himes' friend, novelist Yves

Malartic.

527 Anon. "*Les Elus du Seigneur* de James Baldwin." *La Table ronde* No. 119 (November 1957), pp. 183-84.
Go Tell It on the Mountain is largely autobiographical. European writers cannot reproduce the tone of the novel, which is reminiscent of the "pathetic and exalting" Negro Spirituals. A summary of the plot is included.

528 Anon. "Mais l'homme blanc reste sourd." *France-Observateur* (November 7, 1957), p. 24.
Favorable review of *White Man, Listen!* stressing Wright's expatriation and the importance of his message.

529 Anon. Review of *Les Elus du Seigneur*. *Informations et Documents* (May 13, 1957).
In writing about the French translation of Baldwin's *Go Tell It on The Mountain*, the reviewer praises his picture of black youth trapped between the ghetto streets and an illusory escape through religion; he contrasts the political orientation of Baldwin's characters with those of Wright and Himes. He finds that Baldwin's heroes are rather consistently involved in psychological problems and remain aloof from political and social battles.

530 Anon. "Un monde noir." *Demain* (May 16, 1957), pp. 15-16.
America knows Baldwin mostly through several of his essays. To the French reader of *Go Tell It on the Mountain* he will be known as "the author of one of the finest books published in a long time."

531 Brièrre, Annie. "Preface to *La Troisième Génération* by Chester Himes. Paris: Plon, 1957, pp. i-iii.
Brièrre describes Himes as a successful author who has been awarded a Rosenwald Fellowship and who has had three other books published in France. She characterizes him as youthful with a casual appearance and an obstinate nature. She notes that *The Third Generation* is partly autobiographical and compares it to Thomas Wolfe's *Of Time and the River*. She writes that it deftly explores personal reactions to color within the Negro race, itself; his art reaches far beyond mere social statement and that his psychological approach is universal. She praises the book as "a moving work with a colorful style that is admirably expressed through Yves Malartic's translation."

532 Brièrre, Annie. "Rencontrés à Paris: Chester Himes et James Baldwin." *Les Nouvelles littéraires* No. 1560 (June 25, 1957), p. 4.
An essay based upon an interview, quoting at length the two Negro novelists, who had become popular in France and had firmly established their reputations after a difficult start in the United States. Both Himes and Baldwin, Brièrre feels, are worthy spokesmen for their race and offer interesting analyses of the complex dimensions of the race question in America.

533 Brièrre, Annie. "Un Américain d'Harlem à Paris." *France-U.S.A.* (May 1957), p. 2.
The characters in *Go Tell It on the Mountain* are deeply religious but they are "prey to uncontrollable sexual ardor." Baldwin, one of the best American writers, earned the respect of his peers with *Notes of a Native Son*. *Giovanni's Room*, his next novel, will not disappoint Baldwin's admirers.

534 Daven, Jean-Claude. "USA: Chester Himes: les noirs d'Amérique à la troisième génération." *La Tribune de Lausanne* (May 26, 1957), p. 4.
A brief interview with Himes on the occasion of the publication of *The Third Generation*. Himes characterizes the book as "an autobiographical novel" dealing with racial prejudice within a Negro family, but he denies that it is his own life story. The novel is "a description and an acknowledgement of simple facts." Daven's article includes a photograph of Himes and Regine Fischer, who is incorrectly identified as his wife.

535 Dulck, J.[ean] "Richard Wright - *Black Power*." *Les Langues modernes* No. 51 (May-June 1957), pp. 107-08.
Review of the British edition focusing on Wright's gradual discovery of Africa and the ultimate difficulty he encounters in trying to penetrate non-Western types of knowing. The book mirrors the problems of Afro-Americans when they go to Africa with the illusion that they will establish immediate kinship with Africans. Wright depicts this situation with much deftness and poignancy.

536 Giron, Roger. "Le jour de ses 14 ans, un petit noir de Harlem voit le Seigneur lui apparaître." *France-Soir* (May 14, 1957).
Go Tell It on the Mountain is more an epic than a novel. The characters search for spiritual values. Baldwin's exposition of the individual stories of Florence, Gabriel and Elizabeth "forms a

marvelous picture in which the individual destiny melts into the destiny of a family and of a people." The love story of Elizabeth and Richard is "upsetting" and "sad". It is a "strange book" where revolt remains in the heart. Brief biographical sketch.

537 Glissant, Edouard.   "Le romancier noir et son peuple." *Présence africaine* No. 16 (October-November 1957), pp. 26-30.
In these notes for a lecture on the relationship between the black novelist and his audience, the French West Indian novelist contrasts the urban, proletarian, working-class novel of the United States, best represented by Richard Wright and Langston Hughes, with the "peasant novel" of the West Indies and Haiti.

538 Hesse, Jean-Albert. "Vie douloureuse et mystique des Noirs." *Franc-Tireur* (April 11, 1957), p. 7.
Of all the works by black novelists, *Go Tell It on the Mountain* stands out as the finest work on the life a black people in the United States. Brief comparisons are made with Richard Wright as well as with Victor Hugo. Baldwin, like Hugo, is influenced by Christian notions of justice. Hugo's poor are good because they are poor; Baldwin's characters are chosen because they are oppressed. Plot summary stressing characters.

539 Joly, Pierre. "James Baldwin évoque Harlem, sa patrie." *Paris-Normandie* (April 5, 1957), p. 11.
The introductory remarks frame Baldwin within a new group of "lost generation writers" which includes Henry Miller and Richard Wright. In the interview Baldwin describes Harlem, discusses overt segregation and covert racism, and explains why France has become his new home.

540 Kim Jean-Jacques. "La culpabilité multiple des noirs américains." *Critique* No. 13 (January, 1957), pp. 80-88.
Review of *The Outsider* summarizing the major stages in the development of Cross Damon's awareness of the entanglements of life and his own desires. Kim does not stress Wright's existentialism in the work, but he does comment on the interest manifested in the nature of human relationships.

541 Perrochon, Henri. "*Les Elus de Seigneur* de James Baldwin." *Le Semeur vaudois* (April 27, 1957), pp. 1-2.
Go Tell It on the Mountain, like *Uncle Tom's Cabin* and

"Hallelujah", is a valuable work, which describes the life of black people. Fortunately, racism has not prevented black men and women of merit from emerging. The review contains a plot summary stressing religious ritual.

542 Vallette, J.[acques] *"The Third Generation*, Chester Himes (New American Library, New York)." *Mercure de France* No. 1115 (July 1, 1957), p. 535.
Valette briefly reviews Himes' novel, summarizing much of the plot rather than commenting on it.

1958

543 Anon. "A propos d'*Espagne païenne* par Richard Wright." *Le Journal de Genève* (July 12-13, 1958), p. 6.
Excerpts from a letter by Victor de la Serna, a Spaniard, responding to P.-O. Walzer's review of the translation of *Pagan Spain*. De la Serna attacks Wright bitterly for bias and mendacity. Walzer replies to this and another letter from a Spaniard.

544 Anon. *"Giovanni, mon ami,* de James Baldwin." *Arcadie*, September 1958, pp. 56-58.
Anglo-Saxon digressions puzzle the French reader. Haphazard arrangement of episodes, irregularity in the entrance and exit of characters, slow pace of the action are pointed out. The readers of *France-Soir*, but not the readership of *Arcadie* will find enlightening information on homosexuality. In spite of its "mediocre translation" and stylistic weaknesses, *Giovanni's Room* is "very honorable" and recommended to the French reader. The reviewer's preference is for the American title over the French title.

545 Anon. *"Giovanni, mon ami,* de James Baldwin." *L'Express* (June 5, 1958), p. 27.
A black-American writer writes about a subject that many find difficult to treat: homosexuality. Baldwin tells the story naturally and emotionally. His achievement can be compared to Jean Genet's and André Gide's works on homosexuality. Plot summary.

546 Anon. *"Il pleut des coups durs,* de Chester Himes." *Revue de la police* (July-September 1958).
The reviewer apparently confuses the book under review, *The Real*

Cool Killers, with an earlier work, *The Crazy Kill*. It is noted that the newer novel avoids racial stereotypes by leaving the slums of Harlem behind for the middle-class Sugar Hill neighborhood. The tragicomic adventures of a preacher lead to an investigation by Himes' detectives. The novel is characterized as an excuse for sociological study, and Himes is praised for his zesty style.

547 Anon. "L'Espagne vue par Richard Wright." *Le Figaro littéraire* No. 624 (April 5, 1958), p. 14.
Favorable review of *Pagan Spain*, "a beautiful book, quivering with anger, color and life."

548 Anon. "*La Troisième Génération*, Chester Himes." *Le Figaro littéraire* No. 649 (September 27, 1958), p. 13.
A brief and favorable review of *The Third Generation*, which is regarded as "probably the most poignant and complex novel written by Chester Himes."

549 Anon. "La vie des lettres." *France-Observateur* (November 13, 1958), p. 23.
A brief note announces the award of the Grand prix de la littérature policière to Himes for *For Love of Imabelle*.

550 Anon. "Policiers insolites." *France-USA* (November 1958), pp. 2, 4.
The Crazy Kill is briefly described as taking place "in the exciting Harlem locale" of other Himes books.

551 Anon. "Revue des livres -- Policiers." *Revue de la police* (April-June 1958), pp. 9-10..
Contains an enthusiastic review of *For Love of Imabelle* praising Himes for "an exceptional style that transcends the limits of the genre." Himes is not satisfied with piling up comic or dramatic scenes. Instead, he writes aggressively, with a rare sense of originality that is combined with unusual descriptive power. By far the best of all publications by "Série Noire" this novel goes beyond the limits of the detective genre. It tells of the extravagant adventures of Jackson, whom a bunch of hustlers deprive of his savings. Himes, in *For Love of Imabelle*, is "a writer of originality" and truculence, with the power to evoke people and situations, and a flair for funny, burlesque imagery. "One should also mention his black humor, his quick, cruel poetry, his often Rabelaisian verve." The

book is a dazzling pastiche as well as a masterpiece of the thriller.

552 Anon. "Richard Wright: *Un Enfant du pays*." *Liens* No. 38 (July, 1958), p. 8.
Favorable review of the translation of *Native Son* stressing that black suffering is symbolic of the human condition. In his plea for social justice, Wright achieves the power of a Biblical prophet.

553 Anon. "Voici les écrivains étrangers qui ont choisi de vivre en France." *France-Soir* (September 6, 1958).
A chart of authors from different countries who are then living in France. The greatest number, five, come from the United States. Three are Black. Incorrectly lists Baldwin's birth year as 1931 and the year when he came to France as 1949.

554 Baumier, Jean. "Richard Wright: *Espagne païenne*." *Europe* No. 353 (September 1958), p. 137.
Unfavorable review of *Pagan Spain*. Wright's Spain is a tourist's Spain and his political conclusions are weak.

555 Bonnefoi, Geneviève. "*Espagne païenne*, par Richard Wright, traduit par Roger Giroux." *Les Lettres nouvelles* No. 6 (June 1958), pp. 929-32.
Review of *Pagan Spain*. Bonnefoi analyzes at length Wright's attempt to connect subconscious motivation and cultural trends, especially concerning his perception of the link between Church and State, between the sacred and sexuality. The reviewer praises Wright's angry warning against Franco's political system.

556 Brenner, Jacques. "*Giovanni, mon ami*, de James Baldwin." *Paris-Normandie* (May 9, 1958), p. 11.
In *Giovanni's Room*, David stands out as a remarkable portrait. This makes him, and not Giovanni, the hero. The strength of the characterization overshadows both plot and locale (France). Baldwin shows his puritan education. The novel has a firm moral: true scorn is to scorn the sufferings of others. Both theme and central character remind one of Gide's *La Symphonie pastorale*. Giovanni's deterioration is similar to that of Laurence in *Jocelyn* by Lamartine.

557 Brièrre, Annie. "Classiques et nouveaux venus." *France-U.S.A.* (October 1968), p. 2.

Among half a dozen books, *The Dark Vine* by Hal Bennett is mentioned and *Jubilee* by Margaret Walker is praised as an 'original book that grips you almost continuously." Viry clearly dominates the scene; religious feelings and the natural beauty of Georgia are beautifully evoked.

558 Bucaille, Victor. "*Espagne païenne*, par Richard Wright." *Les Nouvelles littéraires* 34 (May 15, 1958), p. 3.
Mixed review of *Pagan Spain*. Although biased and overly critical, the work is written in a lively and colorful way.

559 Diop, Thomas. "*White Man, Listen* de Richard Wright (Editions Doubleday, New York)." *Présence africaine* N.S. No. 20 (June-July 1958), pp. 128-29.
Short, very favorable review. Mentions Wright's lectures in Western Europe and his wish was to" be useful and constructive" in the framework of a campaign of cultural cooperation. The tone is "neither bitter, nor aggressive."

560   Fol, Jean-Jacques [pseud. for Jean-Jacques Recht]. Introduction to "Probléme de l'intégration des races aux Etats Unis" by W.E.B. Du Bois. *Présence africaine* (January 1958), p. 73.
Mentions that Du Bois gave him this essay in 1957 when he was asked whether he intended to provide a continuation to *The Souls of Black Folk*, which Fol was then translating.

561 Fondeville, Pierre. "James Baldwin, *Les Elus du Seigneur*." *Etudes* No. 298 (July-August 1958), p. 149.
Go Tell It on the Mountain is a fictionalized narrative of the author's experiences. The book revives in a Harlem setting some of the more fascinating aspects of the film "Hallelujah." A sensuous, at times "unhealthy book." In an abrupt but poetic language full of biblical expressions, Baldwin tells of his people's dilemma.

562 Guérin, Daniel. "Controverse autour de l'héritage africain aux U.S.A." *Présence africaine* Nos. 17-18 (February-May 1958), pp. 166-72.
Mentions Wright's change of opinion about cultural retentions in America after visiting the Gold Coast (pp. 171-72).

563 Guette, Jean. "Revues étrangéres: *Partisan Review*, No. 2,

1958." *Les Lettres nouvelles* No. 61 (July 1958), p. 945.
A discussion of the problem of black writing in the U.S. by Stanley
E. Hyman and Ralph Ellison. The latter remarks that black literature
is mostly read by whites. This leads Afro- Americans to rediscover
their history and folklore. "Negro American literature is universal
because it draws upon writers of all colors and cultures." Allusions
are made to T.S. Eliot and Ralph Waldo Emerson. "In brief, the
Negro wants to speak as a man, not as a Negro, and especially not as
the kind of Negro the whites want to define."

564 Joly, Pierre. "Chester Himes, mon pote de Harlem." *Paris-Normandie* (November 7, 1958), p. 5.
Mention is made of the award to *For Love of Imabelle* and of the
ensuing celebration at the Quirinal bar where Himes inscribed books
with tough-guy slang.

565 Las Vergnas, Raymond. "Richard Wright." *La Revue de Paris*
No. 65 (August 1958), pp. 124-31.
After a biographical sketch, Las Vergnas discusses all of Wright's
major works in detail. He considers *The Outsider* a flawed but
important book. Wright needs to develop new territory in his
writing.

566 Lauras, André. *"La Troisième Génération*, Chester Himes."
Etudes No. 296 (January 1958), pp. 140-41.
Himes is a far less colorful personality than Wright and perhaps for
that reason shows less self-confidence in his work. However Himes
is an important witness to the present black generation and *The Third
Generation* is more the lively description of a particular milieu than a
piece of protest fiction.

567 Marchand, Jean-José. "Enquête sur la culture noire." *Preuves*
No. 86 (April 1958), pp.33-38.
Black writers answer half a dozen questions concerning their
relationship to Africa and their culture. What does "black culture"
mean for them? was it whole or divided? what is the influence of the
colonial situation and industriaiization upon it? the role of traditional
religions and languages? the place of black music? the future of black
culture(s) and the move of certain black Americans to accept "white"
values? NAACP official James Ivy thinks that "only ancient African
cultures deserved that apellation." (pp. 34-35). Léopold Senghor,
Cedric Dover and other non-Americans also take part.

568 Marchand, Jean-José. "Enquête sur la culture noire." *Preuves* No. 87 (May 1958), pp. 33-44.
Black writers answer half a dozen questions concerning their relationship to Africa and their culture (continuation).   Ralph Ellison claims "Our struggle proclaims that we are both 'black' and 'American'." (pp. 33-38; repr. in Ellison's *Shadow and Act* as "Some Questions and Some Answers.") Richard Wright declares that "the Negro was created by the whites" (pp 40-41); novelist Richard Gibson defines black culture as the Blacks' "fight for freedom" (pp. 41-43); painter Beauford Delaney ends by declaring that human values are "an amalgamation of the heritage of history." (p. 44).

569 Maslowski, Igor B. "*La Reine des pommes* de Chester Himes." *Mystère-Magazine* (June 1958).
A very positive review of *For Love of Imabelle*, "one of the most extraordinary detective stories I have read since I have been writing this column." One cannot summarize such a book easily, because "it is so filled with surprises." It is going to become a classic.

570 Michel, Pierre-Gérard. "*Giovanni, mon ami*, de James Baldwin." *Le Berri républicain* (July 3, 1958).
The French public knows Baldwin as the author of *Go Tell It On the Mountain. Giovanni' Room*, Baldwin's most recent work, is "very different."   The work is "tolerable" because of its quality of chracterization and modesty in language. Instead of a sordid story, Baldwin presents a story which is "very often upsetting" through its psychological analysis of the characters.

571 Nadeau, Maurice. "*Espagne païenne*, par Richard Wright." *France Observateur* No. 9 (April 24, 1958), pp. 19-20.
Mixed review of *Pagan Spain*. Nadeau concentrates on the paradox of calling so Catholic a country as Spain "pagan." Wright's point of view, emphatically not French, is "inquisitive, inventive, and profoundly human," but it leads him to some distortions, such as the notion that Spain is incapable of change.

572 Naguère, Jean. "*Espagne païenne*." *Le Petit Matin* (March 5, 1958), p. 5.
Favorable review of the translation of *Pagan Spain*. Naguére, agreeing with Wright's method and approach, considers the work a "perfect achievement" uniting warm understanding with a lucid and

fascinating vision.

573   Renaud, P.-A.   "Les Revues: Wright s'adresse à l'homme blanc." *France Observateur* (October 23, 1958), pp. 20-21.
Favorable notice of an extract published in *Les Lettres nouvelles* of the forthcoming French translation of *White Man, Listen!*

574   Tilliette, X.[avier]   "Richard Wright - *Espagne païenne*; Jean Créac'h - *Chroniques espagnoles*; Luis Romero - *Les Autres*; Jesùs Fernandez Santos - *Les Fiers*; Carmen de Icaza - *Avant qu'il soit trop tard*." *Etudes* No. 299 (December 1958), p. 429.
Contains an unfavorable review of the translation of *Pagan Spain* expressing shock and surprise at Wright's distorted picture of the country in question. The image is "partial and false." Does it come from a lack of preparation, ignorance of the language, stubborn prejudice, or a tourist's approach? Whatever the reason, Wright only mirrors his own "sad obsessions, complexes and rancor."

1959

575   Anon.   "*Couché dans le pain*, par Chester Himes." *La Tribune de Genève* (February 10, 1959).
A short but positive appraisal of *The Crazy Kill*, stressing its vivid style and hectic plot.

576   Anon.   "Les éditeurs vous parlent: Gallimard, Série noire: *La Reine des pommes* de Chester Himes." *Mystère-Magazine* (March 1959).
The article notes the award of the Grand Prix de la littérature policière to *For Love of Imabelle* and mentions that it is the first time that a foreign winner of the award has been present at the ceremony. The writer quotes praise by Jean Cocteau, Jean Giono, and Claude Roy and announces the forthcoming publication of *The Real Cool Killers* and *Run Man Run*.

577   Anon.   "Prix de littérature policière." *Mystère-Magazine* (January 1959), p. 123.
The article notes the award to Himes' *Imabelle* for the best detective novel among translated works and also that, for the first time, a foreign winner was present at the ceremony.

578 Anon. "*Tout pour plaire* par Chester Himes." *La Tribune de Genève* (August 1, 1959).
A review of *The Big Gold Dream* includes a detailed analysis of several characters. The plot itself "is only relatively important. It serves as a springboard for a trip into a culture foreign to everything that surrounds it." Himes is praised for the "authentic, unsparing portrayal" of his dark brothers.

579 Baumier, Jean "Notes de lecture: *Ames Noires*." *Europe* Nos. 367-68 (November-December 1959), p. 299.
A brief, favorable review of Du Bois' *The Souls of Black Folk*, published by Présence africaine and translated by Jean-Jacques Fol [Recht]. The "profound authenticity" of this important book is lauded.

580 Baumier, Jean. "Notes de lecture: *Les Noirs dans la civilisation américaine*." *Europe* No. 360 (April 1959), p. 188.
A favorable review of *The Negro in American Culture* by Margaret Just Butcher, which deals extensively with black literature and drama.

581 Dreyfus, Rémy. "*Ecoute, Homme blanc*." *France-Observateur* (July 2, 1959), p. 19.
Favorable review of *White Man, Listen!* analyzing each of the four lectures. Wright's background as a Western black man leads to a duality of perspective which both partakes of, and evaluates the thoughts and aspirations of the Third World.

582 Fol, Jean-Jacques [pseud. for Jean-Jacques Recht]. "A propos de Negroes." *Europe* Nos. 358-59 (February-March 1959), pp. 179-82.
This article discusses Negro spirituals, quoting W.E.B. Du Bois' appreciation of them in *The Souls of Black Folk* several spirituals are quoted and the major themes analyzed.

583 Howlett, Jacques. "Le Livre de la semaine: *Ecoute, homme blanc*, de Richard Wright." *Les Lettres nouvelles* No.7 (May 27, 1959), pp. 9-10.
Favorable review of *White Man, Listen!* Analyzes some of Wright's central arguments, which it defines as liberal humanism as opposed both to racial irrationality and dialectical Marxism.

584 Jouvenel, Renaud de. "Autour de ce numéro." *Europe* Nos.
358-59 (February-March 1959), pp. 17-24.
Speaking of the difficulties of selecting American authors for the
special issue on American literature, the author alludes to the
decision to publish Langston Hughes and exclude Sterling Brown,
"a black American poet who cannot be translated properly because he
writes in a sort of black dialect" (p. 23).

585 Jouvenel, Renaud de. "Preface." *Europe* Nos. 358-59
(February-March 1959), pp. 144-52.
Translator's preface to "Le poète au bigot," "La charrue de la
liberté," and an extract from *Simple Takes a Wife*, printed on pp.
146-52. In this biographical and bibliographical notice, Hughes is
described as "the most important black writer because he is the most
authentic, the firmest supporter of the black cause and the most
unwavering in his attitude, as well as one of the most representative
American writers."

586 Rétif, André. "*Ames noires* par W.E.B. DuBois." *Etudes*
No. 303 (October 1959), p. 123.
Stresses the historical value of the volume but ends on its literary
qualities. "It retains such freshness and poetry, such love for the
black race that reading it remains an enchantment and a benefit. It
belongs to the inheritance of mankind."

587 Rexroth, Kenneth. "L'influence de la poésie française sur la
poésie américaine." *Europe* Nos. 358-59 (February-March 1959),
pp. 43-66.
Dealing with the influence of literature of international social and
political movements, according to the theories of Auerbach, the
author mentions Wright's first works (p. 62). Mentions that
Hughes' works do not show an "obvious French influence" despite
the fact that he has lived in France, speaks "perfect French," and is at
ease with French culture (p. 66).

1960

588 Alter, André. "Noirs pour rire ou pour pleurer?" *Témoignage
chrétien* No. 84 (September 23, 1960), p. 14.
Favorable review of Lorraine Hansberry's *A Raisin in the Sun*
which, in spite of its variety and human warmth, leaves the reader ill
at ease.

589 Anon. *"Un Coup de chance* de Julian Mayfield." *Le Figaro littéraire* No. 769 (January 14, 1960), p. 15.
Review of Julian Mayfield's *The Hit* focusing on the plot of the novel without attempting to provide a judgment on its aesthetic merits.

590 Anon. "C'était le plus grand écrivain noir U.S." *Libération* (December 1, 1960), p. 8.
Obituary notice summing up the highlights of Wright's literary career. Points out that he was an expatriate because he refused to be a propagandist for American "democracy."

591 Anon. "Entretien avec Richard Wright." *L'Express* No. 479 (August 18, 1960), pp. 22-23.
Interview with Wright on a number of topics. He discusses the growing awareness of the world of color and his own fight for a world free of racism. American racism prompted his European exile. Little progress has been made to implement school desegregation. Other signs of continuing racism in the United States are the poor reception of his *Black Power*, the paternalistic attachment of whites to blacks, and Dutch rule in Indonesia. Wright also comments on American expatriates black and white, the liking of the French for Afro-Americans, and sexual freedom in France.   Translated in *Dictionary of Literary Biography, Documentary Series*, Vol. 2 (Gale Research Company, Detroit, 1982), pp. 449-53.

592 Anon. "Il est mort à 52 ans: 'Pour moi il est trop tard...' disait Richard Wright." *Paris-Presse* (December 1, 1960), p. 22.
Obituary quoting a remark made by Wright a few days after the election of President Kennedy. "I won't return to the United States. For me, it's too late." Brief mention of his main books.

593 Anon. "La mort de Richard Wright." *L'Express* (December 1, 1960), p. 36.
Obituary stressing that the themes of Wright's work were always a reflection of the position of blacks in American society.

594 Anon. "Le dernier roman de Richard Wright, écrivain noir U.S. qui vient de mourir à Paris, a été traduit par Mme Bokanowski femme du ministre française des P. et T." *France-Soir* (December 1, 1960), p. 5.
Obituary stressing the hardships of Wright's childhood and his

continuing struggle against racism.

595 Anon. "Mort de Richard Wright." *L'Humanité* (November 30, 1960), p. 2.
Brief notice of Wright's death.

596 Anon. "Mort de Richard Wright." *Le Parisien libéré* (November 30, 1960), p. 6.
Notice of Wright's death explaining his medical condition. Hardly mentions his works.

597 Anon. "Richard Wright, écrivain solitaire." *Combat* (December 4, 1960), p. 9.
Obituary with a favorable assessment of Wright's literary career, especially in regard to its concern with the suffering of American blacks. Includes a photograph of Wright.

598 Anon. "Richard Wright est mort." *La Croix* (December 1, 1960), p. 6.
Obituary emphasizing Wright's struggle for the independence of colonized peoples everywhere and his resolve never to return to the United States to live.

599 Anon. "Richard Wright est mort." *Le Monde* (December 1, 1960), p. 6.
Obituary-eulogy commenting on the irony of Wright's death at a time when blacks are just beginning to liberate themselves. Although he attained personal fame, Wright was never satisfied with the political effect of his writings.

600 Anon. "Richard Wright est mort." *Paris-Jour* (December 1, 1960).
Brief obituary mentioning the influence of Sartre and Simone de Beauvoir upon his writing.

601 Anon. "Richard Wright n'est plus." *Le Figaro* (November 30, 1960), p. 17.
Obituary emphasizing his exile in France. He appealed to the consciences of both blacks and whites.

602 Anon. "Trois acteurs d'*Un Raisin au soleil*." *L'Humanité* No.

5035 (November 7, 1960), p. 2.
A review of Hansberry's *A Raisin in the Sun* with long quotations from an interview of three black actors in the play - Toto Bissainthe, Giséle Baka and Bachir Touré. The play is the story of a Negro family which wants to be emancipated and reach some freedom. "But the reasons for hope vary. The dispute then begins, rough and passionate, although human dignity finally wins."

603 Anon. *"Un Raisin au soleil* de Lorraine Hansberry." *Les Lettres françaises* No. 842 (September 22, 1960), p. 8.
Review of a performance of Hansberry's *Raisin in the Sun* staged by Guy Lauzin. The play is to be seen as one of "those generous works whose ambition it is to make the audience aware of an important social and human problem." The theme is racism and its iniquities. A summary of the plot follows. The French audience "should be especially attentive to those problems."

604 Anon. [Diop, Alioune] "In Memoriam." *Présence africaine* Nos. 34-35 (October 1960-January 1961), p. 247.
Obituary of Wright praising his aid to the magazine, to French-speaking Africans, and to liberty.

605 Anon. [Nadeau, Maurice]. "Avec Richard Wright qui parle de *Fishbelly.*" *France-Observateur* (June 9, 1960), p. 19.
Excerpt of an interview with Wright by his French publisher. Wright stresses the social implications and psychological meaning of *The Long Dream.* See item 635.

606 B., C. "A la Comédie Caumartin: *Un Raisin au soleil.*" *Le Figaro* No. 4987 (September 15, 1960), p. 22.
Review of *A Raisin in the Sun.* It was not easy to find a new perspective from which to deal with the question of the integration of Negroes in the United States. Hansberry, however, managed to write three acts free of the usual stereotypes, laments, and protest. The events mostly serve to analyze the sensitiveness, complexes, ingenuousness, limits, poetry, superstition and peculiar intelligence of the Negro race. Its ancestral instincts have alienated it from modern realism the efficacy of which is nevertheless acknowledged.

607 Baumier, Jean. "Richard Wright: *Fishbelly.*" *Europe* No. 377 (September 1960), pp. 150-51.
Generally favorable review of *The Long Dream.* Wright exaggerates

the bleakness of his subject, however.

608   Beigbeder, Marc. "Rentrée théâtrale." *Les Lettres nouvelles*
No. 5 (December 1960), pp. 194-95.
In an article on Jean Genet's *The Blacks*, a full page is devoted to the
audience reactions to *A Raisin in the Sun* by Lorraine Hansberry.
The play has enjoyed tremendous success in New York; it is
acclaimed in Paris but were the Younger family Algerians, would
there be a single performance of it there? "There are limits to French
eclecticism."

609   Borel, Jacques. "Un noir face à l'Europe." *Beaux-Arts* No. 888
(March 11, 1960).
Favorable review of the translation of *White Man, Listen!* Borel
stresses his agreement with Wright's point that Western aid to Africa
and Asia should be given fraternally, not paternalistically Wright is a
better novelist than polemicist, but *White Man, Listen!* is an
important book.

610   Bosschére, Guy de. *"Fishbelly*, de Richard Wright." *Présence
africaine* No. 31 (April-May 1960), pp. 125-27.
Favorable review of *The Long Dream* with a plot summary.
Emphasis is laid on the themes of dreaming and fear. Focuses on the
compromise achieved by Tyree and its psychic cost, both to him and
to his son. Wright's style is admirable.

611   Bosschére, Guy de. *"Fishbelly*, de Richard Wright."
Synthèses No. 174 (November 1960), pp. 63-66.
Reprint of his *Présence africaine* review of *The Long Dream* with a
preamble on the racial question.

612   Brièrre, Annie. "L'Amérique n'est pas conformiste, elle se
renouvelle sans cesse." *France-U.S.A.* Nos. 141-142 (September-
October 1960), p. 2.
Discusses *The Long Dream* and *The Outsider*. The latter is
Dostoevskian. Quotes Wright as saying that he did not intend *The
Outsider* to be specifically existentialist but to reflect his wider
philosophy. Wright believes that human creativity will triumph over
technology, prefers Dreiser to most other American novelists, and
considers Freud and Marx as poets.

613   C., J-L. "A la Comédie Caumartin: *Un Raisin au soleil."*

Combat No. 5036 (September 5, 1960), p. 2.
A review of "the first play ever written by a black woman," *A Raisin in the Sun* by Lorraine Hansberry. According to Guy Lauzin, who produced the play, the work "is extremely objective in its unfolding. It belongs to American naturalistic drama but its topic is not segregation." It is the story of a family living in a ghetto slum and their reactions when they are told they'll get a huge insurance compensation payment. This is no protest play but "an objective work, mostly through its human variety and emotional suspense." Emmanuel Roblès, who wrote the adaptation, cut everything that could have seemed "too conventional."

614 Clair, Andrée. "*Un Raisin au soleil*: Trois actes de Lorraine Hansberry adaptés par Emmanuel Roblés." *Présence africaine* No. 32-33 (June-September 1960), 214-15.
Prefaced by Langston Hughes' poem, the review focuses on the theme and topic of the play and the evolution of the integration of black Americans into the mainstream. The outstanding success of *A Raisin in the Sun* in the United States is mentioned; reading Harold J. Isaacs' *The New World of Negro Americans* is recommended.

615 Feather, L. "Nouvelles d'Amérique." *Arts, Lettres, Spectacles* No. 788 (September 21, 1960), p. 6.
Short, favorable review of *Tambourines to Glory* by Langston Hughes.

616 G., D. "Richard Wright." *Théâtre* No.15 (January 19, 1960), pp. 1, 3.
Obituary listing Wright's major works, stressing his theatrical activities, and noting the continuing contribution of his work to blacks in the New World and in Africa.

617 Gatinot, Gérard. "*Un Raisin au soleil* (gonflé de tendresse et de dignité)." *L'Humanité* No.4990 (September 15, 1960), p. 2.
The review of Lorraine Hansberry's *A Raisin in the Sun* begins with a mention of Langston Hughes' famous line. The play, whose topic is still very much present in contemporary preoccupations, is commendable because it manages to create a   likeable and mostly believable family. "If good feelings were enough to fill up theaters, the Comédie Caumartin would be sure of prolonged success."

618 Gérard, Albert. "Négritude et humanité chez Richard Wright."

La Revue Nouvelle 10 (October 15, 1960), pp. 337- 43.
Deals with Wright's most important novels, especially *The Outsider*.
Gérard argues that Wright's real concerns transcend race. His
novels focus on the larger dilemma of modern man facing his
existential condition in a world left without traditional values.

619   Hampaté-Ba, Amadou.   "Richard Wright, mon frère."
Démocratie 60 No. 59 (December 8, 1960), p. 26.
Very flowery and passionate obituary extolling Wright as a   fighter
for black freedom and solidarity. It emphasizes Wright's universal
appeal and his commitment to the struggle for African independence.
"Your death makes human culture poorer. Black Africa recognizes
you and claims you back." Reprinted in *La Vie africaine* No. 10
(January 10, 1961), p. 5.

620   Juin, Hubert. *"Fishbelly*, un grand roman." *Les Lettres
françaises* No. 827 (June 2-8, 1960), p. 3.
Favorable, largely descriptive review of *The Long Dream*. Juin
emphasizes Wright's treatment of racism.

621   Julien, Claude. Introduction to *God's Trombones: Sermons
noirs en vers* by James Weldon Johnson. Paris: Editions de l'Epi,
1960.
Brief introduction to "a great Negro poet," capable of preserving the
authenticity and vividness of folk preachers and the spirituals. The
call and response pattern, ecstasy and the climaxing of emotion in
Negro church rituals are mentioned.

622   Julien, Claude. "Richard Wright." *France-Observateur*
(December 1, 1960), p. 18.
Obituary-editorial noting the irony of Wright's exile. In contrast to
the rising hope of the civil rights movement in the United States,
Wright was more violently bitter in *The Long Dream* than in his
earlier works.

623   Julien, C[laude]. *"La Reine des Pommes*, de Chester Himes;
Un coup de chance de Julian Mayfield." *Le Monde* (November 5,
1960), p. 4.
A brief mention of the award of the Grand prix de la littérature
policière to Himes for *For Love of Imabelle* precedes a more in-depth
evaluation of *The Hit*, which is found to be worthwhile reading.

624 Kattan, Naïm. "La saison théâtrale." *Les Cahiers du Sud* No. 355 (April-May 1960).
The reviewer has a favorable opinion of the production of *A Raisin in the Sun* by Lorraine Hansberry and pans a performance of a play by Tennessee Williams.

625 Kessel, Patrick. *"Fishbelly*, de Richard Wright." *France-Observateur* (July 9, 1960), p. 18.
The reviewer defines *The Long Dream* and spells out its message as it being abnormal to be "conditioned" by a society into which one cannot be assimilated.

626 Las Vergnas, Raymond. "Images en noir et blanc." *Les Nouvelles littéraires* 38 (May 26, 1960), p. 2.
Favorable review of *The Long Dream*, with a lengthy plot summary and an analysis of Fishbelly's moral and psychological drama. Includes an account of Wright's literary evolution.

627 Las Vergnas, Raymond. "Un roman de Richard Wright." *La Revue de Paris* (October 1960), pp. 169-70.
Detailed analysis of *The Long Dream* considered as Wright's first novel in which the hero's story is not autobiographical.

628 Lerminier, Georges. "A la Comédie Caumartin: *Un Raisin au soleil*." *Le Parisien libéré* (September 20, 1960), p. 6.
"Nothing is tamer than this portrayal of a Negro American family if one considers dramatic technique only..." Without "ignoring Lorraine Hansberry's talent," the reviewer of *A Raisin in the Sun* considers that "the rather loose way in which the situation is developed and the characters delineated prevents us from feeling any authentic emotion." He would have wished the adapter to have been less concise and faithful; but the staging is realistic and meticulous.

629 Marcabru, Pierre. *"Un Raisin au soleil*: du naturalisme attendri." *Arts, Lettres, Spectacles* No. 788 (September 21, 1960), p. 6.
An unfavorable review of Lorraine Hansberry's *A Raisin in the Sun*. "Everything is there, except for the enthusiasm of drama and the pulsing of the blood."

630 Moget, Marie-Therése. "Richard Wright: *Fishbelly*." *La*

Nouvelle Critique No. 119 (October 1960), pp. 143-45.
Favorable review of *The Long Dream* noting the lack of social opportunities for American blacks. A summary of the plot is included.

631 Nadeau, Maurice. "Portrait: La vérité de Richard Wright." *L'Express* (December 8, 1960), p. 47-48.
Eulogy emphasizing Wright's service in substituting truthful images of race relations for traditional ones. His interest in Africa and Asia was inspired by the same impulses as his earlier works and shared their sense of urgency. Nadeau recalls his first meeting with Wright, explains the importance of Marxism for the writer, and comments on *Uncle Tom's Children* and *Native Son*.

632 Nadeau, Maurice. "Richard Wright s'explique sur son oeuvre et sur *The Long Dream.*" *Les Lettres nouvelles* No. 8 (April 1960), pp. 9-15.
Interview with Wright, who discusses American political pressures on Afro-American literature (which he rejects) and his intentions in *The Long Dream*. Nadeau provides a prefatory note on Wright's career. This interview is included as an introduction to the French edition of the novel (*Fishbelly*, Paris: Lettres nouvelles, 1960).

633 Paget, Jean. "A la Comédie Caumartin: *Un Raisin au soleil.*" *Combat* (September 15, 1960), p. 2.
A review of Hansberry's *Raisin in the Sun* which claims that "the play is rather conventional and often verges on melodrama...it never rises above a tone of temperate protest." This is probably what makes for the mood of bitter acceptance and a resignation stemming perhaps from the Christian influence or else a sort of activism. "The play is immature and seems to condone every prejudice with the black bourgeoises' conventional tears." Mrs Hansberry is very "American" but not very lucid.

634 Pivot, Bernard. "Rencontre avec Richard Wright." *Le Figaro littéraire* No. 734 (May 14, 1960), p. 3.
Presentation of *The Long Dream* [*Fishbelly* in French] as well as of Wright himself. "This man is both sad and optimistic." Wright states that his writings have aided interracial understanding, explains the failure of the stage adaptation [*The Long Dream*, by Ketti Frings] in the United States and mentions his correspondence with a Danish girl who committed suicide.

635 Poirot-Delpech, Bertrand. *"Un Raisin au soleil* adapté de l'américain par Emmanuel Roblès." *Le Monde* (September 15, 1960), p. 13.
A review of Lorraine Hansberry's *A Raisin in the Sun* with a long summary of the plot. "The most emotional and preachy kind of naturalism....The realism of the text and the staging is pushed to the verge of shamelessness...in order to make a guilty voyeur of the spectator to his utter shame and enlightenment."

636 Rétif, André. "Richard Wright - *Ecoute, homme blanc.*" *Etudes* No. 304 (February 1960), p. 279.
Unfavorable review of the translation of *White Man, Listen!* complaining of Wright's lay point of view.

637 Rousseaux, André. *"Fishbelly* de Richard Wright." *Le Figaro* No. 737 (June 4, 1960), p. 2.
Favorable review of the translation of *The Long Dream* analyzing the social and psychological elements of the novel.

638 Schneider, Douglas H. "Le Souvenir de Richard Wright." *France-U.S.A.* No. 144 (December 1960), p. 2.
Obituary-eulogy recalling Schneider's meeting with Wright when the author arrived in Paris: as he was being driven around the city with Gertrude Stein, he responded to its beauty enthusiastically.

639 Stil, André. "Les Livres et la vie: Noir sur noir." *L'Humanité* (July 28, 1960), p. 2.
Unfavorable review of the translation of *The Long Dream*. Although it starts very well, the novel becomes ambiguous and presents a black life so corrupted as to seem almost to justify white racist repression.   It is true that Wright shows where the ultimate responsibility for racism lies, but the latter part of the book is too melodramatic. The CP journalist compares Wright to French popular novelist Eugéne Sue.

640 T., H. "Un grand romancier noir est mort." Paris *Le Populaire du Dimanche* (December 11, 1960), p. 2.
Obituary referring to Wright as "a man liberated from all racial and ideological prejudices."

641 Vernon, Françoise. "Traduit de l'américain." *Informations et*

Documents (September 1, 1960), pp. 34-39.
Contains a highly favorable notice of the translation of *The Long
Dream* (p. 37) calling it Wright's masterpiece and emphasizing its
universal meaning.

642 Vilaine, Anne-Marie de. "Richard Wright: La rééducation des
Blancs est plus urgente que celle des Noirs." *L'Express* No. 463
(April 26, 1960), p. 34.
Interview with Wright commenting on *The Long Dream,* "a novel
about the corruption bred by racism." Crippling the psychological
processes of whites as well as blacks, the affliction is present in Asia
and Africa as well as America. France is comparatively free of
racism, however.

643 Wagner, Jean. "Littérature nègre et littérature américaine."
Rives No. 16 (1960), pp. 16-20.
This essay by Professor Wagner poses the problem of a specific
Afro-American literature and the absence of black authors in white
American (and French) literary histories. Praises Robert Bone's *The
Negro Novel in America* and the beginnings of the American Society
of African Culture. The advent of the paperback era should favor the
reprinting of such major works as those of J.W. Johnson, while
Wright, Ellison, Baldwin, Yerby, Motley and Mayfield are better
publicized. (See the introduction to this volume for Wagner's
protests about cuts in an article submitted to *Informations et
Document*ts.)

1961

644 Anon. "Il y a un an, Richard Wright." *La Vie africaine* No. 20
(December 1961), p. 42.
A commemoration of Wright emphasizing his interest in the
liberation of European colonies and in African economic and political
development.

645 Anon. Note on *Ne nous énervons pas* by Chester Himes. *Les
Lettres françaises* (August 24, 1961), p. 7.
A brief review of *The Heat's On,* which is characterized as merely a
series of events that depict daily life in Harlem, rather than a story.
The reviewer makes note of the humor in the piece and says that

Himes is unique among contemporary authors.

646 Anon. "Votre policier: Chester Himes, *Ne nous énervons pas.*" *Paris Presse* (July 5, 1961), p. 9.
A brief mention of *The Heat's On*, which the reviewer describes as "corpses waltzing around a missing treasure." Himes is said to have reached a peak with his imaginative humor and "literary fitness."

647 Duvignaud, Jean. "Un humanisme naissant: la négritude." *Critique* No. 170 (July 1961), pp. 579-90.
Will literature help societies not based on the written word create a history and reality of their own? Several volumes are discussed, but not exclusively in this perspective: *Les Contes d'Amadou Koumba* by Birago Diop, *Muntu* by Janheinz Jahn, *Fishbelly* by Richard Wright, *Un Nègre à Paris* by Bernard Dadié, *Chemins d'Europe* by Ferdinand Oyono and *Rouge est le sang des noirs* [*Tell Freedom*] by Peter Abrahams. Wright's *The Long Dream* is granted comparatively little space but his style and testimony about the racial situation as it was in the United States are greatly praised.

648 Gérard, Albert. "James Baldwin et la religiosité noire." *La Revue nouvelle* 33, 2 (February 1961), pp. 177-86.
An attack on journalists and critics who in their facile reading of *Go Tell It on the Mountain* call attention only to the "picturesque" and the exotic. A serious study of the religious sensibilities of Blacks is needed at a time when Blacks seem destined to play an important role in the "destiny of the globe." *Go Tell It on the Mountain* has the same role as Dickens' novels and Beecher Stowe's *Uncle Tom's Cabin*, but it has not "received the attention it deserves." Unlike *Uncle Tom's Cabin*, Baldwin's first published book of fiction is not a "humanitarian tract in the form of fiction." It has "eminent literary value." Baldwin shows a "remarkable mastery" of his craft. He presents a purely "ethical and interior theme." Racial conflict is absent. On the level of character, Baldwin "confirms a Faulknerian vision" and his characters, by their intense emotions, are close to Dostoevsky's. The work is extremely original and important.

649 Gérard, Albert. "La Nuit de Jacob." *Synthèses* No. 5 (May 1951), pp. 348-355.
Review of *The God That Failed* discussing Wright's proletarian background and quoting at length from his contribution, especially to indicate his delight and exultation at the time he was writing his

revolutionary poems in the thirties.

650   Gérard, Albert.   "Ralph Ellison et le dilemme noir."   *Revue générale belge* 97, 10 (October 1961), pp. 89-104.
A long review-essay on *Invisible Man*, approached in the wide context of American literature and race relations, but making much of Ellison's art. It was later included in a chapter of *Les Tambours du néant.* (q.v.).

651   Gérard, Albert.   "Vie et vocation de Richard Wright."   *Revue générale belge* 97 (January 1961), pp. 65-78.
Obituary-article summarizing and defining the major trends and characteristics of Wright's career as an embattled writer, stressing his humanistic and existential interests, his political commitment, and the problems raised in his fiction.

652   Jean, Raymond.   *"Fishbelly*, de Richard Wright."* Les Cahiers du Sud* No. 358 (December 1960-January 1961), p. 470.
Highly favorable review of *The Long Dream* in which the reviewer, himself a left-wing novelist, takes up the defense of black Americans.

653   Jokinen, Denise.   "L'art poétique du jazz".   *France-Amérique* (July 2, 1961), p. 4.
Langston Hughes, the star of the Boston Jazz Festival on June 20, 1961, was exonerated of charges of un-American activities. A friend of France, he has visited Paris many times, appreciated French love of jazz, and translated Jacques Roumain's novel, *Masters of the Dew.*

654   Kala-Lobé, Iwiyé.   "Un des vieux amis de *Présence africaine.*" *La Vie africaine* No. 20 (December 1961) pp. 42-43.
Reminiscence on Wright's association with *Présence africaine* magazine.

655   Lemaire, Marcel.   "Fiction in U.S.A.: From the South..." *Revue des langues vivantes* 27, 3 (1961), pp. 244- 53.
Includes a review of *The Long Dream* (pp. 246-48). The novel is melodramatic and sordid but Wright points up the moral problems in Southern racism.

656   M., C.   "Un grand romancier 'noir', Chester Himes."

Carrefour (June 21, 1961).
In a very favorable review of the early Harlem stories, the typical book is characterized as "a thriller containing several crimes at once, and a story that omits the usual baggage of the traditional mystery"; Himes' work nevertheless should be regarded as detective literature. *The Heat's On* has not only an exciting plot but also superb descriptions of people, places, and things. The rich mixture invites the favorable comparison to Victor Hugo. The series is densely packed, brilliant, realistic, and romantic and Himes' protagonists are the stuff of flesh-and-blood policemen, rather than supermen. The reviewer denounces the literary snobbery that has denigrated the Série Noire and suggests that Himes' fiction is comparable to that of Erskine Caldwell and John Steinbeck.

657   Masson, René.   "Un noir dans la 'Série Noire'."   *Candide* (June 15, 1961).
The Heat's On is as fantastic as the other "domestic" stories by Chester Himes. In each story one finds a revelation about life in Harlem and the people who live there. Himes' own life is discussed at some length, but there is no mention of his prison years.

658   Pétrie, Daniel.   *"Un Raisin au soleil."* *La Table ronde* No. 163 (July-August 1961), p. 139.
Review of the film adaptation of Lorraine Hansberry's play *A Raisin in the Sun* with Sidney Poitier and Claudia McNeil. The reviewer quotes George Collar; he concludes that racism is one problem among many others and that "human solutions" have to be elaborated.

659   Rousseaux, André.   *Littérature du vingtiéme siécle.* Paris: Editions Albin Michel, 1961.
Discusses *The Long Dream* with emphasis on the theme of black fear of whites. Whatever Wright's literary limitations, he speaks irresistibly to the white conscience.

660   Sadoul, Georges.   "Noirs Américains de 60".   *Les Lettres françaises* No. 876 (May 18, 1961), p. 6.
Review of the film adaptation of Hansberry's *A Raisin in the Sun*. "The producer...was satisfied with photographing a successful drama." But the play itself is an important event since it reached a wide American audience, certainly wider than Hughes' own great poetry. Quotes Hansberry on the ability of blacks to know whites

and the inability of whites to know blacks. "The film is too long and too rich to be summed up."

661 Vischnegradsky, Dimitri. "Le Blues." *Présence africaine* No. 37 (2nd trimester 1961), pp. 157-88.
This study of the origins, themes and variations of the blues goes into great detail concerning their complexity and variety.   The bibliography refers to Langston Hughes and Arna Bontemps' *The Book of Negro Folklore.*

662 Wagner, Jean. "Langston Hughes." *Informations et Documents* No. 135 (January 15, 1961), pp. 30-35.
A detailed and accurate retrospect of Hughes' career by the author of *Black Poets of the United States*, who provides full information on the poet's evolution and major themes. "Negro," "My Lord," Pride" and "Trumpet Player" are included in bilingual inserts. (See Introduction to this volume for Wagner's letter about the essay.)

1962

663 Anon. "Amer." *Paris-Jour* (February 1, 1962).
A review of *Pinktoes* mentions the swift pace of the story and Himes' humor. It remarks on the bitterness of the protagonist, Mamie Mason, who in spite of her great wealth and position can neither escape racism nor her excessive weight.

664 Anon. Brief note. *Le Populaire du Centre* (December 1, 1962).
The author has high praise for *All Shot Up*, describing it as full of angry humor. Himes is praised for the artful manner in which he works chance and coincidence into his narrative.

665 Anon. "*Mamie Mason*, de Chester Himes." *France-Soir* (March 3, 1962).
A brief but very positive appraisal of *Pinktoes*. "Only Chester Himes could meet the challenge of writing so humorously about the seemingly insoluble Negro problem."

666 Anon. Introduction to *Imbroglio negro* by Chester Himes." *L'Action littéraire* (November 29, 1962).
The first magazine installment of *All Shot Up* is preceded by a few

paragraphs that characterize Himes not only as "one of the best black writers of his generation" but also as "one of the most remarkable American writers of today."

667 Bénot, Yves. "Richard Wright et la condition du romancier noir américain." *Europe* No. 398 (June 1962), pp. 134-43.
Introductory note to William Alphaeus Hunton's essay "Richard Wright et la condition noire américaine," explaining that it is a translation of a lecture delivered at Conakry on January 18, 1961.

668 Bonnichon, André. "*Mamie Mason*, de Chester Himes." *Etudes* No. 313 (June 1962), p. 427.
The reviewer gives a favorable evaluation of this "amazing satire." He finds that the pace of *Pinktoes* is so hectic that he became dizzy after the first 150 pages. He notes that because it is such a bawdy book it is not suitable reading matter for the young but will probably serve to introduce the French reading audience to an unknown part of black life.

669 De Bure, I. "Chronique des livres: *Mamie Mason*, Chester Himes." *La Revue de Paris* (June 1962), p. 169.
Includes a short favorable review of *Pinktoes* which is judged "an entertaining and farcical story about racial segregation." De Bure praises Himes' deeply humorous approach.

670 Gérard, Albert. "Humanisme et Négritude: notes sur le roman afro-américain contemporain." *Diogène* No. 37 (Spring 1962), pp. 121-40.
Gérard discusses many Afro-American writers starting with Richard Wright and Ralph Ellison. He focuses on the extraordinary process "of the acceleration of history" in the 20th Century. Because of the movement of liberation by Blacks in the world, more than at any other time in history, more people will have the possibility of "actively intervening" in global affairs, a fact which is more important historically than the Soviet or nuclear revolutions. These "new" people will inevitably control not only their destiny but the destiny of the world. So important a group, and one which is hardly known by the white world, will move civilization in a new direction. Black literature has not been exploited for the purpose of understanding Black culture, although from year to year numerous books written by Black American authors appear in French and English. He finds that "the Afro-American novel offers a key to the

secrets of negritude, which is destined to contribute to the evolution of civilization in the next century." Also in English as "Humanism and Negritude: Notes on the Contemporary Afro-American novel." *Diogenes* No. 37 (Spring, 1962), 115-33. Reprinted in his *Les Tambours du néant* (q.v.).

671   Guénolé, Jean.   "Le blues dans la maison." *Informations et Documents* (March 15, 1962), pp. 21-29.
A brief panorama of African American music includes the spirituals and mentions the field hollers. Langston Hughes' *First Book of Jazz* is mentioned and Hughes quoted for stressing that humor, not only sadness, is to be found in the blues. Some twenty blues songs are reproduced in translation.

672   Haedens, Kléber.   "Il ne faut jamais dire à une femme qu'elle ressemble à une saucisse de Francfort..." *Paris-Presse* (March 10, 1962), p. 11D.
A detailed analysis of *Pinktoes* which discusses the Harlem backdrop, the well-meaning white characters, the orgies of sex and eating, and the satire of the so-called "promotion of interracial relations."   Haedens feels that Himes' prose is not always on par with his ambitions but that the characters, particularly Mr. and Mrs. Samuels, are engaging, colorful, and alive.

673   Jeanpierre, W[endell] A.   *"Youngblood,* par John O. Killens." *Présence africaine* No. 41 (1962), pp. 186-7.
A favorable review of this novel about the coming of age of a rebellious black youth in racist America. Notes that the style of the novel recalls the Wright of the early forties.

674   Lacouture, Jean and Baumier, Jean. *Le poids du Tiers Monde.* Paris: Arthaud, 1962.
Discusses *The Color Curtain,* noting Wright's experiential qualifications to analyze the political and psychological processes of the oppressed (pp. 32-34).

675   V., L. "Les romans de la semaine. Lu, approuvé, discuté: *Mamie Mason,* de Chester Himes." *Le Figaro littéraire* No. 827 (February 24, 1962), p.5.
This brief review of *Pinktoes* is a mixed one.   Although Himes is characterized as a "black Rabelais," the reviewer finds that the novel is too bawdy and vulgar.   He says that there are too many characters,

too many innuendoes, and too much farce. He concludes, however, that "you won't find another book like it."

1963

676 Amalric, Jacques. "La question raciale vue par un jeune écrivain noir américain." *Le Monde* (August 24, 1963), p. 5.
In the midst of the racial conflict, Baldwin, "one of the most brilliant representatives of the young generation," is trying to fashion a society that can live in interracial harmony. He is in Paris now to spark the solidarity movement in support of the March on Washington. Baldwin responds to questions on the Kennedys, the Black Muslims, the non-violent policy of Martin Luther King, Jr., the ability of the races to achieve racial equality, and the significance of the march.

677 Anon. "Actualités: Un roman policier pas comme les autres." *L'Action* (October 13, 1963).
This brief description of the major detective novels by Himes focuses more sharply on *Cotton Comes to Harlem*, which was then his latest detective story.

678 Anon. "*Black Nativity*." *Les Nouvelles littéraires* No. 1846 (January 17, 1963), p. 11.
Very favorable review of Hughes's play. The author notes the spontaneity of an art that is diametrically opposed to intellectual and "learned" music. Yet, although the singers seem to improvise at the height of enthusiasm, their cohesion is perfect. Praises the "noncommercial" rendering of the songs and jazz rhythms.

679 Anon. "Chester Himes: *La Croisade de Lee Gordon*." *Profils*, No. 3 (April 1963), p. 166.
In this French version of *Perspectives* magazine, a United States Information Service publication, a note indicates that *Lonely Crusade* "describes the life of a black intellectual."

680 Anon. "*Huit Hommes*, par Richard Wright." *Présence africaine* No. 46 (2nd trimester 1963), pp. 240-41.
Favorable review of *Eight Men*. Emphasizes the work's statement against racism, comparing it to the treatment of it in *Black Boy* and

The Long Dream.

681   Anon.   *"La prochaine fois, le feu* et *Personne ne sait mon nom."* *L'Union* (December 10, 1963), p. 10.
Biographical sketch and brief summary of the plots of *The Fire Next Time* and *Nobody Knows My Name* by James Baldwin.

682   Astre, Georges-Albert.   "Poésie noire aux U.S.A." *Les Lettres françaises* No. 988 (June 25, 1963), p. 6.
Descriptive review of Jean Wagner's book on Afro-American poetry from L. Dunbar to Langston Hughes.

683   Baignères, Claude.   *"Black Nativity."* *Le Figaro* No. 5707 (January 7, 1963), p. 16.
Very favorable review of Langston Hughes's play, performed in Paris at the time. "Here is the true and pure blues tradition steeped at the same time in the mysteries of the church, the nostalgia of African rhythms and the dynamic joy of the believers."

684   Beauvoir, Simone de.   *La Force des choses*. Paris: Gallimard, 1963. 686 p.
Mentions Wright several times, especially in connection with the political   activity   of   the   Rassemblement   Démocratique Révolutionnaire. De Beauvoir's friendship with the Wrights began in 1946 and continued though she disagreed with Wright's open anti-communism of the late fifties. His death grieved her. Translated: 1965.

685   Bloch-Michel, Jean.   *"La prochaine fois le feu* par James Baldwin." *La Gazette de Lausanne* (December 7-8, 1963), pp. 1-2.
James Baldwin was catapulted into prominence in America as a "leader" among Afro-Americans by the Civil Rights movement. However, Baldwin is not a "political man" but an "intellectual doing his job." There are too many inaccuracies in the translation of that fine essay. The author points out ways in which Baldwin and Wright differ on the racial issue. Wright saw only the uniqueness of the racial problem in the U.S. while closing his eyes to the plight of the Black Africans at St.Denis [a poor suburb north of Paris]. "Wright was living protected not by the open-mindedness of the French spirit but by his American passport." Having had a more recent encounter with racism, France may be destined to take a lesson from America.   To the reviewer, *The Fire Next Time* is

important because, as an inhabitant of Harlem, Baldwin has witnessed racism in the North. Also, he captures something new in America: "Blacks are now aware of the heavy weight of oppression and will no longer endure it."

686 Bondy, François. "Pour libérer les blancs..." *Preuves* No. 152 (November 1963), pp. 3-18.
The Fire Next Time changed Baldwin from novelist and essayist to spokesman for Black Americans and put him on the cover of big magazines and in many newspapers. Robert Kennedy included him in a list of Blacks called to discuss the racial crisis. In this, one of the most extensive interviews he granted in the sixties, Baldwin is called upon to answer a wide range of questions on the "Black question." Published in English in *Transition* (January 1964).

687 Bosschère, Guy de. "Chester Himes: *Une Affaire de viol.*" *Présence africaine* No. 48 (4th trimester 1963), pp.239-40.
A very favorable review of *A Case of Rape*. De Bosschère notes that although the story is located in Paris rather than in an American city, the topic is still the race problem, something that Himes handles with his usual vigor. He finds that the writing is terse and powerful and that "within the close intimacy of each sentence, one feels a spring uncoiling to deliver a powerful blow." The reviewer also mentions that the protagonist, Roger Garrison, bears a close resemblance to Richard Wright.

688 Breton, Emile. "Chester Himes ou le purgatoire de la Série noire." *Action poétique* No. 22 (October 1963), 40-41.
In a brief retrospective of Himes' career as a crime fiction writer, Breton emphasizes both his art and authenticity with quotes from the various books and interviews.

689 Clancy, Thomas S. "Le problème racial aux Etats-Unis." *Etudes* No. 319 (October 1963), pp. 67-78.
This essay focusing on a century of black resistance and oppression devotes a long development to the Civil Rights movement and Martin Luther King; it stresses the importance of James Baldwin as a novelist and essayist (*Notes of a Native Son, The Fire Next Time*) and ends by quoting Ellison on one's invisibility due to other people refusing to see you.

690. Clarke, John Henrik." *The Fire Next Time*, de James Baldwin

(Dial Press, New York)." *Présence africaine* No. 48 (4th trimester 1963), pp. 245-48.
A long and detailed review of Baldwin's sensational book of essays, seen as "his contribution to his own attempt at self-definition as a black man in his country." After a study of the contents of the volume, Clarke concludes that "better than any other contemporary writer, Baldwin has succeeded in giving the personal essay its place as a creative literary form." He is a highly respected writer who "opens wide onto the whole world."

691   Dadoun, Roger.   "Retour á Richard Wright." *Jeune Afrique* No. 119 (January 28-February 3, 1963), pp. 25, 28.
Favorable review of *Eight Men* tracing Wright's success to his intimate knowledge of both black and white spheres of life. Wright achieves unity through subject matter and imagery. Discusses "The Man Who Lived Underground," "Big Black Good Man," and "The Man Who Killed a Shadow."

692   Dalmas, André.   "L'humeur des lettres: *Personne ne sait mon nom*." *La Tribune des nations* (November 1, 1963), p. 4.
Nobody Knows My Name describes with remarkable accuracy the condition of all Black people in the U.S. and the world. Baldwin "knows how to write what he sees and feels." A brief discussion of only one essay, "Princes and Powers," follows.

693   Fabre, Michel.   "James Baldwin, *La prochaine fois, le feu*." *Rives* No. 26 (Summer 1963), p. 14.
Brief review of *The Fire Next Time* emphasizing the brilliant style and beauty of Baldwin's writing, as well as his message. This book marks the new commitment of Baldwin, who had forsaken detachments in order to replace Richard Wright as spokesman for black writers.

694   Guérin, Daniel. *Décolonisation du noir américain*.   Paris: Editions de Minuit, 1963. 219 p.
Dedicated to Wright, George Padmore, Fanon and Du Bois, this study cites Wright several times in support of particular points about race relations in the United States. Guérin notes that Wright paid tribute to communist support of the black cause in the thirties.

695   Kesteloot, Lilyan. *Les Ecrivains noirs de langue française: naissance d'une littérature*. Bruxelles: Université Libre. 1963.

Pp. 53-63 explore the writings of the Harlem Renaissance in detail;
Kesteloot asserts that the founders of the Negritude movement have
intimate contacts with McKay, Hughes, Cullen and Toomer, "whom
they read and knew personally" in the group of the Nardal sisters.
The works of those writers are analyzed and their possible influence
on Damas, Senghor and Césaire explored. Quotes *White Man, Listen*
and mentions Wright's relationship to *Présence africaine* and his
influence on black writers in French.

696 Le Pape, Pierre. *"La prochaine fois, le feu."* *Paris-Normandie*
(December 20, 1963), p. 9.
The Fire Next Time demarcates an era in the history of Black-
American literature and in the history of Black-White relations.
Baldwin teaches us that racism is endemic to the United States.
Richard Wright thought that racism was contained within Southern
boundaries. "This book frightens us because it comes from a man
and a people who have tried all solutions of reconciliation. ... Will
America listen to Baldwin's pleas for peace? The future of the most
powerful nation in the world depends on it."

697 M., E. and D., J. "L'oeuvre de Chester Himes." *Jazz hot*
(May 1963), p. 17.
This overview of Himes' work emphasizes his career as a writer of
detective fiction but also notes his "more serious writing."
Qualitatively, Himes is ranked just after Wright and Hughes among
black American writers. Himes' work is not only an authentic
picture of the American race relations problem but also a strong
indictment of it. His descriptions of the man on the street compare
favorably with those to be found in the novels of Balzac and
Dickens. The critics regard Himes' writings as "the blues at their
purest." Appended are a list of French translations of his work then
available and a plea for the reprinting of other titles.

698 Masson, Jean-Robert. *"Black Nativity."* *Les Lettres françaises*
No. 960 (January 10, 1963), p. 7.
Brief description of the musical show based upon "a text by the poet
Langston Hughes."

699 Mayfield, Julian. "La mort d'un militant." *Révolution* No. 3
(November 1963), p. 82-83.
A brief summary of W.E.B. Du Bois's career as a militant making
much of his stay in Ghana, when Mayfield met him. Followed by

Du Bois's last message to the world, written on June 26, 1957 and to be published after his death.

700 Mélèze, Josette. "*Huit Hommes* par Richard Wright." *Les Nouvelles littéraires* 41 (January 24, 1963), p. 5.
Favorable review of *Eight Men* commenting specifically on five of the pieces. Méléze notes a lyrical vein as well as the protest mode and praises "The Man Who Saw the Flood" and "The Man Who Lived Underground."

701 Parot, Jeanine. "Nouvelles en noir et blanc." *Les Lettres françaises* No. 965 (February 14-20, 1963), p. 3.
Favorable descriptive review of *Eight Men* by Richard Wright mentioning each of the eight pieces.

702 Prudon, Hervé. "C'est très dur d'être un blanc; entretien avec James Baldwin." *Le Nouvel Observateur* No. 364 (April 29, 1963), pp. 93-94.
This interview of Baldwin, "the author of *Native Son* (sic) and *If Beale Street Could Talk*," deals mostly with his reactions to French racism and xenophobia.

703 Rabi, W. "La prochaine fois, ce sera le feu." *L'Arche* No. 83 (December, 1963), p. 52.
Brief summary of *The Fire Next Time* by James Baldwin. In the black ghetto prevail feelings of anguish and guilt largely created by segregation. Religion is not satisfying but Baldwin refuses to hate all whites and seeks an "American solution."

704 Reiss, Françoise. "*Les Poètes nègres aux Etats-Unis.*" *Arts, Lettres, Spectacles* No. 916 (May 15, 1963), p. 4.
Laudatory review of Jean Wagner's book focusing on the racial and religious inspiration of Afro-American poetry from P.L. Dunbar to Langston Hughes.

705 Rochefort, Christiane. "Postface" to Chester Himes, *Une Affaire de viol*. Paris: Les Yeux Ouverts, 1963, pp. 169-172.
A noted novelist compares the plight of the black American with that of the woman in modern society and finds them to be similar. She believes that Himes' novel deals with both issues by having the plot hinge on the accusation of rape levelled at four black men, while the

separate "case studies" stress the background and social position of Elizabeth, the female protagonist.

706 Sainville, Leonard. Introduction to "Herbert Simmons" in his *Anthologie de la littérature négro-africaine*. Vol. 1. Paris: Présence africaine, 1963.
Simmons, a young author, reminds one of Motley: with sobriety and talent he depicts victims of the social system who turn into outlaws. *Corner Boy* is briefly summarized and excerpted.

707 Sainville, Léonard. Introduction to "Chester Himes" In his *Anthologie de la littérature négro-africaine*. Vol. 1. Paris: Présence africaine, 1963.
Himes is a remarkably fertile writer who, like Richard Wright, has had most of his work translated into French. Sainville praises Himes for not being afraid to broach any subject and also for his limitless zest and rates him among the best writers of his generation. Summaries and excerpts from *If He Hollers Let Him Go* and *Lonely Crusade* are appended.

708 Sainville, Léonard. General introduction to his *Anthologie de la littérature négro-africaine*. Vol. 1. Paris: Présence africaine, 1963.
Mentions that Blacks absorbed Western culture to "sing their grief and their hopes." Alludes to Wright quoting, in *White Man, Listen!*, a number of worksongs, dozens, and poets ranging from Phillis Whiney (sic), George Mose Harton (sic), and James M. Whitfield to F. Ellen Harpe (sic) and P. Lawrence (sic) Dunbar. Advises reading the anthology *The Negro Caravan*, and *The Negro in American Culture* by Margaret Just Butcher (p. 16).

709 Sainville, Léonard. Introduction to the section on "Etats-Unis d'Amérique" in his *Anthologie de la littérature négro africaine*. Vol. 1. Paris: Présence africaine, 1963.
A brief note quotes Billie Holiday to emphasize the continuity of racial endurance, expresses through the blues and spirituals, and the function of literature as vocal. Numerous novelists like Wright, Ellison and Himes emerge. Ann Petry, Ridding J. Saunders [sic], Bruce [McMarion] Wright and Franc [sic] Yerby should also have been mentioned, Sainville acknowledges.

710 Sainville, Léonard. Introductory note to "James Baldwin" in his *Anthologie de la littérature négro-africaine*. Vol. 1. Paris:

Présence africaine, 1963.
The importance of *Go Tell It on the Mountain* is explained by the depth of its psychological analyses, its art, its "colorful, dense, strikingly lyrical style." This young author is more preoccupied with moral misery than with poverty; he is "more a mystic than a militant."

711   Sainville, Léonard. Introductory note to "Arna Bontemps" in his *Anthologie de la littérature négro-africaine*. Vol. 1.   Paris: Présence africaine, 1963.
Arna Bontemps is described as an elder, prolific writer who deserves better recognition in Europe, where he has not appeared in translation. *Drums at Dusk* and *They Seek a City* are excerpted.

712   Sainville, Léonard. Introductory note to "Charles Wright" in his *Anthologie de la littérature négro-africaine*. Vol. 1. Paris: Présence africaine, 1963.
Hardly over 30, Charles Wright is "a remarkable novelist" who, like many in his generation, is "more objective than Richard Wright concerning racial problems." A summary and an excerpt of *The Messenger* follow.

713   Sainville, Léonard. Introductory note to "Claude Mac Kay" [sic] in his *Anthologie de la littérature négro-africaine*. Vol. 1. Paris: Présence africaine, 1963.
Stresses McKay's Jamaican birth, "in spite of the tendency to make him one of the U.S. blacks." He is "a prestigious novelist" and "ranks at the top of the monument which is constituted by the body of Negro-African literature." An excerpt from *Banjo* follows an enthusiastic summary of the novel; the French-speaking black author recalls "it is a Bible...no other novel elicited so much enthusiasm among us when we were young."

714   Sainville, Léonard. Introductory note to "John O. Killens" in his *Anthologie de la littérature négro-africaine*. Vol. 1. Paris: Présence Africaine, 1963.
Youngblood is Killens' only known novel, but a remarkably rich book. It shows objectively that not all whites are racists and ends on a note of hope: only persistent struggle can bring about progress. A summary of the novel and extract follow.

715   Sainville, Léonard. Introductory note to "Langston Hughes" in

his *Anthologie de la littérature négro-africaine*. Vol. 1. Paris: Présence africaine, 1963.

Before the war, Hughes was the best-known Afro-American writer in Europe; he no longer appears to be one of the greatest poets in the world but his varied and immense work is still important. He is a precursor, a master who wrote in order to "become a spokesman, not only of his people, but of all black people in the world in a perspective of human brotherhood." Excerpts from *Not Without Laughter* follow.

716 Sainville, Léonard. Introductory note to "Owen Dodson" in his *Anthologie de la littérature négro-africaine*. Vol. 1. Paris: Présence africaine, 1963.

Judging from his only novel, *Boy at the Window*, Dodson is more preoccupied with moral and intellectual problems than with the social plight of his characters. An extract from the novel follows.

717 Sainville, Léonard. Introductory note to "Ralph Ellison" in his *Anthologie de la littérature négro-africaine*. Vol. 1. Paris: Présence africaine, 1963.

Invisible Man suffices to make Ellison one of the "world's very good writers."   His art, his psychological analysis, his characters are superlative-- "there is only one reservation to make: his depiction of the revolutionary party is likely to alienate left-wing readers."

718 Sainville, Léonard. Introductory note to "Richard Wright" in his *Anthologie de la littérature négro-africaine*. Vol. 1. Paris: Présence africaine, 1963.

Wright is probably the best-known Afro-American writer in the whole world since World War II. Some of "his novels, like *Black Boy*" (sic) and *Native Son*, created a sensation and established him as a spokesman for his race. "If he had not existed, he would be missed as the most violent and the most astute opponents of racism." However, he "hardly mentions the deep causes of the problem he so vehemently denounces." *Uncle Tom's Children, Native Son,* and *Black Boy* [again described as a novel] follow.

719 Sainville, Léonard. Introductory note to "Saunder Ridding" [sic] in his *Anthologie de la littérature négro-africaine*. Vol. 1. Paris: Présence africaine, 1963.

Jay Saunders Redding is described as a contemporary of Charles Wright and Herbert Simmons. His work shows the Présence of alienation and obsequiousness in the black man. His novel, *Stranger and Alone*, which is summarized and excerpted, represents "a step forward toward psychological literature."

720 Sainville, Léonard. Introductory note to "Willard Motley" in his *Anthologie de la littérature négro-africaine*. Vol. 1. Paris: Présence africaine, 1963.
An extract from *Knock on Any Door* (still unpublished in France at the time) does not show Motley to be "one of the best writers of our time" as some critics say he is; his novel is creditable but hardly reflects his being black.

721 Sainville, Léonard. Introductory note to "William Attaway" in his *Anthologie de la littérature négro-africaine* Vol. 1. Paris: Présence africaine, 1963.
Attaway is unknown in France; he could be compared to Chester Himes, but is "a naturalist" along the lines of Caldwell's *God's Little Acre*, Faulkner's *The Sound and The Fury,* or James Hardley Chase's *No Orchids for Miss Blandish. Blood on the Forge*, which attempts to denounce racism in the United States is summed up and quoted at length.

722 Sainville, Léonard. Introductory note to "W.E.B. Du Bois" in his *Anthologie de la littérature négro-africaine*. Vol. 1. Paris: Présence africaine, 1963.
Du Bois needs no introduction as an intellectual and political leader of "immense culture and efficacy. ... A universal thinker, he is no novelist." A summary of *Black Folks, Then and Now* and an extract of the book follow.

723 Vianey, Michel. "James Baldwin parle." *L'Express* No. 637 (August 29, 1963), pp. 8-9.
One day after his participation in the March on Washington, the world press awaits its turn to interview Baldwin. The intellectuals' reception is joined by a public interest in Baldwin following the publication of *The Fire Next Time.* Baldwin's daily movements are a source of news: "Baldwin and second-hand book-dealers, Baldwin pushing the door of the hotel." Americans like Baldwin because he is not threatening, nor violent, nor communist, nor ill-mannered. Parenthetically, Baldwin is described as the author of three novels and three books of essays and two plays. Sidestepping a discussion of Baldwin's newly finished play, the interviewer asks

him about racism.

724 Wagner, Jean. *Les Poètes nègres des Etats-Unis: Le sentiment racial et religieux dans la poésie de P.L. Dunbar á L. Hughes (1890-1940)*. Paris-Strasbourg: Librairie Istra, 1963. 637 p.
A first-rate academic study of black American poetry, including consideration on blacks in the U.S. the oral tradition, the minstrels, Dunbar and his contemporaries, the Harlem Renaissance ideology, and the role of Du Bois and Garvey; with detailed analyses of the themes and art of Hughes, McKay,Toomer, Cullen, J.W. Johnson, Sterling Brown, including biographical sketches. Unpublished poems by McKay, Hughes, Cullen, Brown and Fenton Johnson appear in the appendix. Detailed bibliography. Later published in the U.S. as *Black Poets of the United States* (University of Illinois Press).

725 Wintzen, René. "Pour que l'homme reconnaisse sa véritable identité." *Témoignage chrétien* (December 19, 1963), p. 30.
Review of *Nobody Knows My Name*, by James Baldwin. The strength of the work lies in Baldwin's discussion of writers like Faulkner, Hemingway, Fitzgerald and Dos Passos. "Will America ever cease to consider herself a white nation? ... [It] considers itself the most civilized, the most generous, the richest [nation] in the world."

1964

726 Achille, Louis, T. "*Les poètes nègres des Etats-Unis* par Jean Wagner." *Présence africaine* No. 49 (1st trimester 1964), pp. 144-150.
Analyzes the major theme in Wagner's dissertation [later published in the U.S. as *Black Poets of the United States*] which deals specifically with the racial and religious feelings in black poetry from P.L. Dunbar to L. Hughes and also discusses many major aspects of Afro-American ideology and writing. Achille stresses the continuity in the religious component of blackness; he mentions the first-rate bibliography and the inclusion of 23 unpublished poems by Sterling Brown, Hughes and others.

727 André, Robert. "*La prochaine fois, le feu* et *Personne ne sait mon nom*, par James Baldwin." *La Nouvelle Revue française* No. 136 (April 1964), pp. 722-24.

Since racial segregation does not exist in France, understanding the "Black Problem" seems difficult. *Nobody Knows My Name* and *The Fire Next Time* complement each other. "Deep honesty" and "intelligence" are the merits of the essays. Baldwin sheds light on that mysterious negritude "which can only have a negative definition." For the first time the reviewer senses his own color. The most remarkable essay is "Princes and Powers."

728 Anon. *"Un Autre Pays* par James Baldwin." *Arts, Lettres, Spectacles* (November, 1964), p. 7.
The translation of *Another Country* is an important event after that of Baldwin's *Nobody Knows My Name* in 1959. As well as being the spokesman for the Black protest movement in the United States, he is a talented and passionate writer. The contents of the novel are briefly summarized.

729 Anon. "Ecrivains américains à Paris: James Baldwin, un progressiste éclairé." *L'Algérien* (October 1, 1964),p. 14.
Certainly the works of James Baldwin are dominated by the racial issue, but that does not put him in the same category as Martin Luther King, Jr. Baldwin speaks for the man who suffers, not particularly for Black Americans. In *Another Country* Baldwin shows that partners in interracial relationships "are condemned to destroy each other." His novel tries to explain the "Black problem." *Giovanni's Room* is classified as a book of essays.

730 Anon. "James Baldwin." *Bulletin de l'Association des bibliothécaires français* No. 45 (1964).
Baldwin, spokesman on the condition of Black Americans, now has two books of essays, *The Fire Next Time* and *Nobody Knows My Name*, both recently published in France. He is the only Black novelist who appeals to a wide American public on the moral crisis in America. "A radical change in the minds of the white man" will change the racial situation. Baldwin wanted to supersede Wright, but succeeded instead in taking another direction. He demystifies the Black man. *Go Tell It on the Mountain* is a long and "pathetic Negro spiritual that does not escape being "engagé." In *Giovanni's Room*, the theme explored is that man in a corrupt society is unequipped to establish relationships. *Another Country* is the most "ambitious," "powerful" and outstanding work of the "young American literature": "violence, rage, anger are in abundance." Baldwin makes one aware that beyond the confines of sex and race, people love each other and

suffer and are full of passion and anger. Baldwin, like Bernard Malamud and Saul Bellow, would like to "express his own affirmation of life in his rediscovery of America." Biographical sketch. Error in the year of Baldwin's birth.

731 Anon. "James Baldwin parle." *Notre République* (September 25, 1964).
Baldwin's place was recognized in France long before reporters began to inundate him and long before Robert Kennedy summoned him to the White House. Before the upcoming Goldwater-Johnson election, Baldwin's role is to fight for the rights of every man. "Would you say that the United States is in the midst of a moral crisis?" "How does one activate the whole social structure?" "Aren't some Black leaders advocating total separation from the United States?" "Would you say that the problem is that everyone must admit the existence and rights of the other?" Most questions focus on the socio-political aspects. One, "Are Blacks exotic?," does not.

732 Anon. "James Baldwin, *Personne ne sait mon nom.*" *Les Livres* (November 1964),p. 27.
Some of the essay in *Nobody Knows My Name* are autobiographical, some are of an international character. Critical of Wright and Faulkner, Baldwin "seems to see in a political engagement less an adjuvant than an obstacle to the success of his mission as a writer." Baldwin in the "cadence of a paternal sermon" guides his readers into "another promised land." The translation is creditable.

733 Anon. "*La prochaine fois le feu* et *Personne ne sait mon nom* par James Baldwin." *Le Témoin de la vie* (March 7, 1964).
This review of *The Fire Next Time* and *Nobody Knows My Name* states that the United States is feeling the weight of the wrong it committed in bringing people by force and by violence from another continent. The title *Nobody Knows My Name* "could well be the complaint of a Negro Spiritual."

734 Anon. "*La prochaine fois, le feu* par James Baldwin." *Cahiers du clergé rural* (June-July 1964).
Brief summary of *The Fire Next Time*.

735 Anon.[?] "*Le Messager* par Charles Wright." *Le Figaro littéraire* No. 946 (June 4, 1964), p. 5.

A brief, favorable review of *The Messenger* noting that "this is a novel of loneliness--it is often anguished and stifling but its tone has a particular quality."

736 Anon.[?] "Le romancier noir Chester Himes: à Harlem, cet été, il fait très chaud." *Paris-Presse* (July 23, 1964), p. 4.
An interview with Himes, who is described as the author of "breathtaking, realistic thrillers." Himes explains the frustrations of and emotional damage done to the black Americans. He says that they ask for redress of their grievances but are unable to stage the revolution that would bring about such redress.

737 Anon. "*Personne ne sait mon nom* par James Baldwin." *Arts, Lettres, Spectacles* (November 1964), p. 7.
The talented author of *Nobody Knows My Name* reveals much about himself and deserves credit as a spokesman for integration.

738 Anon.[?] "*Retour en Afrique*, par Chester Himes." *Le Nouvel Observateur* No. 726 (April 2, 1964), p. 19.
In an enthusiastic review of *Cotton Comes to Harlem*, the critic describes the idea for the plot as excellent. The characterizations are praised, and Himes' style is described as being as "pithy as ever." The only complaints are about the banal title and the small typeface used in printing the book.

739 Anon. Review of "*La prochaine fois le feu* et *Personne ne sait mon nom* par James Baldwin." *Bulletin du Centre* (March 1964).
The historical and political study of black Americans by Daniel Guérin and several other books published in recent times confirm the interest of the French in the "Black problem" in the United States. *La Révolte noire* by Louis Lomax completes Guérin's work. The two works by Baldwin, recently translated, have placed him at the head of Black intellectuals and made him one of America's spokesman.

740 Anon.[?] "*Un Autre Pays* par James Baldwin." *La Libre Belgique* (November 27, 1964), p. 7.
Another Country is yet one more novel on the same boring theme. Both the Algerians in France and the educated Blacks in the United States look for their place in the white world and give up the attempt. In more than four hundred pages, Baldwin pleads unrelentingly for integration. Publishers exaggerate the measure of Baldwin's talent.

741 Anon. "Wright (Richard)." In *Grand Larousse encyclopédique*.
Edited by Claude Dubois. Paris: Librairie Larousse, 1964.
Detailed biographical notice.

742 Anon. [Bondy, François] "Interview de James Baldwin."
Congrés d'information pour la liberté de la culture (March-May
1964), p. 10.
A reprint of a small portion of the Baldwin-Bondy interview in
October 1963 which explores Baldwin's perception of himself as a
Black leader.

743 Astre, Georges-Albert. "Harlem et Langston Hughes." *Les
Lettres françaises* No. 104 (August 20, 1964), pp. 1,8.
The article deals mostly with the political and ideological causes and
results of the black protest movements and marches; it also focuses
on black literary expression as a vehicle both for a rebellion and for
the glorification of Negro life, analyzing works by Langston Hughes
and quoting some statements made to Astre, who met him in New
York City.

744 Astre, Georges-Albert. "Rencontre avec James Baldwin." *Les
Lettres françaises* No. 1047 (September 30, 1964), pp. 1, 4.
Baldwin must be read because he is a "key author in order to
understand Black people in the United States." Baldwin had just
been interviewed on French television and announced that Gallimard
will soon publish *Another Country*. Baldwin would have preferred
as French title "Une autre planéte" [Another Planet]. Questions:
What are your current plans? What role are Black intellectuals
playing in the United States? Don't you find singularly important the
dialogue begun between white intellectuals and the minorities:
Blacks, Hispanics and Indians? Do you agree that literary works like
your *Blues for Mister Charlie* are decisive in demystifying America?
Do you feel in any danger now that you are a popular American
writer?

745 Bhély-Quénum, Olympe. *"La prochaine fois, le feu* et
Personne ne sait mon nom, par James Baldwin." *La Vie africaine*
(February 1964), p. 43.
The racial problem of Black Americans dates from several centuries
ago, but the recent liberation movement of black African countries
and the "hard struggle" of Algeria make men   naturally more
sensitive to the racial struggle in the United States. Africa and

Europe became better informed about racism through Richard Wright than through W.E.B. Du Bois. Richard Wright attempted to understand Africa and its problems; while Baldwin, clutching vehemently to America, remained "impervious" to issues concerning Africans. Therefore it is curious to find the essay in *Nobody...* on the conference of Black writers and artists, "Princes and Powers." Baldwin excels in his criticism of Faulkner's exploitation of Black characters. *Nobody Knows my Name* written with nervousness and concision, upsets. In *The Fire Next Time* Baldwin captures Harlem's environment and people with astonishing accuracy. The work by a man who has close links to Blacks and Whites has prophetic qualities.

746 Blair, Thomas. "DuBois et le siécle de la libération africaine." *Présence africaine* No. 49 (1st trimester 1964), pp. 184-91.
This general essay on the Pan-African initiatives and action of "the great Afro-American leader" emphasizes his political involvement and influence upon African readers and statesmen. A complete bibliography of his works lists his literary achievements. Du Bois is paralleled with Frantz Fanon and George Padmore because of his diasporic perspectives.

747 Borvel, Bernard. "Les heures noires de l'Amérique." *Forces nouvelles* (January 23, 1964), p. 9.
Thirty years before the Civil War, Alexis de Tocqueville perceived the racial situation as the worst of America's evils. Today, America's number one problem is still racism. The essay stands out for its "vigor" and "elegance of style." *The Fire Next Time* sings the Negro spirituals without abandoning the "authenticity of the voice." The simple and convincing language of *Nobody Knows My Name* makes clear the cruel hopelessness of the different phases of a reality which one would rather not see. Biographical sketch of Baldwin.

748 Bosquet, Alain. Foreword to *Le Tombeur* by Alston Anderson. Paris: Calmann-Lévy, 1964. pp. 7-8.
Contrary to committed writers like Richard Wright and James Baldwin, Anderson is "more elegiac" in *Lover Man*. Is such tenderness due to his birth in the tropics (Panama)? He claims that "being black means nothing to me, what matters above all is to be a human being." His language includes the liveliest expressions; Bosquet then argues in favor of adapting the book rather than translating it.

749 Bott, François. "Chester Himes: 'Il n'y a dans aucune autre ville du monde...' " *Adam* No. 296 (November 1964), pp. 74-75.
Bott presents Himes not only as a well-known author of thrillers but also as an elegant, somewhat ascetic man with perfect manners and wry wit who lives in the Latin Quarter. Bott shows how Himes' books emphasize both his racial and social concerns. Himes is quoted as saying that he writes "domestic" rather than detective novels, a factor that helps him to reach a wider audience. This essay-interview is a companion piece to "La colère noire," a ten-page essay on Harlem by Himes himself.

750 Bourniquel, Camille. "James Baldwin." *Esprit* No. 327 (April 1964), p. 681-85.
Baldwin's place among those struggling for civil rights has been decided by two different polls. In each case he was ranked lower than Black entertainers like Harry Belafonte, Lena Horne and Dick Gregory. Baldwin's place in American literature is due to his three novels. As an essayist he is a witness picking up where Faulkner stopped. Baldwin reacts above all as a writer rather than simply as a spokesman. Puritanism has "heavily burdened racial relations in America." The tone of *The Fire Next Time* and that of *Lettre sur le Colonialisme* by Aimé Césaire are similar. The sting of racism is felt beyond the South of Richard Wright.

751   Brodin, Pierre.   "James Baldwin." In his *Présences contemporaines: écrivains américains d'aujourd'hui.* Paris: Nouvelles Editions Debresse, 1964.
Baldwin's life is briefly retraced, preceding summaries of *Go Tell It on the Mountain*, truly great in spite of its sentimental atmosphere; *Another Country*, filled with too typical characters; and *Giovanni's Room.* Baldwin is at his best as an essayist; his style then becomes animated by passion and at times uncontrolled fury and rhetoric (pp. 20-28).

752   Brodin, Pierre.   "Ralph Ellison." In his *Présences contemporaines: écrivains américains d'aujourd'hui.* Paris: Nouvelles Editions Debresse,1964.
A single paragraph sums up Ellison's career. *Invisible Man* is then analyzed, from its "dazzling prologue" to the hibernation of the protagonist. It is "a novel of salvation, a salvation hard won through innumerable trials." Ellison is a gifted novelist, able to make the reader visualize things but his characters are far from real,

embodiments of invisibility. His strong sense of humor, of absurdity and the grotesque, his liking for puns reconcile human dignity and irony. "Closer to us than Richard Wright, a better novelist than Baldwin," Ellison occupies a unique niche in contemporary American fiction (pp. 50-56).

753 Cazemajou, Jean. "*Personne ne sait mon nom* par James Baldwin." *Les Livres* (December, 1964).
The French public knows Richard Wright better than James Baldwin.   Nevertheless, Baldwin champions the cause of all minorities, "transcending the black racial problem" in *Nobody Knows My Name*. Biographical sketch.

754 Chedel, A. "*Un Autre Pays*, par James Baldwin." *L'Impartial* (December 3, 1964).
Baldwin's *The Fire Next Time,* a book of great literary and human quality, is important and valuable. *Another Country*'s theme is "expectedly" the segregation of the races. The novel is realistic with "picturesque" characters. Rufus Scott, portrayed in the first one hundred pages, reaches a tragic end. And the rest of the plot, prolonged throughout the last three hundred sixty pages, adds very little. The novel is as "literary" as it is documentary. The fact that the novel was written in slang presented no difficulty in the translation.

755 Copans, Simon. *Chansons de revendication, reflets de l'histoire américaine.* Paris: Lettres modernes / M.J. Minard, 1964.
Volumes I and II, pp. 165-334, are devoted to African American songs.   Vol. I quotes many Negro spirituals as expressions of protest as well as hope; vol.II comments more extensively on the blues which depict hard times during the Depression, racism and segregation, from "Jim Crow Blues" to "Black, Brown and White." Many blues songs are reproduced and translated. Richard Wright and James Baldwin are cited on the function of the blues as a vehicle of social protest.

756 Davis, Charles. "*The Stone Face* de William Gardner Smith." *Présence africaine* No. 49 (1st trimester 1964), pp. 255-56.
A favorable review of a novel by W.G. Smith dealing with an Afro-American artist in Paris and his discovery of French anti-Arab racism. The similarities between racist attitudes in France and in the United States and between the plights of the different groups of

"colored people" are emphasized.

757 Dodat, François. *Langston Hughes*. Paris: Seghers, 1964, 190 p.
A 70-page introduction precedes a selection of Hughes' poems and a bibliography of his works. Dodat sketches "the Birth of the Poet" and considers "the Enraptured Traveller" and "the Writer" before analyzing the themes and forms of his poetry. Jean Wagner's book on Afro-American poets is often quoted.

758 E., P. "Noirs et blancs aux Etats-Unis." *L'Illustré* (May 1964), p. 32.
Baldwin's prophetic voice in *The Fire Next Time* denounces the myth of white supremacy. Baldwin gives an account of the inhuman treatment of Blacks in the United States. Nonetheless, it is not farfetched to conclude that we are all accomplices in the American racial drama.

759 Elsen, Claude. Review of *Nobody Knows My Name* and *The Fire Next Time*, by James Baldwin. *Ecrits de Paris* (January, 1964), p. 120-21.
The two collections of essays present a "very personal" view of the life of Black Americans. *The Fire...* is a manifesto and a "kind of reporting on the famous Black Muslims." Baldwin's description approaches delirium but it has a profound "psychosociological" interest. In *Nobody...*, "a chronicle of things seen and remembered," 190 pages out of 200 are devoted to a discussion of racism. His literary subjects, his criticism of Faulkner and [Norman] Mailer are tiresome because of the limited subject matter which diminishes his judgments. Simone de Beauvoir commits a similar sin with her topic, feminism. Unfortunately, this gifted writer "loses himself in a cloud of neo-racism more fanatical than anything else." The novels of Wright are those of a writer; Baldwin is a "monomaniac obsessed with a problem that has no probable solution." Quotes from the preface by Albert Memmi.

760 Franck, Jacques. "James Baldwin et le problème noir." *Revue générale belge* (1964), pp. 120-23.
President John F. Kennedy's speech of June 11, 1963 and the content of *The Fire...* and *Nobody...* are remarkably similar. Blacks are now ruling countries in Africa. But Blacks in America cannot buy a cup of coffee where they choose. The psychological

effect of this paradox should not be taken lightly. The intelligent study of Baldwin is enriching although other analyses of the situation may be more meticulous.

761 Franklin, André. "La Saison vivante: *Another Country*." RTB, [Radio-Télévision belge francophone] Radio Program (November 1964).
With Baldwin, the Black writers' wait for a leader since Wright is over. The role that made Richard Wright famous has been taken over by Baldwin, but the works of these two writers do not resemble each other. However, since Wright, Baldwin stands alone in analyzing the "profound motivations of the racism of white people." *Another Country* "very subtly" mirrors the "Black condition." Its style and "psychological penetration" are the strengths of the novel, the ending of which is weak. Excerpts are read.

762 Grauss, E. Review of *Nobody Knows My Name*, by James Baldwin. *Centre protestant d'études et de documentation* No. 96-97 (1964), p. 95.
Summary of the essays in the volume.

763 Gresset, Michel. " James Baldwin, *La prochaine fois, le feu*." *Mercure de France* No. 1206 (April 1964), p. 653-55.
A review of *The Fire Next Time*. A favorable estimate of Baldwin's attempt to define American identity and its problems. His major contribution consists in trying to make social and psychological reality coincide with the theoretical framework of U.S. institutions. He shows that Faulkner's conceptions about the racial situation are obsolete.

764 Gresset, Michel. " L'Amérique en noir et blanc: *Un Autre Pays* par James Baldwin." *Le Nouvel Observateur* No. 7 (December 31, 1964), p. 22.
Review of *Another Country* including a 20 line quote from the novel. Gresset stresses the originality of Baldwin's voice. He quotes at length from the novel. "It is a book which shocks, wounds and upsets us in the comfort of our decolonization... The novel dramatizes a limited number of ideas, but they are ideas which must be stressed again and again."

765 Hunton, William A. "W.E.B. Du Bois." *Europe* No. 425 (September 1964), pp. 148-54.

Yves Bénot's translation of the essay emphasizes the four major causes advocated by the late Afro-American leader: the fight against colonialism and racism; Pan-Africanism; the struggle for peace; and socialism.

766   Irele, Abiola. "*Poems from Black Africa* de Langston Hughes." *Présence africaine* No. 49 (1st trimester 1964), pp. 263-66.
Joint review of Hughes' anthology and Gerald Moore's *Modern Poetry from Africa*. Both volumes were quite necessary because of the appearance of a new school of poetry formed by English-speaking African poets. Without the négritude movement the new consciousness of J.P. Clark, Christopher Okigbo and Kofi Awoonor would have existed in a different way. It is regretted that Césaire, Damas and West Indian poets are not included, as they are part of the same black whole.

767   Juin, Hubert. "Negro Spirituals." *Les Lettres françaises* No. 1059 (December 17, 1964), p. 7.
A brief, very favorable review of a collection of spirituals prepared by Marguerite Yourcenar: *Fleuve profond, sombre rivière* (Deep river, dark river). Seven poems are included in translation.

768   Kanters, Robert. "La tragédie américaine." *Le Figaro littéraire* No. 947 (June 11, 1964), p. 4.
The review discusses William Goyen's *Savannah* and Charles Wright's *The Messenger*. The latter is favorably considered as "more than fiction... a kind of journal" and "a tragic statement which attempts to awaken the conscience of the world."

769   Kanters, Robert. "Le Négre qui chante." *Le Figaro littéraire* No. 975 (December 24, 1964), p. 4.
This essay on Afro-American songs and spirituals retraces their genesis and the influence of Christianity. The author shows the continuity of religious inspiration from Johnson's *God's Trombones* to the sermons of Martin Luther King. As a supplement, a very favorable review of M.L. King's *Strength to Love* is added.

770   Krief, Claude. "Réflexions sur la question noire." *L'Express* (January 16, 1964), pp. 24-30.
Four books which complement each other have just been published on the racial issue: two by Baldwin, *Nobody Knows My Name* and

The Fire Next Time, one by the Marxist Daniel Guérin, and one by the Black American Louis Lomax. Baldwin translates the feelings of Blacks into writing which moves to a level of revolt "in spite of himself." Baldwin is "less" a spokesman and rarely, in a strict sense, reaches the political domain. He surpasses the role of spokesman because as literature his work attains the universal. The essays are "emotional." Daniel Guérin cannot rival the works by Lomax and Baldwin, but he writes about racism using terms that appeal to the European intellectual. Those to whom emotions and "lyricism" appeal should read Baldwin.

771 Lacote, René. "Poésie américaine." *Les Lettres françaises* No. 1045 (September 10, 1964), p. 2.
The essay deals in part with the works of Tennessee Williams and Langston Hughes.

772 Las Vergnas, Raymond. "Lumière noire." *Les Nouvelles littéraires* No.1900 (January 30, 1964), p. 5.
In a review of novels by Erskine Caldwell, Anthony Shafton, Ring Lardner and James Baldwin, the Sorbonne professor provides a very detailed summary of The *Fire Next Time*. He discusses Baldwin's approach, rhetoric and style favorably on the whole.

773 Las Vergnas, Raymond. "Visions insolites: *Un Autre Pays*." *Les Nouvelles littéraires* No. 1939 (October 29, 1964), p. 5.
The weakest aspect of Baldwin's *Another Country* is its homosexual theme accompanied by the same Mediterranean setting used in *Giovanni's Room*. *Another Country* compels by the "deep sincerity" with which Baldwin treats the racial problem. Between Baldwin's objectivity and Wright's revolt a considerable gap exists.

774 Lauras, André. "James Baldwin, *Personne ne sait mon nom* et *La prochaine fois, le feu*." *Etudes* No. 320 (June 1964), p. 877.
Review of *Nobody Knows My Name* and *The Fire Next Time*, emphasizing Baldwin's embattled stance. "These pages are one and the same outcry, that of Black Americans in the throes of a slow and difficult phase of desegregation in the U.S."

775 Le Clec'h, Guy. "James Baldwin: les Noirs sont l'espoir de l'Amérique; je suis enragé par notre sort actuel." *Le Figaro littéraire* No. 962 (September 24-30, 1964), p. 4.
From this interview it appears that there are two Baldwins in *The*

Fire Next Time and *Nobody Knows My Name*, the writer and the politically committed black man. Discussion of *Blues for Mr. Charlie* and biographical sketch.

776 Le Clec'h, Guy. "Les Américains de Paris à la recherche de la Génération perdue." *Le Figaro littéraire* No. 944 (May 21, 1964), p. 4.
This report of a round-table held in Paris on the theme "Americans in Paris: Then and Now" mentions the participation of James Jones, Maria Jolas, Virgil Thompson, John Levee, Man Ray and William Gardner Smith. Each participant explains his reasons for coming to France and what he found there.

777 Lemaire, Marcel. "William Faulkner et James Baldwin: deux conceptions de la mission de l'écrivain." Brussels *Le Soir* (April 30, 1964), p. 9.
The Biblical echoes of *The Fire Next Time* reveal a "pathetic document on the life of Afro-Americans." To Faulkner, the writer uses his craft as a weapon in the service of his "moral convictions." In spite of Baldwin's "ardent conviction" in this "poem of iron and fire," his moral outlook is as "vaguely sentimental" as Dickens'. But his "aggressive" voice concerns everyone.

778 Lescaut, Sonia. "James Baldwin: En France, la couleur ne colle pas à ma peau." *Arts, Lettres, Spectacles* No. 974 (September 30, 1964), p. 4.
Baldwin has a world-wide reputation and is the leading Black writer in the United States. Lescaut questions Baldwin on his youth, his relationship with France, the effect of fame on him, and the interracial relationship of the characters in *Another Country*. Biographical sketch.

779 Maunick, Edouard J. Review of a Radio Program on James Baldwin. *Les Bonnes Feuilles* (February 29, 1964).
This Black American has in important place in United States literature, as well as in World literature. Reading from the third part of *Another Country*. The novel describes despair but leaves the reader with a feeling of hope. Baldwin continues a long tradition of Black writers who are for the "advancement of Black Americans:" Claude McKay, Countee Cullen, J.W. Johnson, Edwin Campbell, Jean Toomer and especially Langston Hughes, writers of the Harlem Renaissance. This program on Baldwin will certainly interest those

who are sincerely concerned with the status of Blacks in the United States.   A poem by Edwin Campbell prepares the audience for the "spirit" of the essays.   His passionate description of Harlem is the most beautiful.   Baldwin raises the consciousness of the reader: "that is already a lot."   Baldwin's criticism of Richard Wright is "a very important point to remember."   [Adequate but literal translation by Jean Autret.]

780 Médaz. "La Décolonisation de Noir." *Voix ouvrière* (April 29, 1964).
After Louis Lomax, Baldwin documents the era of racism in the United States with "concision" and "sometimes admirable lyricism." It seems that Baldwin has replaced Richard Wright as spokesman of Black Americans.   Several passages from *The Fire Next Time* are quoted.

781 Médaz. "*Personne ne sait mon nom*, par James Baldwin." *Voix ouvrière* (March 15, 1964).
A Black American author is entitled to use any subject in order to explain the difficulty of being Black in America.   In *Nobody Knows My Name*, penetrating articles on Norman Mailer, William Faulkner and André Gide illustrate the point. Baldwin and Louis Lomax discuss the Black Muslims who represent the "emotional aspirations of three quarters of all American Blacks."

782 Merton, Thomas. "La Révolution noire." *La Revue nouvelle* 39, 2 (February 15, 1964), pp. 113-22.
A reprint in translation of Merton's pages in *Seeds of Destruction* dealing at length with the moral issues in William M. Kelley's *A Different Drummer*.   His satirical and mythopoeic approach is contrasted with Richard Wright's open protest.

783 Mohrt, Michel. "Il veut que les Etats-Unis ne soient plus seulement un pays blanc." *Le Figaro littéraire* No. 925 (January 9, 1964), p. 3.
Baldwin's personal political engagement exemplifies his desire to do more than denounce with his pen the racial conditions in the United States.   Four days before participating in the March on Washington, Baldwin led a March on the U.S. Embassy in Paris to protest against segregation.   *Nobody Knows My Name* shows him fighting with choices and remorse.   *The Fire Next Time* explains the origins and goals of the Black Panthers whose extremist philosophy attracts

Baldwin; but he cannot accept it, perhaps because of his "sentimental attachment to his white friends." Baldwin seems to be advocating war when he wants everything immediately. He and his friend William Styron have the "same Puritan conscience tortured by remorse, the same recourse to a vengeful God." [Repr. in Mohrt's *L'Air du large*, Paris: Gallimard, 1970.]

784 Ngango, Georges. "*Les poètes nègres des Etats-Unis*, par Jean Wagner." *Présence africaine* No. 49 (1st trimester 1964), pp. 178-83.
This review of Wagner's important dissertation on the racial and religious feeling in Afro-American poetry from Dunbar to Hughes focuses on the difficulty of reconciling what Du Bois called "the twoness" of the black soul. The author analyzes how different were the answers provided by McKay, Cullen, Sterling Brown, J.W. Johnson, and Hughes, and concludes that Africa is in its turn experiencing the same kind of conflicting loyalties to traditional cultures and the West.

785 Parisse, Jacques. "Sur la question raciale deux essais d'un jeune écrivain noir: James Baldwin." *Combat* (January 21, 1964).
Baldwin captures our attention more than any other writer on the subject of racism. *Nobody Knows My Name*, although made up of disparate parts, has a unique voice in its "passionate desire" to serve the Black race "with a calm and noble assurance, without hiding the truth."

786 Penel, Alain. "Amours en noir et blanc." *La Tribune de Genève* (November 6, 1964).
Baldwin's *Another Country* is added to the list of books available in Europe on the racial problem in the United States. Baldwin's novel does not give a precise and objective view of racism. However, the nature of racism cannot be expressed in precise formulas or statistics. The characters in this novel are frustrated by barriers other than racism. Oppression in this case is felt not only by the Black man but all men. Pierre Koralnik's "remarkable" television program on Baldwin revealed the kind of artist and man Baldwin is. "The work and the man appear to have been created for combat." Embodied in the work are modern and eternal themes. "The essence of the novel is a sort of gigantic development of a jazz theme."

787 Penel, Alain. "Les écrivains noirs existent-ils?" *La Tribune de*

Genève (March 30-31, 1964).
Black American literature is in a "literary ghetto" because of tag words like "anger, hate, rage, protest, revolt" used to describe it. Outside of music, Blacks have not "substantially" contributed to American art. Replacing Wright, Baldwin's *The Fire Next Time* and *Nobody Knows My Name* exemplify how Black American literature imprisons itself. In spite of efforts by Wright and Baldwin, lack of organization and unity dilute the cultural impact Black writers have and hamper attempts to bring about the desired solution to the racial issue. In contrast, the Black Muslims' goals and politics are "precise." To a great degree Baldwin and to a lesser degree Charles Wright [*The Messenger*] extract Black literature from its "rut." Hoping to become a part of America, Black writers must write more universally; this would also make "such literature" more accessible to Europeans.

788   Penel, Alain. "Une saison en littérature." *La Tribune de Genève* (December 11, 1964), p. 13.
It seems that "in the country of Descartes, reason has killed inspiration." The "avalanche" of books published in France in the last decade has come from abroad. Baldwin's *Another Country* on the "formation and disintegration of couples" describes the condition of Black people in the United States. But other aspects of American life are seen. Baldwin with *The Fire Next Time* succeeds Richard Wright as spokesman of Black Americans.

789   Périer, Denis. "Alston Anderson; *Le Tombeur*." *La Nouvelle Revue française* No. 148 (May 1964), p. 943.
Brief review, rather critical of the novel *Lover Man* and of Anderson's position.

790   Renaud, Tristan. "Chester Himes, 'homeless.' " *Les Lettres françaises* No. 1020 (March 12, 1964), p. 5.
An interview/essay discusses Himes' writing against the backdrop of the changing racial situation in the United States. Himes is more than just a successful writer of thrillers, "one of the best American novelists" because of his unconventional view of society.

791   Rivier, Robert. "*Un Autre Pays*, par James Baldwin." *La Fauche* (November 14, 1964).
Baldwin, known in France only by to volumes of essays, now has published his first novel, *Another Country*. The style of the novel

greatly distances the reader from the assured style of Richard Wright. The story's plot "dominates the book and gives to it a resonance which goes beyond its literary value." The article contains a brief discussion of the characters Rufus and Ida.

792 Ruff, P. *"Un Autre Pays*, par James Baldwin." *Fiches bibliographiques* (1964).
A novel with a "rich human density." The characters are lifelike. "We would like to help them in their quest without a solution."

793   Salomon, Michel.   "Juifs et noirs dans l'Amérique d'aujourd'hui." *L'Arche* No. 89 (June 1964), pp. 22-26, 61.
An interview with Himes that is mainly concerned with the relationship of American blacks and American Jews. Himes says that black anti-semitism is the result of economic competition and exploitation by Jews. He insists that the role of the Black Muslims in the black community should not be regarded as predominantly negative since they channel much of their latent hatred into non-violent, constructive activity. He feels that blacks are in a much more critical situation than Jews, and believes that the only possible way to achieve change in America is through a violent revolution.

794 Sauvage, Léo. "James Baldwin, prophète noir de la colére." *Le Figaro littéraire* No. 925 (January 9-15, 1964), p. 3.
Delayed for several months, this interview was originally planned for the day John F. Kennedy was assassinated. At that time, the discussion would have been on *Blues for Mr. Charlie*. Baldwin and the Black political movement cannot be separated. The majority of the questions are on the assassination. Baldwin concludes "I would like to be a writer only, but how can I shut my door to life?"

795 Séjourné, Philippe. "La carrière littéraire de Richard Wright et l'évolution du problème noir aux Etats-Unis." *Annales de la Faculté des lettres d'Aix-en-Provence*, 41 (1964), pp. 133-54. Reprinted in *Travaux du Centre d'études anglaises et nord-américaines*, Université de Provence. Tome III. 1966, pp. 139-60.
This academic essay retraces Wright's political and literary career in the light of the racial situation in the United States.

796 Senghor, Léopold Sédar. "La poésie négro-américaine." In his *Liberté I: Négritude et Humanisme*. Paris: Editions du Seuil; 1964. Pp. 104-121.

In this 1950 lecture, Senghor uses again much of his essay in *Poésie 47*. He examines the socio-cultural roots and political context of black poetry in the U.S., deals with folk poetry, mostly with the spirituals and the blues, then turns to the poetry of the "New Negro", which was made fashionable by white interest in jazz, African art, etc.; this allowed a "Negro Renaissance" about whose ideology Hughes ["The Negro Artist and the Racial Mountain"] is quoted. The "dialect school" of Dunbar and James Weldon Johnson leads Senghor to focus on the style and the "Negro features" of those poets; "the essential quality of Negro poetic style is rhythm" (p. 111). Nothing is codified, nor rigid in the poetry of Joseph Cotter, Dunbar, Hughes, Sterling Brown and others. Religion and humor often go hand in hand. McKay, Cullen, Toomer are the best representatives of "learned poetry." The poems in which negritude is proclaimed are not the "blackest" ones, since "negritude resides in style and emotion (p. 119). At the end, Senghor quotes from "I Have Seen Black Hands" and comments briefly on the proletarian poetry of Wright: "The poem is beautiful and its inspiration epic...Yet proletarian poetry is not the most beautiful one. Maybe because we feel that proletarian solidarity is postulated rather than lived."(p. 120)   He ranks Wright with Hughes and McKay among leading poets attempting to transcend racial themes.

797 Senghor, Léopold Sédar. "Le problème culturel en A.O.F." in his *Liberté I: Négritude et Humanisme*. Paris: Editions du Seuil, 1964.
In this lecture delivered in Dakar on December 10, 1937, Senghor claims that vernacular languages are as beautiful as recognized literary tongues. Dunbar, McKay Hughes, and Sterling Brown have turned "the Negro American dialect, that poor faltering speech of uprooted slaves, into a marvel -- *a thing of beauty*."(p. 19)

798 Thelwell, Mike."James Baldwin." *Présence africaine* No. 52 (4th trimester 1964), pp. 14-26.
The essay attempts to see beyond Baldwin's image as a public figure and committed activist to see him as "one of the truly great artists in this country, in the words of Edmund Wilson."

799 Van Peebles, Melvin. "Chester Himes, l'invaincu." *Le Nouvel Observateur* No. 720 (February 20, 1964), pp. 13-14.
An interview with Himes on the occasion of the publication of *Cotton Comes to Harlem*. Himes asserts that there remains no non-

violent solution to the race problem in America. The general hostility
of American critics to *Lonely Crusade* in the late 1940s is given as
the reason for Himes' move to Europe. He names *The Primitive* as
his favorite novel and notes that he would prefer his thrillers to be
called "domestic novels." He believes his work is no more anti-
American or racist than Zola's was anti-French. He comments
favorably on the work of Wright, Baldwin, and Van Peebles
himself.

800 Villard, Léonie. *Panorama du théâtre américain*. Paris:
Seghers, 1964.
Pages 294-97 are devoted to a summary of *A Raisin in the Sun*, "the
first play of the 'black' theater, written by a young woman of African
descent." Lorraine Hansberry's play avoids too strident militancy in
the case of residential segregation. It was welcomed as the first
authentic Negro venture into a portrayal of the life of the black
bourgeoisie.

801 Yourcenar, Marguerite. Introduction to her *Fleuve profond,
sombre rivière*. Paris: Gallimard, 1964.
In the spirituals the Afro-American folk poets express their dreams
and resignation, secret revolt and sense of God. Their spirit is that
of a lyrical sermon: Jerusalem and the banks of the Jordan River
become mythical and reminiscent of small Southern river towns;
performers tend to dilute Africanisms. A major theme is Exodus; the
crossing of the river means both evasion from slavery and the
revivalism of the river of death. Since they are part of an eternal
Christian monologue, the spirituals are not exclusively about the
pains and frustrations of oppressed blacks.

1965

802 Abirached, Robert. "L'Autre Amérique." *Le Nouvel
Observateur* No. 53 (November 17-23, 1965), p. 36.
A review of *Dutchman* and *The Slave* by Le Roi Jones, adapted by
Eric Kahane. The author seems to be shocked and fascinated at the
same time by the violence which emerges from Jones' plays,
although he refrains from passing judgement on them. *The Slave* is
called "a fable for the future." A description of the plot of *Dutchman*
concludes it is "certainly the most violent play I ever saw on stage."

803 Anon. "A déconseiller: *Un Autre Pays.*" *Notes bibliographiques* (March 1965), p. 295.
This novel on the theme of racism in the United States is not recommended. *Another Country* is amoral and Baldwin describes disgusting behavior.

804 Anon. "*Bon sang de bonsoir* de R. Wright." *Panorama chrétien* (October 1965).
Favorable review of *Lawd Today* noting especially Wright's success in creating sympathy for a brutal protagonist.

805 Anon. "*Bon sang de bonsoir* de R. Wright." *Syndicalisme* (July-August 1965).
Short notice of *Lawd Today*. A black man, the protagonist has not found his place in American society and isa prey to unpredictable violence.

806 Anon. "*Bon sang de bonsoir* de Richard Wright." *Sélection des libraires de France* (July 1965).
Review of *Lawd Today* pointing out its welcome humor and lack of didacticism in depicting Jake's appalling condition.

807 Anon. "*Bon sang de bonsoir.*" *L'Echo de Lanion* (October 23, 1965).
Favorable review of *Lawd Today*. Revealing Wright's forceful technique, it deals with twenty-four hours in the life of a black man in racist America. Of intense topical interest, it shows that Wright was many years ahead of his time.

808 Anon. "*Bon sang de bonsoir.*" *Reflets du Luxembourg* (July 1, 1965).
Although *Lawd Today* shows traces of crudity, the novel affirms our basic conception of Wright's message and his art. Jake is involved in the existential confrontation with being but he is the victim of himself as well as society.

809 Anon. "Des livres pour vos vacances..." *L'Epicerie française* (July 17, 1965).
Brief review of *The True American* by Melvin Van Peebles. The plot is summed up and the book praised for its "humor, zest, and contemporary relevance."

810 Anon. "Femme de ministre et femme de lettres." *Candide*
(February 25, 1965).
Mme Hélène Bokanowski, the wife of the Ministre des PTT, has
translated Richard Wright's *Lawd Today*. The novel is the story of a
lower middle class black who lives in the ghetto and, unable to face
the odds, turns to evasion and self-destruction.

811 Anon. "L'enfer est trop petit: *Un Américain en enfer*." *Le
Figaro* (April 24-25, 1965), p. 8.
The reviewer praises the diversity in the writing of Melvin Van
Peebles. The "Negro problem" is seen with some perspective and
balance. "Hell is too small because God is too optimistic," such is
the conclusion derived from *The True American*.

812 Anon. "Les livres du mois: *Un Américain en enfer*." *Bulletin
critique du livre français* (May 15, 1965).
Brief summary of *The True American* by Melvin Van Peebles
described as a work full of "lashing humor". The black American
protagonist manages to be happy in Hell where Satan uses blacks to
plague white people.

813 Anon. "Lettres: *Un Autre Pays*." *Le Nouvel Observateur* No.
16 (March 4, 1965), p. 30.
Tony Richardson and James Baldwin meet to discuss the possibility
of making a film adaptation of *Another Country*.

814 Anon. "Melvin Van Peebles: *Un Américain en enfer*." *Notes
bibliographiques* No. 739 (July-August 1965).
Short summary of the novel: Hell is easier to bear for a black man
than the earth, where injustice reigns. Reading *The True American* is
not an agreeable experience because farce is blended with religion,
and the realistic depictions are violent and raw. But the cruel satire of
American democracy is worthwhile.

815 Anon. "Mercuriale - Revues." *Mercure de France* Nos. 1221-
22 (July-August 1965), p. 510.
Mentions an essay by "that fine novelist, Herbert Gold" in the
Winter-Spring issue of *The Hudson Review*. Gold deals with the
"career of Ralph Ellison, a remarkable Negro writer whose *Invisible
Man* has remained, for 12 years, his first and only novel. His
collection of essays, *Shadow and Act*, provides a moving
explanation for that fact."

816 Anon. "Nous avons reçu: *Un Américain en enfer.*" *Les Echos* (May 14, 1965).
Brief, favorable review of *The True American* by Melvin Van Peebles. "The novel is an unrelenting indictment of racism across the Atlantic..., and a success."

817 Anon. "Richard Wright. *Bon sang de bonsoir.*" *L'Epicerie française* (November 26, 1965).
Favorable review of *Lawd Today*, actually by Germaine Pinot. The plot is briefly evoked and the hero found both pitiable and likeable although he has to find in violence a kind of escape for aspirations baffled by his social environment.

818 Anon. "Revue de livres et des revues." *Afrique contemporaine* No. 37 (May-June 1965), pp. 31-36.
Contains a notice of the translation of Wright's *Lawd Today*. Its style is that of an apprentice work.

819 Anon. "Un roman posthume de Richard Wright." *France-Soir* (June 17, 1965).
Brief review of *Lawd Today*, the first novel written by Richard Wright, the publication of which was discouraged by the CPUSA which expected an "exemplary hero." The plot is summarized. The lower middle-class protagonist is "intelligent but lazy and attempts to take refuge in violence."

820 Anon. "*The Amen Corner.*" *La Table ronde*; No. 212 (September 1965), p. 139.
Mentions the performance of Baldwin's play in English at the Théâtre des Nations .

821 Anon. "*Un Américain en enfer* de Melvin Van Peebles." *La Vie des livres* (Summer 1965).
Brief review of *The True American*. "It is difficult to recommend reading this book, which may shock some readers."

822 Anon. "*Un Américain en enfer* de Melvin Van Peebles." *Nous, les garçons et les filles* (September 1965), p.64.
The True American first appeared in French translation. This review praises the book with moderation: "the starting point is fine but the novel lacks scope. It is too simplistic in spite of the present echoes

of the black revolt in the United States."

823 Anon. "*Un Autre Pays* par James Baldwin." *Bulletin critique du livre français* (January 1965), p. 18.
The reader has no sympathy for the characters in *Another Country*. Baldwin treats the racial issue from the perspective of sexual relationships in the bohemian environment of the Village in New York City. In relief is the difficult coexistence of Blacks and whites in the United States. This novel has helped Baldwin forget his negritude.

824 Anon. "*Un Autre Pays* par James Baldwin." *Clartés* (January 1965), p. 41.
Amidst violence and passion the characters in *Another Country* do not defeat segregation. The author, James Baldwin, is known to the French as the "eloquent spokesman" for Black Americans.

825 Anon. "Une colère noire." *Candide* (May 16, 1965), p. 26.
Favorable review of *Lawd Today* by Richard Wright. It is a courageous book which does not spare the Blacks in the ghetto although it is full of compassion. Retraces Wright's own personal itinerary and ends by suggesting that Wright's pessimism on racial issues is probably the "incurable pessimism of all true novelists."

826 Anon. "Un inconnu en tête." *Le Figaro littéraire*. No. 1017 (October 14, 1965), p. 2.
Mentions that *Invisible Man* has been awarded the distinction of being "the best American novel since the end of World War II" by a group of American critics and intellectuals. [In spite of a first translation, *Au-dela du Regard,* Ellison's novel was then unknown to French readers.]

827 Anon. "Un survol rapide: *Un Américain en enfer*." *Droit et Liberté* (December 15, 1965 --[reprinted January 25, 1966].
Brief summary of *The True American* by Melvin Van Peebles: "the devil makes the whites suffer through his use of the black people...a friendship between black and white cannot withstand real life on earth."

828 Anon. [Neuvéglise, Paule?]. "Roman posthume de Richard Wright." *France-Soir* (June 17, 1965), p. 12.

Review of *Lawd Today* placing it in context of Wright's development and quoting Hélène Bokanowski's introduction on the way the novel reveals Wright's technique. Also states that the Communist Party discouraged publication of the novel when it was written.

829 Astre, Georges-Albert. "James Baldwin: Ne plus dire 'Amen' au Théâtre des Nations." *Les Lettres françaises* (June 24-30, 1965) p. 8.
The Amen Corner performed at the Théâtre des Nations received neither public nor critical acclaim. However, because it explains black life in the United States, it is significant. European audiences would look for an "intellectual message" and "dramatic movement" and be disappointed. Baldwin has attempted a difficult task in projecting "Black sensibility" theatrically. The French grasp this in the spirituals and jazz. The first two acts are too long, but the play exudes power.

830 Aubert, Serge. "James Baldwin: un chat noir de Harlem." *Nouvelle Frontière* (May-June 1965), pp. 56-59.
In 1963, Baldwin's popularity, already "astonishing" in the United States, also reached Europe. His essays saw "constant" reprintings. Readers value his three novels, but the essays, "in which he reveals a remarkable mastery of the American language," are valued the most. To some critics Baldwin seems a unique Black man because he "dissects" his experience as a Black man. Long quotation from *The Fire Next Time*.

831 Bokanowski, Hélène. Introduction to *Bon sang de bonsoir* by Richard Wright. Paris: Mercure de France, 1965.
The translator of the novel analyses *Lawd Today* in detail and construes it as a work characteristic of Wright in theme and technique.

832 Boris, Mireille. "Pamphlet loufoque: *Un Américain en enfer*." *L'Humanité* (April 27, 1965), p.8.
The True American by Melvin Van Peebles is found "somewhat farcical but very useful" along the lines of American comedy. In this original novel, Hell is not only an image of America. It really exists: "Hell and Heaven are the inverted and transformed reflections of what is taking place in the United States ... The author vents his frustrations."

833 Bourniquel, Camille. *"Un Autre Pays."* *Esprit* (February 1965), p. 434-38.

As Marc Saporta reports, American literature does not fall into readily researchable movements and categories. "Avant-garde" literature does not mean the same thing in America that it does in France. In *Another Country*, Baldwin illustrates in a striking way "the extraordinary violence of the attack and breadth of evil." To escape from the "chaos" which emanates from segregation, Baldwin's characters gravitate towards partners who both fascinate and destroy each other. The exasperated tone of the novel resembles the works of Styron. Previous works labeled scandalous are far beneath *Another Country*'s level of language.

834 Brièrre, Annie. *"Le Messager*, de Charles Wright." *La Table ronde* No. 204 (January 1965), p. 132.

This brief review emphasizes the "powerfully evocative style" of Charles Wright's *The Messenger*, but states that it contains unjustified criticism of American society. The fault lies with the strange sensibility of the protagonist who choses to indulge in evil and not in society itself.

835 Brulé, C. *"Bon sang de bonsoir."* *Elle* (August 12, 1965).

Lawd Today, written well before the war and the current racial struggle, is a moving and painful anticipation of black self-hatred by Richard Wright.

836 Cabau, Jacques. "La peau n'est qu'un masque." *L'Express* (September 6-12, 1965), p. 50.

Contains a favorable review of *Lawd Today* emphasizing its realism and commending Wright's achievement. "This hard-hitting novel, influenced by the behavioristic techniques of Dos Passos is a truthful novel which does not hide the faults of black people."

837 Cabau, Jacques. "Traduit de l'américain: la satire désamorcée." *Informations et Documents* No. 219 (September 1, 1965), pp. 35-36.

The Negro problem greatly interests French readers, yet *Lawd Today*, Richard Wright's first novel, did not create a stir. "A hard, realistic novel, influenced by the behaviorism of Dos Passos," this novel does not conceal the blemishes of black people, their chauvinism, their antisemitism, their vanity and sloth. This is why Wright hesitated to publish it before World War II.

838 Cendrars, Miriam. *"Un Américain en enfer."* *Elle* (May 27, 1965), p. 88.
Brief mention of *The True American* by Melvin Van Peebles. "The Negro problem is narrated without partiality and without melodrama after the fashion of one of Voltaire's philosophical tales."

839   Copans, Sim. "Le Problème noir aux Etats-Unis." *Les Langues modernes* No. 59 (July-August 1965), pp. 66-72.
Contains a review of Herbert Hill's anthology *Soon, One Morning* mentioning Richard Wright, Chester Himes, and other black American contributors.

840 D., P. "Gens de Harlem, l'ingénu et le pasteur." *La Tribune de Lausanne* (March 26, 1965).
The reviewer of *The Best of Simple* by Langston Hughes and of a novel by Bruce Kenrick compares the two as ways of depicting marginal people. The career of Hughes is briefly summarized. Simple, his protagonist, makes Hughes "a Carl Sandburg in black skin." Hughes makes us smile and laugh, yet he manages to depict everyday life in Harlem in a most convincing way.

841   Damas, Léon-Gontran.   "Nouvelle somme de poésie; présentation afro-américaine." *Présence africaine* No. 57 (December 15, 1965), pp. 353-56.
A panorama of Negritude insists upon Hughes's pioneering role in "The Negro Artist and the Racial Mountain" and on the impact of his statements upon Nicolas Guillen and Jacques Roumain. The role of Claude McKay is also emphasized. The Cuban poems included in this selection are a result of a common situation within the scope of the worldwide black diaspora.

842 Darnar, P.-L. "Destin noir et Maison blanche: *Un Américain en enfer*." Grenoble *Le Dauphine libéré*, (June 15, 1965).
This short review of *The True American* by Melvin Van Peebles finds his black humor regrettably too realistic: "one can't even hurry to laugh about it to keep from crying."

843 Dassart, André. *"Un Américain en enfer* de Melvin Van Peebles." *Fiches Bibliographiques* (1965) No. 11363.
The True American is summed up carefully. It is praised as a "strange and terrifying novel. Humor is an efficient weapon in this relentless and fierce plea against injustice, cruelty and lack of

humanity."

844 Dejardin, André. "*Un Américain en enfer.*" *Vers l'avenir* (June 16, 1965).
Brief review of *The True American* by Melvin Van Peebles. The plot is summarized and its originality praised, but the general impression is negative: "There are some brilliant pages, ... some useless belaboring of other passages; the erotic side is also useless." Van Peebles cannot be compared with Richard Wright, but he is a witness of the bad conscience of white Americans.

845 Dommergues, Pierre. *Les Ecrivains américains d'aujourd'hui.* Paris: Presses universitaires de France ("Que-sais-je?"), 1965. 128 p.
LeRoi Jones is described as "the boldest of the beat poets, making poetry with whatever can be taken from the garbage of life." The section "The Invisible Man according to Ralph Ellison" (pp.107-108) provides a summary of Ellison's novel. "Contradiction according to James Baldwin" (pp. 109-110) focuses on the *The Fire Next Time, Giovanni's Room* and *Another Country*: "[Baldwin's] works are the extreme point of a literature consciously immersed in absurdity; his tone recalls that of court rhetoric; his themes are racism, love, communication." The style of the novels is colorless and pale. Baldwin writes "white novels" whereas his essays are "black." He is the opposite of Willard Motley, who wrote black novels while attempting to write "white" ones, and of Wright, whose fiction is moving when it does not attempt to deal with ideas.

846 Esnor, Henri. "La négritude américaine vue par Richard Wright: *Bon sang de bonsoir.*" *Le Drapeau rouge* (September 25, 1965).
Favorable and thoughtful review of *Lawd Today* also published as "La Négritude américaine" under the name Henri Ronse in *Courrier du littoral* (September 24, 1966).

847 Fabre, Michel. "Où en est l'écrivain noir aux Etats-Unis?" *Arts, Lettres, Spectacles* No. 1003 (April 25, 1965), pp. 5-7.
A survey of the problems encountered by Afro-American writers, the article deals mostly with the interaction between society and the artist: American publishers want "violent, raw material; American critics are satisfied with "one major black writer per generation"; Blacks are largely excluded by compilers, anthologies and the media; most

important, writers have to resist the temptation of exotic writing; no wonder, under such circumstances, that many of them should choose protest and social criticism.

848 Fléouter, Claude. "*L'Esclave*, c'est la rencontre de Sartre et de Malcolm X." *Le Monde* No. 6471 (November 3, 1965), p. 16.
An interview of Antoine Bourseiller, who directed LeRoi Jones' *Dutchman* and *The Slave* in Paris, quotes him as saying that "these two plays affected me because of their violence. You feel bitterness in them, a subdued kind of hatred. It is a theater of aggression and warning."

849 Foote, F.G. "Thérapeuthique de la haine." *Preuves* No. 170 (June 1965), pp. 70-73.
Review of *Blues for Mr.Charlie* by James Baldwin. The reviewer feels that Baldwin falters in objectivity in the play. "Never in the past did Baldwin abandon himself to the subjective impulses of furor and despair." His central character, a total failure, affects the overall quality of the play. Perhaps this play can be justified "by presenting it as a therapeutic and public expression of hate." Whether "therapeutic" or whether "polemic," the play must be judged according to "intellectual and artistic criteria" which Baldwin himself spoke of in *Notes of a Native Son.* Foote also traces the image of Richard in *Go Tell It on the Mountain, Another Country*, and *Blues for Mr. Charlie.* He warns that a white critic must take precautions "in judging and generalizing" problems and situations pertaining to Black Americans.

850 Freustié, Jean. "Chicago Story." *Le Nouvel Observateur* No. 30 (June 10, 1965), pp. 21-22.
Favorable review of *Lawd Today* including a detailed plot summary. Expressing indebtedness to Hélène Bokanowski's excellent introduction to the novel, Freustié points out that the unflattering portrayal of the blacks caused the Communist Party to advise Wright not to publish it. But the work conveys forcefully, with the aid of auctorial objectivity and techniques derived from Dos Passos, the idea that American society is responsible for the degradation of blacks.

851 Galey, Mathieu. "De Harlem au 'Village'." *Arts, Lettres, Spectacles* No.988 (January 18, 1965), p. 5.
Rather unfavorable estimate of Baldwin who has caught the attention

of a large public audience because of his active role in the racial struggle. The reader feels "a certain malaise" in reading *The Fire Next Time* because Baldwin criticizes white America "without the least effort to excuse if not defend those whom he must call the enemy." *Another Country* is laborious reading while *Nothing Personal* is a splendid and instructive album. Baldwin's description of Greenwich Village is superficial but devoid of exoticism.

852   Gautier, Jean-Jacques.   *"The Amen Corner."* *Le Figaro* No.6469 (June 17, 1965), p. 30.
Review of *The Amen Corner* by James Baldwin. Introductory remarks explain the title and describe the religious ritual of churches outside of "official religions." "Long, monotonous and fastidious," *The Amen Corner* shows actors who can sing better than they act.

853   Gresset, Michel. *"Sans allusion."* *Mercure de France* No. 1218 (January-April 1965), p. 715-16.
Certain facts of American society have been magnified in *Nothing Personal*, a luxurious photograph album. Description of many of the personalities: Governor George Wallace, Marilyn Monroe, Linus Pauling, etc.

854   Herlemont, Maurice. "De l'humour noir." *Le Peuple* (May 25, 1965).
Review of *The True American* by Melvin Van Peebles. This dossier of black and white relationships in the United States is presented in a humorous, even pungent fashion.   Jesus, ill-informed about an American black, sends him to hell where he makes friends with a white man while the Devil allows blacks to become cultured. Abe comes back to earth with new intellectual weapons in order to help his black brothers, but nothing has changed and he is killed again.

855   Kyria, Pierre. "Derniers parus, derniers lus." *Aux Ecoutes*; (April 15, 1965).
Notice of the translation of *Lawd Today*. A social document as well as an individual confession, the novel allows Wright to speak of the difficulties of American cities, using Harlem as an example.

856   Kyria, Pierre. "Noirs contre Blancs." *Combat* (October 20, 1965), p. 9.
A review of *Dutchman* and *The Slave* by LeRoi Jones, performed at the Théâtre de Poche-Montparnasse.   There is no attempt to

summarize the plays but they are defined as "the closed battlefield for the most terrible struggle: Whites against Blacks." What matters is words, reality breaking up and bursting into dialogue, the faith and belief which are embodied in language. Jones goes far beyond cautious rationalizations and sings "a long and fiery hymn to violence." His stance is similar to the prophecies of Malcolm X or James Baldwin in *The Fire Next Time*.

857   Lambert, Gilles.   "Malcolm X et son autobiographie."   *Le Figaro littéraire* No. 984 (February 25, 1965), p. 3.
A mixed review of the black leader's career and tactics, stating that Malcolm X "became less and less picturesque and more and more disquieting." The book itself is hardly mentioned.

858 Las Vergnas, Raymond. *"Bon sang de bonsoir* par Richard Wright." *Les Nouvelles littéraires* 43 (August 26, 1965), p. 5.
Favorable review of *Lawd Today* with a detailed plot summary. "A fine naturalistic novel," it is also invaluable as a document: it shows the emerging talent of the great Afro-American novelist.

859 Laude, André. *"Langston Hughes*, par François Dodat." *Présence africaine* No. 54 (2nd trimester 1965): pp. 275- 77.
The reviewer analyzes Dodat's study, which deals not only with Hughes's art, but also with his background and the literary and political scene in America throughout his career. Part II focuses on Hughes's poetry: "he is no thinker ... but he can beautifully convey the confused sensations that constitute the collective consciousness of the folk." A thematic study is followed by a discussion of the role of music in black literature.

860 Le Clec'h, Guy. "Lu, approuvé, discuté: *Bon sang de bonsoir* par Richard Wright." *Le Figaro littéraire* No. 1004 (July 15-21, 1965), p. 4.
Favorable though brief review of *Lawd Today*. it is a brutal document "fraught with bitter irony." Although American blacks today have more political awareness than in 1938, the novel is otherwise timely.

861 Le Clec'h, Guy. "Wright, Richard (1909 [sic]-1960)." In Georges-Emmanuel Clancier (ed.), *Ecrivains contemporains*. Paris: Editions d'art Lucien Mazenod, 1965.
Brief biographical sketch on p. 608.

862 Lebel, J.[ean] J.[acques] *La Poésie de la Beat Generation.*
Paris: Denoël, 1965.
A translation of "Poems from Prison" by Bob Kaufman is included
(p. 136) and an a development "Notes supplémentaires concernant
ou ne concernant pas l'abomunisme" [comments on "The
Abomunist Manifesto"] appear on pp. 142-44.

863 Lemarchand, Jacques. *"Le Métro fantôme."* Le Figaro littéraire
No. 1022 (November 18, 1965), p. 16.
Adverse review. "Hitler did not speak differently and one feels that
Mr. LeRoi Jones is, in heart and spirit, much closer to the Ku Klux
Klan than to any anti-racist league." This short and bitter review
admits that there is great straightforwardness in *Dutchman* and *The
Slave.*

864 Lerminier, Georges. *"Le Métro fantôme* et *L'Esclave*, de LeRoi
Jones." *Le Parisien libéré* (November 11, 1965), p. 6.
 Review of *Dutchman* and *The Slave,* "the two most Sartrean plays I
have seen in a long time." Jones is more truthful that Jean Genet, a
"Strindberg of apartheid" and racial war, a dynamiter; his drama is
one of "aggression and wild lyricism, full of punch and even
shocking." A sort of "theater of liberation" which is extremely
provocative.

865 Le Six-Quatre-Deux [pseud.] "La voix au chapitre: *U n
Américain en enfer*." *Le Canard enchaîné* No. 2323 (April 28,
1965), p. 6.
A brief review of Melvin Van Peebles' *The True American.* "A black
American, Abe Carver, was lucky enough to be in Hell. He asked
for a chance to go back to the United States, poor man..."

866 Harnat, Marcel. "Masques blancs désemparés." *Les Lettres
françaises* No. 1111 (December 23, 1965), p. 12.
Review of three volumes which are "likely to alarm the reader about
the depth of the Negro Problem." These are *Black Skin, White
Masks* by Frantz Fanon, *The African* by Colin Turnbull and *Nous,
les nègres*, a collection of interviews of James Baldwin, Malcolm X,
and Martin Luther King, Jr.

867 Maunick, E.[douard] J. *"Bon sang de bonsoir* de Richard
Wright." *Les Bonnes Feuilles* No. 46 (December 8, 1965). 3 p.,
mimeographed.

Notice of *Lawd Today* serving as a introduction to a radio presentation. Wright's premature death removed a writer who achieved universality through his desire to rectify injustice wherever found. A summary of a few episodes in the novel follows and the character of Jake Jackson is briefly analyzed. A short extract of the translation is read.

868 Médaz. "Le Probléme noir américain dans un roman." *Voix ouvrière* (January 6, 1965), p. 18.
Contemporary America has one of its most "passionate" writers in James Baldwin, who is also a spokesman for the integrationist movement.   *Another Country*, a violent novel, is unsettling especially in the first part. His realistic portrayal of Harlem and its role in shaping the Black man is very forceful. Baldwin masters a difficult task, describing the miserable existence of Blacks in the United States. The reader is touched by this novel which is "more than a novel presenting a thesis." Baldwin's work is powerful and "filled with bitter poetry."

869 Memmi, Albert. Introduction to *Nous, les nègres,* a collection of interviews of James Baldwin, Malcolm X, and Martin Luther King by Kenneth B. Clark. Paris: François Maspéro (Cahiers libres 70), 1965. Pp. 7-28.
The essay contrasts the three men as stages in protest: Memmi met Baldwin, "an emotional and sincere intellectual, torn and passionate;" King "is the noblest figure, the least disturbing one;" and Malcolm X is "violence that accuses." They do not represent three possible historical solutions. Mentions Wright's *Black Boy*, "the best black protest to date," and his claim that he is an American first; also his own *Portrait du colonisé*.   Analyzes stereotypes and myths elaborated by racist thought.

870 Micha, René. "Les paroissiens de Chester Himes." *Les Temps modernes* No. 225 (February 1965), pp. 1507-23.
Micha's long article is the major study of Himes' detective fiction to appear in French during the 1960s, and an excellent one. In the Harlem Domestic Series Himes finally gives free rein to his delight in the gold mine of vitality and eccentricity found among the people of Harlem. Here he has been able to exercise his sense of fantasy and Rabelaisian verve and at the same time have fun with his writing. Micha finds the Harlem books clearly superior to Himes' earlier protest fiction, a form of writing he regards as being too visibly

geared to socio-political theses and too reminiscent of the worst aspects of the nineteenth-century novel.

871 Olivier, Claude. "Théâtre-choc." *Les Lettres françaises* No. 1105 (November 11, 1965), pp. 18-19.
The reviewer of *Dutchman* and *The Slave* disagrees with LeRoi Jones's position on racial and ideological grounds: Jones believes that the Negro problem is a white problem and wants to restore the power of the colored majority in the world. "His starting point seems to me to be downright erroneous. ... I stated my disagreement with the dramatist's thesis, which is no reason to reject the very high quality performance."

872 Paget, Jean. "Quand Bourseiller arrache les masques: *L'Esclave* et *Le Métro fantôme*." *Combat* (November 6, 1965), p. 8.
A review of *Dutchman* and *The Slave*. "These are two fascinating plays...similar to the revolt of Edward Albee and William Burroughs, i.e., they criticize with linguistic violence hitherto unequalled in Europe, with a teeming, halting and possessed sort of poetry. Jones has rejected his formative years and courageously affirms his blackness. His rebellion is upsetting since he ends up preferring the fanaticism of racial hatred."

873 Pierre, Roland. "Los Angeles dans les livres: *Un Américain en enfer*." *L'Humanité-Dimanche* No. 25 (August 22, 1965) p. 12.
The True American by Melvin Van Peebles is a book against segregation and racism. "Its satirical tone is close to black humor. ... Imagination is let loose but everything is tragically real." This philosophical and fantastic tale stresses two points: black despair is quite satisfactory to the white power structure --they can speak as long as they don't act-- and attempts at rebellion end in lynching, as in the case of Abe. "It is not a coincidence that the defenders of American democracy in Vietnam and the racists of the Ku Klux Klan are the same people."

874 Pini, Richard. "Melvin Van Peebles, *Un ours pour le F.B.I.*" *Les Langues modernes* No. 59 (July 1965), p. 490.
A Bear for the FBI is the story of a young middle-class Negro told in such a platitudinous way that it soon becomes boring. The reasons the author gives for telling about the first day he saw a woman's breasts or when he beat up one of his schoolmates are far from clear.

The book closes on the father's ramblings. One would be tempted to say "Like father, like son."

875 Pivot, Bernard. "Un Américain bien joyeux: *Un Américain en enfer.*" *Le Figaro littéraire* No. 992 (April 22, 1965), p. 2.
A short review of *The True American* emphasizing the diversity of Van Peebles talent; his dedication of the book to members of his family and friends; the acknowledgement of the novelist's talent; and the great laughter provoked by the book.

876 Poirot-Delpech, Bertrand. "Spectacle de LeRoi Jones en version originale." *Le Monde* No. 6474 (November 6, 1965), p. 16.
Review of *Dutchman* and *The Slave.* "The drama of cruelty recommended by Artaud seems a light entertainment when compared to the shouts of deep-seated anger uttered by today's black theater." Jones has so much faith in racial war and the victory of his people that he imagines the white man will eventually be the slave.

877 Poirot-Delpech, Bertrand. "*The Amen Corner.*" *Le Monde* No. 6352 (June 17, 1965), p. 16.
Baldwin's world-wide audience waited for the "first presentation of his theater in France." *The Amen Corner* lacks the appeal of *Blues for Mister Charlie.* Unfortunately it does not show Black alienation. Its maudlin quality diminishes its "documentary interest." Stylistic and formal qualities which contribute to the reputation of works like *Another Country* and *The Fire Next Time* are absent from *The Amen Corner.* The play's movement is so slow and poor that not even the actors' creditable performance can rescue it.

878 R., E. "*Un Autre Pays*, par James Baldwin." *Lettres culturelles* (May-June, 1965).
Brief summary of *Another Country*, a "fine book."

879 Randall, John H. "Ralph Ellison, *Invisible Man.*" *Revue des langues vivantes* 31,1 (1965), pp. 24-44.
A detailed discussion of the themes and intentions of *Invisible Man* noting the novel's insights into the interrelatedness of the black and white experiences in America.

880 Richter, Charles de. "La Chronique littéraire de *La République.*" *La République du Var* (July 16, 1965).

Notice of *Lawd Today* by Richard Wright. The protagonist is so unattractive in his violence and insolence that he seems to constitute a reason for racism.

881 Ronse, Henri. "La négritude américaine." *Le Courrier du littoral* (September 24, 1965).
Favorable and thoughtful review of *Lawd Today* noting Wright's contemporary relevance in the context of the Watts riots. A summary of the plot follows, and the reviewer retraces Wright's strained personal and ideological relationship with the CP, alluding to Bertold Brecht. The analysis focuses on the political and social context of oppression but aesthetic concerns are also addressed: the cinematic technique is praised. Jake Jackson suffers from alienation and self-hatred but Wright places him in a frame of reference wider than psychological. See Esnor, Henri (1965).

882 Santerre, François de. "Langston Hughes au théâtre des Champs-Elysées." *Le Figaro* No. 6342 (January 19, 1965), p. 22.
Review of *Black Nativity*. The author praises the bare expressionism "of the show which calls for the complete adherence of the audience." As a result "No one can remain cool in front of the warmth and enthusiasm of such expressions of faith."

883 Santerre, François de. "Version française de *L'Esclave* avec Gaby Sylvia." *Le Figaro* No. 6556 (September 27, 1965), p. 20.
Brief notice: "*The Slave*, by LeRoi Jones, directed by Antoine Bourseiller, takes place in the year 2000; the leader of the black liberation army is confronted with his ex-wife."

884 Saurel, Renée. "Humanisme et violence." *Les Temps modernes* No. 235 (December 1965), pp. 1112-14.
A long, detailed and balanced review of *The Slave* by LeRoi Jones, addressing its themes, language and militancy.

885 Shavey, P. "Notes de lecture: *Sans allusion*." *Le Lion* (February 1965) p. 17.
Brief review of *Nothing Personal*, a book of photographs by Richard Avedon with text by James Baldwin.

886 Shavey, P. "*Un Autre Pays*, par James Baldwin." *Le Lion* (February 1965), p. 17.

The French reader turns to American literature to learn about the racial problems because American treatments of them are more realistic. In *Another Country*, Baldwin shows that interracial love relations are very difficult. "Baldwin's novel is deliberately realistic and hard."

887 Timsit, Pierre. "Simple et le jazz." *Cahiers du jazz* No. 12 (1965), pp. 62-68.
With quotations and dialogues taken from Hughes's Simple stories, this essay illustrates the thorough knowledge of jazz music evinced by the protagonist and the criticism he levels against pseudo-amateurs of black music.

888 V., P. "*Un Autre Pays*, par James Baldwin." *Informations dieppoises* (February 5, 1965).
In *Another Country*, Baldwin describes a racism which has no geographical confines and is creeping into French society. Baldwin surpasses Richard Wright in his use of language that is "crude, strong and full of imagery."

889 Venaille, Franck. "Notes de lecture - *Un Autre Pays* par James Baldwin." *Europe* Nos. 431-32 (March-April 1965), pp. 333-34.
A vain attempt is made to overturn racism and sexism in *Another Country*. The malevolent effects of segregation cause Rufus Scott to commit suicide.

890 Viatte, Auguste. "*Un Autre Pays*, par James Baldwin." *Livres et Lectures* (September 1965), p. 39.
Baldwin in *Another Country* and Sartre in *Les Chemins de la liberté* weaken their characters' position by placing them in irrelevant settings. Morbid scenes and obscenities pain the reader. On the other hand, Baldwin's essays remain interesting although he is one of the spokesmen of the integrationist movement.

891 Wagner, Jean. "Les noirs et leur musique." *Cahiers du jazz* No. 12 (1965) pp. 116-17.
A review of *Blues People*. The publication of the book is an important event: LeRoi Jones is the foremost Black essayist; he uses a sociological perspective to show that the universalization of jazz music is a purely sociological phenomenon. A long analysis of the blues ends on an aesthetic judgment which shows that Jones is deeply conversant with black music. "This volume opens up a new

and fruitful way."

892   Wagner, Jean.   *Les poètes noirs des Etats-Unis*.   Paris-Strasbourg: Librairie Istra / Nouveaux Horizons, 1965. 282 p.
This condensed version of Professor Wagner's study of black poetry published in 1963 was done by Simon Copans, although his name is not mentioned. The "Nouveaux Horizons" series was subsidized by the USIS African Bureau for distribution in African countries.

893   Willy, Renée. "*Un Américain en enfer* --pour les aînés." *Revue du secrétariat et de la comptabilité* (June 1965) p. 347.
Brief review of *The True American* by Melvin Van Peebles. This is "A book tinged with humor with extremely rich reverberations." Recommended for adults only.

894   Yambo [Ouologuem}. "*Un Autre Pays*, par James Baldwin." *Présence africaine* No. 53 (1st trimester 1965), pp. 260-62.
A long, appreciative analysis of this "novelistic *opus magnum*." Black life is probably not as gloomy as Baldwin presents it in this novel. Nevertheless, *Another Country* is a "beautiful work," expressing the desire to live fully in spite of all odds.

1966

895   Anon.   "Des mots et des rythmes: Une source d'inspiration pour les écrivains." *Informations et Documents* No. 230 (August 1, 1966), 38-41.
A few instances of literary treatment of jazz themes and the use of jazz forms in writing are provided in a special issue devoted to "Jazz in the U.S.A."   Henry Miller, Le Corbusier, Boris Vian, Jack Kerouac, Langston Hughes, Bernard Wolfe, Malcolm Braly, Jean-Claude Albert-Weil are featured. Hughes is introduced as "probably the greatest black American poet." (p. 40) and his "Weary Blues" poem reproduced. Dorothy Baker's *Young Man with a Horn* is mentioned.   Chester Himes' detective novels, from *For Love of Imabelle* to *The Real Cool Killers* are all said to be "remarkable pieces of reporting."

896   Anon.[?]   "Malcolm X, *Autobiographie*."   *France -Eurafrique* (November 30, 1966) .

A favorable estimate of the book, focusing on the causes and evolution of the black leader's militant stance.

897 Anon.[?] "Malcolm X, *Autobiographie.*" *Le Magazine littéraire* No. 1 (November 2, 1966), pp. 20-21.
A detailed review, generally favorable. The first part of the book is found most exciting, the second less so but the narrative of the political struggle of Malcolm X is fascinating. "The book is a sort of *chanson de geste*, " an epic narrative.

898 Anon.[?] "Malcolm X, *Autobiographie.*" Lyons *Le Bulletin des lettres* (December 15, 1966), p. 31.
Mixed review. "In spite of its sincerity, the book leaves one ill at ease. By publishing it "Malcolm X did more harm than good to the cause he claimed he supported. "In sum, one must say, regretfully, that he spent part of his life in debauchery and the rest in error."

899 Anon.[?] "Malcolm X, *Autobiographie.*" *Le Républicain Lorrain* (November 26, 1966).
A brief, rather favorable review, centering on the value of the book as a document and testimony about the evil consequences of racism and hatred.

900 Anon.[?] "Richard Wright, *Bon sang de bonsoir.*" *Les Livres* (March 3, 1966).
Brief notice of *Lawd Today*, stressing its rigorous technique, its fine structure, and remarking that the translation is not very competent. In this violent narrative a la Dos Passos, some sections "sound somewhat outdated."

901 Anon. "*Solitudes*, de Bob Kaufman." *L'Arche* (June 1966), p. 26 [?].
Brief mention of the volume by the black abomunist poet.

902 Anon. "Une esthétique du cri." *Le Nouvel Observateur* (October 19, 1966), p. 30 [?]
On the same page as "La nouvelle chose à Paris" (an article by Yves Buin on "the new thing" in jazz and Archie Shepp), LeRoi Jones is described as "a fiery proselytizer for avant-garde New-York jazz." He is quoted for saying that his friend Shepp is one of the most committed musicians, "one of the most lucidly aware of the social

responsibility of the black artist."

903   Anon.   "Carlene Polite, *Les Flagellants*." *Centre-Matin* (November 8, 1966).
Brief review of *The Flagellants* by Carlene Polite, called "a vision of American life and its racial problems."

904 Anon. "Des mots et des rythmes--une source d'inspiration pour les écrivains." *Informations et Documents* No. 230 (August 1, 1966), pp. 38, 40-41.
In a montage of extracts showing the influence of jazz on several American and French writers, Langston Hughes's "The Weary Blues" is quoted, p. 40. Hughes is said to be "probably the greatest black American poet."

905 Anon. "Granby Blackwood, *Un Sang mal mêlé*." *Bulletin critique du livre français* No. 251 (November 1966): p. 62.
The novel deals with the narrator's quest for his own identity in the style of philosophical tales. It derives its strength from its quiet, almost classical writing, while dealing with the dramas of mixed blood and identity.

906 Anon. "La négritude américaine: *Un Sang mal mêlé* de Granby Blackwood." *Bulletin critique du livre français* Nos. 248-49 (August-September 1966), p. 41.
Describes the novel as the story of a mulatto torn between the black world and the white.

907 Anon. "La petite fille d'une esclave noire américaine, écrivain vedette d'une nouvelle maison d'édition parisienne." *Bulletin de la Nouvelle Agence de presse* No. 135 (October 17, 1966), pp. 1-2.
The article reviews Carlene Polite's *The Flagellants*, which was first published in French. The topic of the novel is not the conflicts between blacks and segregationists; nor is it a love story between black people that ends in tragedy and hatred. The review emphasizes the fact that Editions Bourgois wants to promote books where style expresses anguish better than content does.

908 Anon. "*Les Flagellants* de Carlene Polite." *Afrique-Revue* No. 62 (1966),p. 40.
Review of *The Flagellants*, the theme of which is the conflicting

relationship within a couple. The communication which existed between Ideal and Jimson breaks down and deteriorates until they hate each other without being able to break away from each other. Their life together becomes a living hell, a mutually accepted "flagellation."

909 Anon. "Malcolm X, *Autobiographie.*" *Beaux-Arts* (December 17, 1966).
A favorable review. This book can only "be read feverishly... It is an introduction to black despair and black revolt, and it exposes the hateful drama of segregation."

910 Anon. "Oh, mon révérend!" *Minute* (October 6, 1966), p. 19.
Briefly mentions, in the caption to two photographs of ex-bunny Carlene Polite, that the author of *The Flagellants* had been the secretary of Martin Luther King.

911   Attoun, Lucien. "Le Théâtre: *L'Esclave, Le Métro fantôme.*" *Europe* Nos. 441-42 (January-February 1966), p. 231.
A review of the performance of the two plays by LeRoi Jones. *Dutchman* is praised as fascinating and for the minute progression of the plot and dialogue. *The Slave* is found interesting but open to a charge of reverse racism.   Med Hondo gives a very creditable performance.

912 B., C. "Tous les bistrots du monde." *Arts, Spectacles, Loisirs* No. 83 (December 7, 1966), p. 21.
Brief review of Melvin Van Peebles' collection of short stories in French, *Le Chinois du XIVeme*, commending the diversity of the stories and the vivaciousness of the writing.

913 Bénot, Yves. "La nouvelle Afrique et les lettres." *Europe* No. 449 (September 1966), pp. 212-16.
In a review of several school books dealing with African literature, the author disagrees with the inclusion of Richard Wright in an anthology recently prepared by P. Vésinet and a group of African teachers under the title *Pages africaines* .

914 Bernard, Pierre. "Un monde sauvé." *La Quinzaine littéraire* No. 4 (May 2, 1966), pp. 8-9.
Detailed and favorable review of *Solitudes* by Bob Kaufman. Kaufman belongs to the beat generation and "he is black, Jewish,

and a junkie --enough to take away your desire to live in America."
He is an "undisciplined gardener; he should pull himself back
together and not be content with verbal erosion. Poetry can only be
born from such lightning-like inspiration."

915 Cabau, Jacques. "Autant en emportent les blancs." *L'Express*
No. 892 (August 12, 1966), p. 58.
A very unfavorable review of Margaret Walker's *Jubilee*. "A century
of integration has swept over *Uncle Tom's Cabin* and the Negroes
in *Jubilee* are whitewashed, polite, and conventional like the sheep of
Queen Marie-Antoinette. Margaret Walker is the very kind of Uncle
Tom Negro writer of which Washington dreams: integrated and
sterilized, her only link to black culture is her color."

916 Cabau, Jacques. *La Prairie Perdue; histoire du roman
américain.* Le Seuil, Paris; 1966, p. 353.
None of the "14 novels which made America" according to Cabau
was written by a black man. He only briefly mentions Richard
Wright, opposing him to Steinbeck as a proletarian ideologist
wanting to explode the American dream: Ralph Ellison's *Invisible
Man* is used to highlight the study of Bellow: "it expresses the link
between new novel forms and spiritual unrest." (p. 319)

917 Clarke, John Henrik. *"The Autobiography of Malcolm X*
(Grove Press, New York)." *Présence africaine* No. 58 (2nd
trimester, 1966), pp. 248-253.
Retraces the evolution of Malcolm X in detail. Concludes that this
book could have been the "foremost autobiography of our era." It is
regrettable that the author died before he could make cuts and
organize its rich material.

918 Depestre, René. "Langston Hughes, ou la main sur la charrue
de la poésie." *Présence africaine* No. 58 (2nd trimester 1966), pp.
189-93.
Abundantly illustrated with quotations from Hughes' poetry and
Dodat's study of it, the article emphasizes the universality of his art.
Certainly inspired by Whitman and the British Romantics of
Shakespeare, it is rooted in folklore without being regional; although
is expresses rebellion it is essentially lyrical, and Hughes' point of
view remains broadly humanistic.

919 Descargues, Pierre. "Du nouveau dans le jeune roman." *La*

Tribune de Lausanne (October 9, 1966), p. 7.

A short, rather favorable review of *The Flagellants* by Carlene Polite. The "hysterical" story comes close to becoming poetry. There is a brief mention of biographical details (Polite had been a "bunny" in a nightclub and lives in Alvin Ailey's apartment), followed by a laudatory analysis of the style of the novel: "the young woman (in the novel) discovers that one is always somebody's inferior and the only language that allows communication is the whip: man is looking for something greater than himself and woman for her master."

920 Dion, Georges. "Deux prix Nobel... et deux romans." *Le Phare belge* (October 30, 1966), p. 5.

A review dealing, among other books, with Carlene Polite's *The Flagellants*. The novel is rhetorically described as "the wild outcry, luxurious and luxuriant, of a race and of an era" in which negritude is expressed spasmodically.

921 Dommergues, Pierre. "La négritude américaine." *Les Langues modernes* No. 60 (May-June 1966), pp. 94-98.

After a panorama of the social and cultural situation of Blacks in the U.S., LeRoi Jones is mentioned as the embodiment of the tendency to move away from the false values of the West. His plays, now being performed in Paris, evince strong revolutionary leanings in their violent confrontations and language. But integration is taking place on the cultural level if one is to believe the "new humanism" of Ralph Ellison, whose *Invisible Man* will be translated again. Jones and Ellison meet, however, in their common respect for the militant action of SNCC. "The problem is simple for the black man: he must assume his negritude (Jones) in order to transcend his recovered blackness (Baldwin) and discover his identity as a person (Ellison)." Also published in *Le Monde* (April 13, 1966).

922 Dommergues, Pierre. "LeRoi Jones au théâtre." *Les Langues modernes* No. 60 (May-June, 1966), pp. 102-04.

The essay begins with the development of the new American theater, the initial career of LeRoi Jones in Greenwich Village and his creating BARTS. He refuses the sham values of the U.S., eschews non-violence, and calls for "an honest attempt at social and economic reconstruction." *The Slave* is analyzed and Walker is taken as proof that political drama does not exclude nostalgia and whites are not consistently the villains.

923 Duvignaud, Jean. "D'un ghetto à l'autre." *Le Nouvel Observateur* No. 103 (November 2, 1966).
Review of Claude Brown's *Manchild in the Promised Land* from a psychological rather than sociological perspective. "A splendid document...however complacently Brown may describe violence at times, ...his talent and the richness of his language are the result of his own reforming and adaptation through schooling." The French sociologist notes that the black man must use his own action to make himself free from "inhumanity."

924 Fabre, Michel, ed. and transl. "Table ronde: Le problème noir aux Etats-Unis." *Les Langues modernes* No. 60 (May-June 1966), pp. 108-16.
A round table on Blacks in the United States with the participation of Langston Hughes, William Melvin Kelley, Paule Marshall, Simon Copans, Pierre Dommergues and Fabre. Deals with many aspects of black writing, notable exile, commitment and the need to fight stereotypes, and racism in the American context. Discusses Wright, Baldwin, Ellison and LeRoi Jones as well as Faulkner and verbal creation in the ghetto. [This piece is reprinted in Pierre Dommergues, *Les USA à la recherche de leur identité* (Paris: Grasset, 1967), pp. 142-56.]

925 Fabre, Michel. "Panorama critique: Caliban à l'heure du destin." *Les Langues modernes* No. 60 (May-June 1966), p. 123.
A Different Drummer by William M. Kelley is summarized but its plot is less important than its symbolical meanings. This neo-Faulknerian parable erects the myth of a black superhuman ancestor. The apocalyptic finale of black disappearance from the South is seen not as an act of destruction but an exodus. The form of the novel itself is experimental although influenced by Faulkner.

926 Fabre, Michel. "Panorama critique: Cécité et négritude." *Les Langues modernes* No. 60 (May-June 1966), pp. 123-24.
A Drop of Patience shows the progress of William M. Kelley towards starkness of style and terseness. It is the story of a blind jazz musician, his unhappy marriage and dazzling affair with a white girl until he finds "salvation" in a black church. Ludlow is a powerful character, both full of compassion and able to deride himself in the role of the black minstrel. At bottom, he is a tragic figure, like the protagonist of John A. Williams' *Night Song* or Professor Unrat in "The Blue Angel."

927   Fabre, Michel.   "Panorama critique: L'odyssée de Bronzeville." *Les Langues modernes* No. 60 (May-June 1966), pp. 125-26.
Detailed analytical review of *Lawd Today* by Richard Wright. Fabre points out the novel's indebtedness to Dos Passos and Joyce. The 24-hour odyssey of a black postman allows a vivid, humorous depiction of ghetto life lighter than is usually the case with Wright's fiction.

928   Fabre, Michel.   "Panorama critique: La jeune fille de Brooklyn." *Les Langues modernes* No. 60 (May-June 1966), p. 128.
This review of *Brown Girl, Brownstones* by Paule Marshall focuses on the growth of Selina in her West Indian immigrant Brooklyn environment. Marshall's writing is reminiscent of the convolutions, minute accretions and slow progress which characterized both Virginia Woolf and V.S. Naipaul. Her world, however, is a tough one. "This novel makes her one of the most accomplished writers of her generation."

929 Fabre, Michel. "Panorama critique: Salinger dans le ghetto." *Les Langues modernes* No. 60 (May-June 1966), pp. 124-25.
Dancers on the Shore by William M. Kelley contains short stories related by recurrent characters, but each individual story tends to work through the revelation of "epiphanies." Some are entertaining; some overly moving, like "A Good Long Sidewalk;" but humor always intervenes. "Connie" is the most successful story and the Dunford family is closer to our hearts than Franny and Zooey.

930 Fabre, Michel. "Panorama critique: Une Vie." *Les Langues modernes* No. 60 (May-June 1966), pp. 128-29.
Horace Cayton could have succeeded in the in-between area of bohemian or literary life; he could have been satisfied as a sociologist professional. With clearsightedness, he explores the reasons for his dissatisfaction and his "crack-up" in terms of social and racial pressures but also in terms of personal background. *Old Long Road* is a valuable biography because of his tremendous sensitivity and attempt to be honest. The style is clear and simple, with occasional poetic touches amidst a good deal of detailed analysis generally brought into focus by a broadly sociological approach.

931 Fabre, Michel. "Panorama critique: Voter ou mourir." *Les*

Langues modernes No. 60 (May-June 1966), p. 127.
If We Must Die by black Junius Edwards is a more powerful novel than *Look Away, Look Away* by white Ben Haas which also deals with integration and civil rights in the South. The protagonist is an ex G-Man who achieves every kind of victory over the many obstacles placed on his road towards voter registration except physical violence: the finale leaves us uncertain of his survival after a bloody beating. The terseness of this sad story evinces "certain beauty and the promise of talent."

932 Fontaine, André. *"L'Autobiographie de Malcolm X." Le Monde* (December 24, 1966), p. 16.
A favorable review of "one of the most extraordinary books" published in many years. Malcolm X is a man of "exceptional mettle," and the Black Muslims benefited indeed from an overwhelming propagandist.

933 Gouhier, Henri. *"Le Métro fantôme, L'Esclave." La Table ronde* Nos. 216-17 (January-February 1966), pp. 120-21.
This review considers the plots and style of LeRoi Jones' *Dutchman* and *The Slave*, which are characterized by violence and the nostalgic remembrances of friendship in a context of hatred, doubt and anger. The directing by Antoine Bourseiller is praised.

934 Guérin, Daniel. "Préface", in *L'Autobiographie de Malcolm X*. Paris: Grasset, 1966.
The Marxist historian mostly analyzes the political action and thought of the black leader in the context of his tempering, and his final evolution from racialism and nationalism to a wider, international, class-oriented perspective. Alex Haley's part in writing the book is hardly mentioned.

935 Hahn, Pierre. *"Harlem ou la terre promise." Arts, Spectacles, Loisirs* No. 46 (August 10, 1966), p. 24.
A very favorable review of Claude Brown's *Manchild in the Promised Land* emphasizing the human (not the sociological) aspects of the book. "It is the story of the hero's dreams and sufferings, of his anger and constant struggle, ... of his quest, vindictiveness, hatred and disappointments."

936 Hanga-Golden, L., and O. Melikian. "Une figure scientifique et publique: William E.B. DuBois." *Présence africaine* No. 60 (4th

trimester 1966), pp. 67-82.
This article by an Afro-American student in the USSR and a Soviet Africanist deals with the life, literary career and political activities of the Panafricanist leader. His major ideological positions are explored but not his specific literary achievements.

937 Hardellet, André. Preface to Melvin Van Peebles, *Le Chinois du XIVeme.* Paris: Jérome Martineau, 1966. Pp. 7-9.
Although he does not write in his native tongue, Van Peebles sounds like an authentic Parisian talking about ordinary folks in the 14th arrondissement. His "Chinois" apparently does not refer to a Chinese character but designates a potpourri of quaint and very humane tales.

938 Hervé, Julia. "Carlene Polite, ou l'école du feu et du soufre." *Jeune Afrique* No. 306 (November 20, 1966), p. 75.
An interview with the author of *The Flagellants.* She declares that "we are all born at the bottom of the ladder;" talks about ghetto life; insists upon the importance of the black mother and the force of black women; and mentions that she favors Malcolm X's perspectives. To the free-flowing rhapsodies of Henry Miller, she prefers L.-F. Céline and she writes out of the fire and brimstone brand of religion in which she has been brought up. The novel is called "a haunting testimony to the collective fantasies engendered by racism."

939 Hervé, Julia. "Le furieux itinéraire de Malcolm X." *Le Nouvel Observateur*, No. 102 (November 29, 1966), pp. 42-43.
A review of the *Autobiography* by the daughter of Richard Wright focuses on the political career of the slain leader and devotes some space to the narrative itself. It is rich in detail and astonishing color, full of "earthy, direct images" and couched in a "style just as spontaneous as his vibrant speeches." The book brings an element which is essential to our understanding of Malcolm X, an unceasing dialectical motion between "the inside" and "the outside", by which revolutionary strategy is nurtured.

940 Hughes, Langston. Preface to his *La Poésie négro-américaine.* Edition bilingue. anthologie réunie et préfacée par Langston Hughes. Paris: Seghers, 1966. Pp. 7-14.
The preface was never published in English and provides a short historical panorama of Negro poetry in the U.S. Not love, nor

moonlight, nor even despair and death characterize this poetry but "race and color and the plight of black people." To such a point that James Baldwin who "attacked *Uncle Tom's Cabin* in an essay published with that of Richard Gibson [in the USIS-sponsored publication] *Perspectives* (2, 1952)], now writes only protest literature." Hughes mentions Gwendolyn Brooks as the only black recipient of a Pulitzer prize. The selection ranges from New Orleans Creole poets in *Les Cenelles* to such contemporary names as James Emanuel, Jay Wright, SNCC militant Worth Long, and Jamaica-born Lebert Bethune.

Sim Copans (who suggested the anthology should be done) his son Jean, and Professor Jean Wagner were largely responsible for translating the poems and preparing the notices.

941 Josselin, J.-F. "Le lapin et son trèfle." *Les Nouvelles littéraires* No. 2041 (October 13, 1966), p. 2.
Brief mention of a new novel by Carlene Polite to be published by Farrar, Straus and Giroux [probably *Sister X and the Victims of Foul Play*].

942 Jouffroy, Alain. "Le `bang' de la pensée." *L'Express* No. 769 (March 14, 1966), pp. 92-93.
Review of a poetry collection by Ferlinghetti and of *Solitudes* by Bob Kaufman. Kaufman is "a Poet, i.e., someone who illuminates, lightning-like, the farthest reaches of thinking," far away from any state-sponsored, rational, psychological activity. All his poetry comes out of the bomb-like impact of the present day. Jailed under the pretense that he was taking drugs, Kaufman embodies the "sequestration of the human spirit."

943 Julien, Claude. "Préface à l'édition française" in Malcolm X. *Le Pouvoir Noir* Paris: Maspéro. 1966. Pp. 8-30.
Based on the *Autobiography of Malcolm X*, this introduction retraces in detail the evolution of Malcolm X, notably his conversion to the Black Muslim type of Islam. The author recalls the accommodationism of Booker T. Washington, the decisive action of W.E.B. Du Bois and the impulse given by Martin Luther King, Jr. to the Civil Rights Movement; he mentions James Weldon Johnson's collections of spirituals and quotes Countee Cullen's "Simon the Cyrenian" and Langston Hughes' "I too sing America."

944 Kattan, Naïm. "Rencontre avec Ralph Ellison;" *Les Langues*

modernes No. 60 (May-June 1966), pp. 99-101.
A brief introduction mentions the publication of *Shadow and Act* and
the Irving Howe-Ralph Ellison controversy concerning Richard
Wright. Ellison does not refuse to fight for the cause but he does so
as a citizen, not as a writer; the blues are not the music of a defeated
people but violence is the easy way, which explains why Martin
Luther King has such a large following. The Black Muslims are
desperate people; the racial problem is above all a question of
political power. The black writer is an American writer and his role
consists in expressing the complexity and ambiguity of the American
situation.

945   Lacote, René. "La Poésie négro-américaine." *Les Lettres
françaises* No. 1129 (April 28, 1966), p. 30.
A descriptive review of *La Poésie négro-américaine*, an anthology
compiled by Langston Hughes.

946   Las Vergnas, Raymond. "Terres promises: Claude Brown,
Harlem ou la terre promise." *Les Nouvelles littéraires* No. 2030
(July 28, 1966), p. 5.
A brief mention of the newly-translated novel by Claude Brown,
Manchild in the Promised Land, whose autobiographical contents
overshadows its writing.

947   Lemarchand, Jacques. "Le Théâtre." *Le Figaro littéraire* No.
1046 (May 5, 1966), p. 16.
An announcement concerning a new series of performances of
Dutchman by LeRoi Jones at the Théâtre des Mathurins is followed
by a post scriptum: "This play has already enjoyed a very honorable
career and a well-deserved success" [which contradicts the
reviewer's earlier judgment in the November 18, 1965, issue of the
same newspaper.]

948   Lindenberg, Daniel. "Un théâtre militant." *Les Temps
modernes* No. 239 (April 1966) pp. 1918-20.
Review of Paris performances of *Dutchman* and *The Slave*. Jones is
seen as expressing a form of black racism and attacking white
people, yet more for aesthetic than ideological reasons.

949   Marchou, Chantal. "*Un Sang mal mêlé* par Granby
Blackwood." *La Vie des métiers* (November 1966), p. 7.
Review of the novel considered as "a pain-filled autobiography," an

exploration of the mechanisms of the soul that lead to depression. The cause is to be found in the social and individual malaise of the black hero, who remains anonymous to the end. His partners lack intelligence and express themselves in a superficial way. The protagonist is seen as "the prototype of the self-taught man endowed with enough lucidity to suffer." At times the novel is touching because of its fine analysis and sincerity.

950 Pelayo, Donato. "Malcolm X, *Autobiographie*." *Le Populaire de Paris* (December 13, 1966).
Favorable review supporting an estimate of Malcolm X as a wise, somewhat moderate leader "whose image the French press and media have fashioned in such a way that he appeared to be a sort of 'black Hitler.'"

951 Pini, Richard. "Théâtre américain à Paris." *Les Langues modernes* No. 60 (May-June 1966), pp. 106-07.
Our Little Town by Thornton Wilder and *Love* by Murray Schisgal are reviewed in the same essay as *Dutchman* and *The Slave* by LeRoi Jones. The latter's plays are inspired by the principles of Brecht and Antonin Artaud. *Dutchman* creates a welcome shock, but *The Slave* is a trite sentimental story about a "poor black revolutionary leader who must kill the children he loves to take them out from the sway of white villains."

952 Pinot, Germaine. "Dans votre bibliothèque: *Bon sang de bonsoir*." *Fédération française des Postes et Telecommunications* (January 16, 1966).
Favorable review of *Lawd Today*. Wright is one of the great American novelists and this novel is an important addition to his canon. Wright testifies about the life of his colored brothers in a society where they find no room. These twenty four hours in the life of Jake Jackson are reviewed in detail, and the changing mood of the protagonist stressed. The final episode, especially forces us to "confront moments of nearly unendurable tension." In spite of his violence against his sickly wife, the protagonist is human and even likeable; he is the victim of a ruthless society and his problems are still present today in the most powerful nation in the world.

953 Pouzol, Henri. "*Bon sang de bonsoir* (R. Wright)." *Présence des lettres et des arts* (1966).
Review of *Lawd Today* noting that all the novelistic material of the

great writer is contained in this book, written in the 1930s. A long summary of diverse episodes follows, focusing on scapegoating scenes. Wright condemns both white racism in the North and black submission to it. All must accept responsibility for the racial situation. The tone is reminiscent of Chester Himes' "domestic" novels.

954 Saporta, Marc. "L'ombre blanche." *La Quinzaine littéraire* No. 4 (May 1, 1966), p. 8.
Brief favorable review of *La Poésie négro-américaine*, an anthology compiled by Langston Hughes. This is no bland, neutral selection but a true manifesto and the preface already expresses Hughes' main theme: "Negro-American poetry can only expose and denounce." This reflects today's Black militancy. Also Hughes accumulates lyrical poems celebrating the African heritage of black Americans. "The collection constitutes a remarkable lyrical and documentary whole."

955 Timsit, Pierre. "Essai analytique sur deux poèmes de Langston Hughes." *Cahiers du jazz* No. 13 (1966), pp. 19- 33.
A detailed, line-by-line textual and stylistic analysis of "Blues in Stereo" and "Jazz Muted." The accent is placed upon the ideological commitment as well as the musical composition of the first poem; as for the second, the many allusions to free jazz are emphasized.

956 Tournier, Jacques. "Carnet de théâtre: *Métro fantôme.*" *Etudes* No. 324 (January 1966), p. 79.
Review of *Dutchman* by LeRoi Jones. The essential element of the play is not the language, although it is violent, direct and raw; it is the nature of the relationship between the black man and the white woman. "There is no ambiguity in the playwright's intentions; he resorts to the stage as a tribune for social satire and political demands.

957 Wagner, Jean. "Lettre à un provincial à propos d'un papou." *Cahiers du jazz* No. 13 (1966) pp. 70-78.
An unfavorable review of *La Bataille du jazz* by French critic Hughes Panassié. Several paragraphs are devoted to defending James Baldwin and LeRoi Jones against accusations of shoddy anti-conformism leveled against them. Richard Wright is quoted and the conversion of Jones from beatnik to black nationalist militantism is retraced.

958 Wagner, Jean. "Le mur invisible." *La Quinzaine littéraire* No.12 (September 15, 1966), pp. 23-24.
Review of *Dark Ghetto* by Kenneth Clark and *Manchild in the Promised Land* by Claude Brown. The two books are complementary although one is a sociological study and the other a story of childhood and youth in the ghetto. Better than Clark, Brown demonstrates the evolution of Harlem blacks since their migration from the South. Clark tries hard to be deceived by the American "solution" while Brown refuses to be duped.

959 Wagner, Jean. "Pouvoir noir." *La Quinzaine littéraire* (November 15, 1966), pp. 49-50.
In a postscript to his review of *Pouvoir noir*, a collection of speeches by Malcolm X, Wagner adds that he had just completed the review when he received *L'Autobiographie de Malcolm X,* published by Grasset in Paris. He notes that his present analysis of the black leader's career coincides with Daniel Guérin's introduction to the autobiography; this is proof that men of good faith see alike. The autobiography "is a document of prime magnitude for those concerned by racial issues in the U.S." Malcolm paradoxically appears very black and American to the utmost; one learns much about the methods and involvement of the Black Muslims, also about their ability to fight drug addiction without any medical therapy. Malcolm was shot when he had just written to a friend: "I am above all a human being, and I support whatever is good for mankind as a whole."

1967

960 Achille, Louis, T. "Les Negro Spirituals." *Présence africaine* issue on "Colloque sur l'art négre" Vol. 1 (1967), pp. 363-77.
Excludes all secular songs from the definition of the "spirituals," with the exception of "Freedom songs." Analyzes the tendency of Afro-American thinking to refer constantly to God. Ends on a survey of Negro spirituals in contemporary times.

961 Albert-Lévin, Marc. "Cassius le Grand ou l'envers de Polly Magoo." *Les Lettres françaises* No. 1185 (June 1, 1967), p. 23.
Mentions at length the *Autobiography* of Malcolm X.

962 Anon.[?] "Un texte remarquable." *Le Figaro littéraire* No. 1112 (August 7, 1967), p. 3.

After the publication of the July 31, 1967 interview with Baldwin in this newspaper, a reader expresses his full agreement with his views.

963   Anon.[?]   "Dixieland, terre sauvage." *Le Provençal* (April 2, 1967).
A rather favorable review of Langston Hughes' *The Best of Simple*, stressing the ingenuity and common sense of the ghetto-dwellers and the violence of American racial oppression.

964   Anon.[?]   "Granby Blackwood, *Un Sang mal mêlé.*" *La République du Centre* (March 28, 1967).
A mostly descriptive review emphasizing the hatred between the protagonist and his lighter-skinned brother the sight of whom revives his memory. Also states the types of conflict that take place within the hero's soul.

965   Anon.   "Granby Blackwood, *Un Sang mal mêlé.*" *Notes bibliographiques* (February, 1967), pp. 19-20.
Long summary of the novel: the protagonist suffers from amnesia at the beginning but recovers his memory in the Canary Islands, where he spent his childhood. Of mixed blood, he is devoured by jealousy and hatred of his lighter-skinned brother who finally succumbs. The novel is more the study of a neurosis than of the racial problem. The atmosphere is oppressive and only "forewarned and well-balanced adults" should attempt to read it.

966   Anon.   "James Baldwin." *La Quinzaine littéraire* No. 36 (October 1-15,1967), p. 10.
An announcement of the publication of Baldwin's latest work in the United States, *Tell Me How Long the Train's Been Gone.*

967   Anon.   "Je pense que c'est grâce à Maupassant que j'ai réellement souhaité devenir écrivain..." *Arts, Spectacles, Loisirs,* June 1967.
Briefly hails the publication of Langston Hughes' book of short stories, *L'Ingénue* [sic] *de Harlem*, and quotes his mention of Maupassant's influence upon his becoming a writer.

968   Anon. [?]   *"L'Autobiographie de Malcolm X." L'Arche* (January 1967).
A favorable review emphasizing the tone of the narrative; it is often

"truculent" and "the fervor is nearly prophetic."

969 Anon.[?] *"L'Ingénu de Harlem* de Langston Hughes." *Détective* (May 18, 1967), p. 32.
Brief introduction to Hughes' *The Best of Simple*, through which "the people of Harlem are vividly seen and, beyond them, the whole of U.S. social life."

970 Anon. *"L'Ingénu de Harlem* de Langston Hughes." *L'Est républicain* (June 28, 1967).
Brief review of *The Best of Simple*, whose protagonist is seen as a symbol for the folklife of Harlem and mainstream America too.

971 Anon.[?] *"L'Ingénu de Harlem* de Langston Hughes." *Le Magazine littéraire* No. 6 (April 1967), p. 23.
Mention of *The Best of Simple,* introducing Simple and labeling Hughes "the most famous black writer in the U.S."

972 Anon.[?] *"L'Ingénu de Harlem*, nouvelles par Langston Hughes." *Jeune Afrique* No. 331 (May 14, 1967), pp. 60-61.
The review praises the character of Simple who has nothing in common with Voltaire's Candide except his ingenuousness. Simple authentically reflects the joys and griefs of the Harlem community: he is neither a never-do-well nor a drunkard nor an Uncle Tom nor a revolutionary. He cannot be easily labeled. He is not a symbol either, but merely possesses the qualities required for survival in Harlem.

973 Anon.[?] *"L'Ingénu de Harlem*." Montréal *Le Soleil* (December 16, 1967).
The French Canadian newspaper presents *The Best of Simple,* by Langston Hughes translated into French; includes biographical information on the author.

974 Anon.[?] *"L'Ingénu de Harlem* par Langston Hughes." *Le Courrier d'Aix -en-Provence* (November 4, 1967), p. 6.
A review of *The Best of Simple* stressing the funny and pathetic sides of the personality of Simple, and the linguistic richness of his speech and verbal creations.

975 Anon.[?] *"L'Ingénu de Harlem* par Langston Hughes." *Le Jardin des modes* (July 1, 1967).

Brief mention of *The Best of Simple,* a collection of stories.
"Hughes was one of the greatest black poets; his Simple is an
extraordinary drunkard, as candid and quiet as Soldier Schveik."

976 Anon. "Langston Hughes et son *Ingénu de Harlem.*" *Le Droit
de vivre* (May 1967).
Short article introducing Hughes as "one of the most authentic poets
of our time, of whom his white compatriots should be proud." His
Simple stories are praised for their cunning and authenticity.

977 Anon.[?] "Langston Hughes: *L'Ingénu de Harlem.*"
Humanité-Dimanche No. 121 (June 25, 1967), p. 42.
Brief mention of Langston Hughes' collection of stories, *The Best of
Simple*. "Under the guise of vivid and original humor, the book is a
vehicle for the forceful accusations leveled by Blacks in America."

978 Anon.[?] "*Les Elus du Seigneur* de James Baldwin."
L'Express (April 19, 1957).
The inspiration of *Go Tell It on the Mountain* comes from the
condition of some Blacks in the United States. The novel embodies
the universal "mournful poetry of immobile revolt." The reviewer
elaborates on, and gives examples of the peripheral and anonymous
appearance of whites in the novel. It displays a "troubling mixture"
of religion and sensuality which appears in the best works of Richard
Wright, or in Alan Paton's *Cry, the Beloved Country*. Such mixture
seems to "belong to the art and nature of Blacks."

979 Anon.[?] "Le héros de Langston Hughes, *L'Ingénu de
Harlem.*" *Le Méridional* (July 16, 1967).
Brief evocation of Hughes' hero, whose adventures reflect "a life
which is both funny and pathetic because Simple's way of looking at
the world is lucid, even (and especially) when it becomes tinged with
humor." Simple has become a real character for millions of
Americans and he represents the people in the streets of American
cities. "They are depicted with biting talent in these sketches, where
the finesse of a Hogarth goes hand-in-hand with the precision of a
Maupassant."

980 Anon.[?] "Malcolm X, *Autobiographie.*" *Jeune Afrique* No.
64 (February 1967), p. 41.
A very favorable review; the book is "fascinating... warm... full of

dramatic ups and downs."

981 Anon.[?] "Malcolm X, *Autobiographie*." *Les Echos* (January 6, 1967).
A favorable evaluation concluding that Malcolm X was "one of the most authentic African-American leaders."

982 Anon.[?] "Malcolm X, *Autobiographie*." *Le Peuple* (February 7, 1967).
A mixed review. "It is certainly necessary to take into account a certain romance in a book by the adept of a sect who wanted to leave, if not a gospel at least a legend behind him."

983 Anon "Polémique théâtrale à Montpellier". *Le Figaro* No. 7218 (November 11-12, 1967), p. 2.
Concerning the banning of *Dutchman* by LeRoi Jones by the mayor of Montpellier, it is stated that the play was not really prohibited but that due to its erotic boldness and its political violence, it could not be included in the performances officially sponsored by the city and given with its financial support. [The play was performed in the nearby and rival city of Sète to which the audience was bused.]

984 Anon. "Une anthologie présentée par Langston Hughes: *La Poésie négro-américaine*." *Esprit* No. 356 (January 1967), p. 208.
Review of Hughes' anthology of Afro-American poetry [a sort of sequel to *The Poetry of the Negro*, compiled with Arna Bontemps]. The author emphasizes the difference between "this new kind of literature" and African poetry. One can find in it the heritage of slavery and the voice of rebellion.

985 Anon. "*Un Sang mal mêlé* de Granby Blackwood." *Bulletin critique du livre français* No. 254 (February 13, 1967), p. 114.
This novel, first published in French by a black American, is described as the narration of the frustrations experienced by a mulatto whose conflict with his brother leads him to kill him at the end. The analysis of emotions and the passion and violence of the novel inspire pages which reflect the poetry of the Canary Islands.

986 Anon.[?] "*Un Sang mal mêlé*: Granby Blackwood." *Jeune Afrique* No. 64 (February, 1967), p. 41.
The review sums up the novel as the inner adventure of a mulatto

who attempts to recover his memory; it emphasizes the interest of the mental processes of the awakening of memory. The book is lauded as "the painful quest for one's past recounted like a poem."

987 Anon. "*Un Sang mal mêlé* par Granby Blackwood." *Droit et Liberté* No. 264 (July-August 1967), p. 32.
The review notes that the mulatto protagonist reacts to his mixed blood so badly that he loses his memory. He thus has to undertake a discovery of himself. His quest is hindered by the hated *présence* of his brother, whose skin is lighter that his and who cannot pass for white because of his own presence.

988 Arsenijevic, Drago. "Deux livres sur le problème noir." *La Tribune de Genève* (January 25, 1967).
A review of *Dark Ghetto* by Kenneth Clark and *The Autobiography of Malcolm X*, contrasting the staid tone of the sociologist and the fervor of the political activist and religious leader. "Malcolm's book grips you by the guts."

989 Attoun, Lucien. "Le Théâtre: *Les Voisins*." *Europe* Nos. 454-55 (February-March 1967), pp. 367-80.
In this review of James Saunders' *Neighbors*, the author makes a comparison with LeRoi Jones' *Dutchman*: for Saunders, the black man starts and leads the conflict. He goes further into violence than Jones, whose play depends upon sex.

990 Bergues, Valentine. "Dixieland, terre sauvage." *Le Provençal-Dimanche* (March ?, 1967).
Retraces the political career and racial involvement of Malcolm X, "this black man with a prophet's aura, and nearly raving verbal violence."

991 Bhély-Quénum, Olympe. "*L'Ingénu de Harlem*, par Langston Hughes." *Afrique actuelle* No. 21 (1967), p. 28.
Favorable review of *The Best of Simple*. The book is praised for its vividness and charm. The protagonist does not openly care about politics but he reveals many aspects of daily life in America through his witty, although somewhat candid, perception and recounting of commonplace events.

992 Buenzod, Emmanuel. "La dernière chronique." *La Gazette de*

Lausanne (May 20, 1967).

Review of *The Best of Simple* by Langston Hughes, stressing the "incredible truthfulness of the character of Simple" with his big heart and brotherly approach to human problems. Jesse is endowed with great lucidity and the reader is led to conclude that the advent of justice will not take place soon.

993 Cazemajou, Jean. *"L'Autobiographie de Malcolm X."* *L'Education nationale* (June 15, 1967).

A detailed commentary on the career of the black militant.

994 Copans, Simon. "James Weldon Johnson et le patrimoine culturel des noirs américains." *Cahiers de la Compagnie Renaud-Barrault* No.61 (May-June 1967), pp. 42-48.

Discusses the role Johnson played as a propagandist and promoter of black American music and poetry and analyzes the African origins of black music.

995 D., Mary. "Tout ou rien." *Le Figaro littéraire* No. 1113 (August 11, 1967), p. 2.

A black woman from Chicago passing through Paris, writes to the editor after reading the July 31, 1967 interview of Baldwin in the *Figaro littéraire*. She disapproves of the author's ideas and claims: "I am of the opinion that our race cannot make progress separate from the whites."

996 Diakhaté, Lamine. "Langston Hughes, conquérant de l'espoir." *Présence africaine* No. 64 (4th trimester 1967), pp. 38-46.

This homage places Hughes' poetry within the context of the Negritude movement; recalling that he did not only go back in search of his cultural roots but "attempted to impose Africa on white America and on the black bourgeoisie whose major preoccupation was to pass." He restored the rhythms of Africa, which jazz had preserved. "He has now gone to join Garvey and McKay Du Bois and Dunbar."

997 Dodat, François. "Situation de Langston Hughes." *Présence africaine* No. 64 (4th trimester 1967), pp. 47-50.

Homage to "a citizen of Harlem" who had chosen to remain in the United States without forsaking any of the genius of his race. The essay stresses his quest for equality along the lines of the NAACP and his attempt to promote racial reconciliation. An examination of

Hughes' poetry also reveals a strong influence of black music and jazz rhythms.

998 Dommergues, Pierre. *Les USA à la recherche de leur identité: Rencontres avec 40 écrivains américains*. Paris: Grasset, 1967. See p. 343-47, 486.
This book is largely a montage of interviews with and essays by the writers concerned. Chapter four, "The White Problem," provides excerpts from a round-table discussion held in 1966 with Langston Hughes, William M. Kelley and Paule Marshall as well as texts written by Malcolm X, Martin Luther King, LeRoi Jones and Ralph Ellison, and the October 1963 interview of James Baldwin by François Bondy. Chapter eight dealing with "The Theatre Caught between Two Alienations," includes a manifesto by LeRoi Jones on the aims and functions of "Revolutionary Theatre".

999 Fabre, Michel. *Les Noirs américains*. Paris: Armand Colin: 1967; new edition, 1970.
This volume is both an anthology and a sociological-historical survey of Afro-Americans from slavery to the Black Power Movement. See pp. 112-26.
In a general introduction to African Americans, Fabre includes a brief panorama of their literature as an expression of self-affirmation and cultural resistance. Beginning with folk forms (the blues, spirituals, dozens, and so forth), he eventually focuses on the Harlem Renaissance and the protest fiction of Wright, Petry, and Himes. He also discusses the success of Baldwin and Ellison and the perspectives of the "black aesthetics." He states that books like *The Fire Next Time* and other works of Baldwin and Black authors like Langston Hughes, Claude McKay, and Richard Wright would shake up the average university student, who continues to "grow up under the egalitarian myth." *Nobody Knows My Name* may be added to the list of books in Afro-American literature which carry the theme of the "non-existence of the Black man." Baldwin, Ann Petry, William M. Kelley, Wright and others write in a "tradition of humanism, of social criticism." Pp. 112-16. (New ed. 1969)

1000 Fauchereau, Serge. "La poésie des Noirs américains: du jazz à la révolte." *Critique* No. 236 (January 1967), pp. 203- 09.
Rooted in folklore, black American poetry is faced with specific problems which are different from those of negritude. Until recently

it has been "restricted to propaganda, protest, or folklore. Having no American Negro tradition, the poets must be contented with producing complaints in the folk style or inspired by the spirituals." LeRoi Jones is breaking new ground, however, in *Preface to a Twenty Volume Suicide Note*. Ray Durem shows dignity and courage; Bob Kaufman wields derision and burlesque but suggests no solutions in *Solitudes*. Only Jones carries the critical debate further. Langston Hughes (though "not a first-rate artist"), Kaufman and Jones all see jazz as central to black poetry and their rhythms are sometimes akin to the poetry of Césaire. Included in Fauchereau's *Lecture de la poésie américaine* (Paris: Editions de Minuit, 1968).

1001 Galey, Mathieu. "La foi ne suffit pas." *Les Nouvelles littéraires* No. 2075 (June 8, 1967), p. 13.
Review of "Trumpets of the Lord," a recital of Negro spirituals by an Afro-American group. Traditional spirituals were sung and some of James Weldon Johnson's sermons were performed. The result does not equal Hughes'*Black Nativity* but it is "a continuous enchantment."

1002 Gautier, Jean-Jacques. "Au Théâtre des nations: 'Trumpets of the Lord.' " *Le Figaro* No. 7078 (June 1, 1967), p. 30.
An extremely favorable review of a performance of Negro spirituals including a few sermons by James Weldon Johnson. Great detail is provided on lighting and voice effects, on the artist Jane White, and on the masterful interpretation of Lex Monson uttering the sermon on the death of Reverend Bradford Parham.

1003 Gilles, Serge. "*L'Ingénu de Harlem*, de Langston Hughes." *France nouvelle* No. 1129 (June 7, 1967), p. 21.
The review of *The Best of Simple* quotes Hughes speaking of Simple: "He is my knight and lucky charm..." He would never have been created were not Harlem full of people who manage to keep cool and smile within the hell of segregation. Following the review are poems by Hughes: "Parfois dans la nuit de Georgie," "Lamento pour les peuples noirs," "Po' Boy Blues," "Le poéte au bigot," "Brigades internationales." (p. 24)

1004 Gouhier, Henri. "Trumpets of the Lord." *La Table ronde* No. 236 (September 1967), p. 125.
Very favorable review of the performance of an adaptation of James Weldon Johnson's *God's Trombones* at the Théâtre des Nations.

1005   Guérin, Daniel.   "Malcolm X, force ou fragilité?" *Présence africaine* No.62 (2nd trimester, 1967), pp. 31-35.
Analyzes the political ideology and development of Malcolm X in terms very comparable to those used in his introduction to the French translation of *The Autobiography of Malcolm X* He was "a thorn in the foot of the oppressive Western power structure" and perished like Patrice Lumumba and J.F. Kennedy.

1006   Guillen, Nicolas. "Le souvenir de Langston Hughes." *Présence africaine* No. 64 (4th trimester 1967), pp. 34- 37.
Guillen evokes his encounters with Hughes in 1930 in Cuba, in 1937 in Spain, and again in New York. From *The Weary Blues* to his last poems, all of Hughes' writings express his struggle for black equality and liberation; most of his short, moving pieces wherein laughter mostly serves to hide tears are formally structured after the blues. "His drive, sincerity and endurance in furthering the cause of his people deserve the deepest reverence."

1007   Hahn, Pierre.   "*L'Autobiographie de Malcolm X*." *Arts, Spectacles, Loisirs* (June 10, 1967), p. 25.
A favorable review emphasizing the human more than the political aspects of the book. It destroys the legend which makes of Malcolm a "racist black leader. It is the story of the growth of self-awareness and a spiritual and political itinerary."

1008   Han, J.-P. "*Le Métro fantôme, L'Esclave*." *Europe* No. 464 (December 1967), p. 309.
The plots of the two plays are summarized. Both of them have a documentary value after the racial riots in the United States. *Dutchman* is preferred because LeRoi Jones seems to go further in his "visceral hatred of the white man."

1009   Hervé, Julia and Jean Duflot.   "James Baldwin: ' Il y a plusieurs maniéres de tuer un noir.' " *Jeune Afrique* No. 340 (July 16, 1967), pp. 30-34.
The author of *The Fire Next Time* is very open in his comments. Meanwhile, bricks are flying in the ghettos and suburbs of the United States. Baldwin responds to some questions on Martin Luther King, Jr., the Black power movement, racism, and urban riots.

1010   Hervé, Julia. "Un noir et une blanche." *Jeune Afrique* No.

334 (June 4, 1967), p. 62.
Melvin Van Peebles, shooting the film "La Permission" [The Three-
Day Leave], is interviewed about interracial sex relations in America,
on the occasion of the French publication of Calvin Hernton's *Sex
and Racism.* .

1011 J., M. *"L'Ingénu de Harlem,* par Langston Hughes." *France-
Eurafrique* (August 30, 1967).
A summary of Hughes' career precedes the review of *The Best of
Simple.* Simple is "naive but lucid." His "funny and pathetic life" is
similar to that of millions of Americans and thus he stands as a
symbol for a whole social class.

1012 Joski, Daniel. *"L'Ingénu de Harlem,* par Langston Hughes."
[Addis Abbeba] *Addis-Soir* (July 29, 1967).
This Ethiopian newspaper reviews favorably *The Best of Simple* in
French .

1013 Jouffroy, Alain. "LeRoi Jones, théâtre de la révolution noire."
Cahiers de la Compagnie Renaud-Barrault No. 63 (Oct., 1967), pp.
43-54.
Briefly evokes New York memories and concludes that Dutchmen is
"not theater but lived experience." Jones' struggle is the
revolutionary struggle of Malcolm X and Stokely Carmichael (who is
quoted extensively). *The Slave* addresses itself to the practicalities of
guerilla warfare. This theater speaks to blacks not whites: "Jones
shows that the black revolutions is taking place, " with our weapons
and with language. Reference is made to Bob Kaufman as a militant
poet. Adrienne Kennedy is briefly introduced by Lewis Funke.
Reprinted from the *New York Times.*

1014 Kala-Lobé, Iwiyé. *"L'Autobiographie de Malcolm X,* avec la
collaboration de Alex Haley (Trad. Anne Guérin)." *Présence
africaine* No. 64 (4th trimester, 1967), pp. 182-186.
A long review retraces the evolution of Malcolm X in great detail,
chapter after chapter; the co-editor of the periodical concludes that
"no other method could render this story"... it is authentically true
and "as fascinating as the mindboggling interview dictated by
Malcolm X to Haley" in which Malcolm X declared he would die of
violent death.

1015 Kesteloot, Lilyan. *Anthologie négro-africaine: panorama*

critique des prosateurs, poètes et dramaturges noirs du XXe siécle.
Verviers, Belgium: Marabout, 1967.
Literary voices like Baldwin and Louis Lomax, more "bitter" than
Richard Wright, clamor after the independence of African nations
signifying a lesser degree of tolerance for racist conditions. By and
large, negritude literature has changed its tone. Mentions Baldwin's
other works such as *The Fire Next Time* and *Nobody Knows My
Name*. Quotes extracts from Baldwin's "penetrating analysis" of
Richard Wright.

1016 Kourilsky, Françoise. *Le Théâtre aux Etats-Unis.* Bruxelles:
La Renaissance du Livre, 1967.
The book mentions Wright's *Native Son* and *Blues for Mr. Charlie*,
"a melodrama by Baldwin on the racial problem" (p. 61).
Hansberry's *A Raisin in the Sun*, often cited by critics as a
courageous and earnest play," is found to be in fact rather
conventional (p. 49); but LeRoi Jones's *The Toilet* and *Dutchman* are
interesting experimental plays. Two pages are devoted to the
activities of the Free Southern Theatre.

1017 Kyria, Pierre. "Langston Hughes: Candide à Harlem."
Combat (June 1, 1967),p. 11.
Review of *The Best of Simple* introducing Hughes as "the poet of
the American Negro condition." Simple's adventures are seen as the
thousand incidents of daily life and the explanation of the
protagonist's name shows that Hughes wants to give a lesson in
humor and humanity. "This is true literature." Hughes is quoted as
stating that Simple is drawn from life in the streets of Harlem.

1018 Lambert, Gilles. "James Baldwin nous parle de l'explosion
noire de l'été 67." *Le Figaro littéraire* No. 1111 (July 31, 1967), pp.
6-7.
Baldwin describes the condition of the ghetto which caused the urban
riots. The interviewer interrupts Baldwin's long monologue with
one question: Have you accepted violence because you no longer
believe in a peaceful solution? Text illustration: a riot scene in
Detroit, July 24, 1967.

1019 Las Vergnas, Raymond. "L'oiseau rare: *Un Sang mal mêlé* de
Granby Blackwood." *Les Nouvelles littéraires* No. 2056 (January
25, 1967), p. 5.
A detailed summary of the plot stressing the traumatic events which

lead the protagonist to suffer from a sort of split personality because of his dual racial background. His brother, who is also his enemy because his skin is whiter, stands as a symbol of the white man. The novel is not devoid of clumsy and weak passages nor of overly sophisticated and contrived pages. "But the attempt to raise the conflict of a double heritage onto the symbolical level" has an originality that captures our attention.

1020   Las Vergnas, Raymond.   "Plongeur de grands fonds: Langston Hughes." *Les Nouvelles littéraires* No. 2087 (August 31, 1967), p. 5.
Brief review dealing with Hughes' career and *The Best of Simple.* The author notes Hughes' wit and commitment also his capacity to evoke straightforward and poetic situations.

1021 Lattés, Jean-Claude. *"L'Ingénu de Harlem."* *Le Figaro littéraire* No. 1102 (May 29, 1967), p. 35.
Shortly after Hughes' death, the author evokes his career as a writer and as a black militant intellectual. He is "a brother to Mark Twain and Ernest Hemingway, the color of his skin coming only second..." The collection of stories, *The Best of Simple,* is reviewed favorably and the protagonist labelled a "kind of 1967 Candide with sadness, humor and tenderness added."

1022 Lauras, André. "Claude Brown, *Harlem ou la terre promise." Etudes* No. 326 (January 1967), p. 138.
This book must be read in order to understand how few can escape the vicious circle which the author managed to break. *Manchild in the Promised Land* reveals a rising new generation of blacks, to whom Richard Wright's books seem already to belong to the past along with *Uncle Tom's Cabin.*

1023 Léger, François. "Malcolm X: *Autobiographie." Aspects de la France*, February 2, 1967, p. 6.
A long review of *Pouvoir noir* (collected speeches) and the autobiography in the right wing weekly focuses on Malcolm X's career and on his hatred for whiteness. A long argument is levelled at the Black Muslims and all forms of black nationalism like him. Léger concludes that "he died in time to retain his high reputation."

1024 Les "3" [pseud.]. "Le sang mal mêlé de Granby Blackwood." *Le Pélerin du 20eme siécle* (April 2, 1967).

The novel depicts the painful life of a mulatto suffering from amnesia after a traumatic conflict with his white brother; but above all he is plagued by his own inner conflict about his own mixed heritage.

1025 Le Bris, Michel and Bruno Vincent. "La littérature noire: de Wright et Baldwin à LeRoi Jones et William Kelley." *Le Magazine littéraire* No. 12 (November 1967), pp. 30-32.
This essay focuses on the new orientations of Afro-American writing, mostly from a thematic angle: the protest writing of Wright and Baldwin's plea for social justice and interracial love are being superseded by violent diatribes, a rejection of whites, and reverse racism. Short review of W.M. Kelley's *A Different Drummer*.

1026 Maunick, Edouard J. "Barbara Simmons." *Présence africaine* No. 64 (4th trimester 1967), pp. 97-110.
An interview of the Afro-American poet by a Mauritian poet, followed by four poems by Simmons. "Soul" is defined as "representing, in its most religions sense, our spiritual being, our goodness" and is seen, in relationship to Negritude, as "whatever we, as black people, use to create the true picture about our innermost selves."

1027 Monod, Martine. "*L'Ingénu de Harlem* et la leçon de Maupassant." *L'Humanité-Dimanche* No. 108 (March 26, 1967), p. 44.
Very detailed review of a collection of Hughes' *The Best of Simple,* explaining the origin of the protagonist's name. The book is a plea for social justice. Langston Hughes is quoted as saying that reading Maupassant really prompted him to become a writer, to write about black people but be read the world over even after his death.

1028 Olivier, Claude. "Etats-Unis et Tchécoslovaquie au Théâtre des Nations." *Les Lettres françaises* No.1187 (June 15, 1967), p. 23.
Review of "Trumpets of the Lord" based on *God's Trombones* by James Weldon Johnson, performed by the "Circle in the Square" troupe and staged by Donald McKayle. A mixed review: the singers may not be first-rate but the actors are stupendous.

1029 Olivier, Pierre. "Langston Hughes, poète déchirant de l'àme nègre." *La Presse* (June 10, 1967).
The Montreal newspaper publishes one of Hughes' Simple stories

included in the collection *The Best of Simple,* published in French as
L'Ingénu de Harlem. It is preceded by a commentary on the author
whose tone is perceived as less "politically demanding" than
Baldwin's.

1030 Pélieu, Claude. "Bopology." In *Burroughs, Pélieu, Kaufman.*
Special issue of *L'Herne* No. 9 (1967), p. 306.
Pélieu's ideological and stylistic comments on the presentation and
inspiration of black beat poet Bob Kaufman follow a translation of
extracts from *Golden Sardine* and a number of unpublished pieces.
Kaufman exerted an important influence on the generation of Claude
Pélieu and contemporary French surrealist poets.

1031 Pivot, Bernard. "Lettres: Cette semaine..." *Le Figaro littéraire*
No. 1120 (October 2, 1967), p. 18.
Baldwin borrows a line from a blues song for the title of his new
book, *Tell Me How Long the Train's Been Gone.* It reveals "the
problem of winning civil rights in the U.S."

1032 Pludovski, Georges. "*Sardine dorée* de Bob Kaufman." *Les
Nouvelles littéraires* 45 (March 12, 1967).
Kaufman is, with Ginsberg and Ferlinghetti, one of the major poets
of the Beat generation. His poems reveal a distance "art of lyrical
state-setting where despair is felt underneath the brilliance of myth."
His use of language is superlative and few poets could "hold out for
so long."

1033 Poirot-Delpech, Bertrand. "Trumpets of the Lord." *Le
Monde* No. 6961 (June 1, 1967), p. 17.
A review of "a gospel concert" based on J. Weldon Johnson's *God's
Trombones-* where enthusiasm and rhythm seem to predominate,
making up for an outdated backdrop and voices which could be
improved upon.

1034 Ransan, André. "Au Théâtre des Nations: 'Trumpets of the
Lord' de James Weldon Johnson." *L'Aurore* (June 1, 1967), p. 8.
The reviewer notes the reconstruction of a religious service lacking in
solemnity. "The sermons are interspersed with pleasant, if not
funny, reflections." The Bible is interpreted very freely. This never
shocks the audience because such adaptations are very skillfully
achieved. "An unusual performance."

1035   Reynolds, Paul R.   "Premier roman."   *Informations et Documents* (April 15, 1967), pp. 22-25.
This essay by Carlene Polite's literary agent is illustrated by seven photographs of her but does not deal with *The Flagellants*; rather, it is a somewhat technical discussion of problems concerning sales and publishing the first novel by an unknown author. Mentions that the novel appeared in Paris before Farrar, Straus published it. Polite is now working on a second novel.

1036   Richter, Charles de.   "Chronique littéraire."   *La République du Centre*, undated clipping [early 1967].
Review of *The Flagellants* by Carlene Polite. Polite is "a poet of the weird, an angel of the bizarre and the decrepit in an unknown world."

1037   Rosset, Pierrette.   "Le Sancho Pança noir."   *Candide* (April 10, 1967).
A brief retrospect of Hughes' career precedes a summary of the character of Simple, who is "cunning, lazy and naive" at the same time.   "His confidence permits so may detailed, mischievous sketches, which never verge on drama or thrive on misery (one is far from Négritude in the Schwartz-Bart style), that as a result the stories are very efficient." A story about liberal whites is reprinted from *The Best of Simple*.

1038   Sabatier, Robert.   "Noir c'est noir."   *Le Figaro littéraire* No. 1120 (October 2, 1967), p. 22.
A review of *L'Ingénu de Harlem*, i.e. *The Best of Simple*, comparing Hughes with Sammy Davis, Jr.: "both of them have the same aim-to shed light on the many aspects of the racial drama in order to attract allies while discarding prejudice, resentment and hatred." Simple, a poor Negro, remains moving and manages to teach the reader a lot in his "direct, comical, colorful and naive language."

1039   Sabatier, Robert.   "Sang noir, blouse blanche, rideau rouge: *Un Sang mal mêlé*."   *Le Figaro littéraire* No. 1048 (February 26, 1967), p. 6.
A summary of the plot insists upon the rearing of the hero and his lighter-skinned brother by a strange couple: their incestuous uncle and aunt. The fight between the brothers is emphasized. This confession and narrative is full of suspense, intrigue and

psychoanalytical allusions. Granby Blackwood's book is an important one, equally moving on the human and literary levels.

1040   Saporta, Marc. "Entre Prévert et Art Buchwald." *La Quinzaine littéraire* No. 26 (April 15-30, 1967), p. 20.
According to this review of *The Best of Simple*, Hughes "no longer is the vehement denouncer of social injustice but a sarcastic moralist. He is not Walter Lippman turned poet but Art Buchwald transformed into a performer. ... Simple finds the right note and the accurate tone of voice."

1041   Saporta, Marc. "Un poéte est mort." *Informations et Documents* (June 15, 1967), p. 24.
An homage to Langston Hughes, "whose mixed racial origins are probably the cause for his openness of mind." Mentions *Fine Clothes to the Jew* and the Simple stories. Hughes is black and a Harlemite. No one else has managed such a close synthesis of Anglo-Saxon poetry and jazz." Even in his darkest works he was a "blues poet."

1042   Serreau, Geneviéve. "Trois romanciers noirs: Melvin Van Peebles, *Le Chinois du 14eme.*" *La Quinzaine littéraire*, No. 19 (January 1-15, 1967), p. 6.
Melvin Van Peebles' short stories reveal he is a born storyteller and above all a wonderful listener, reinventing what he hears and blending it with his own fantasy. This black American is "one of the first to take black American literature out of the ghetto of the Negro problem." These stories about unimportant, commonplace people are full of tenderness and humor; they stand comparison to J.D. Salinger's because of "their sensitiveness to everyday reality and their sense of life and death." "The Tale of the Black American" is one of the best: in it the narrator tells of riding in a train across the whole state of Virginia, with the head of an unknown white woman resting on his shoulder as she slept, and of the irrepressible fear that he might be lynched for that. But there are revealing stories about the French too. The situations are always intriguing and extraordinary --exactly the stuff a good yarn is made of-- but people are keenly observed in their cultural differences and their common humanity, with tremendous humor and respect.

1043   Smet, Michel de. "Un Sang mêlé." Brussels *Le Soir*

(February 16, 1967).
Review of *Un Sang mal mêlé* by Granby Blackwood, believed to be "an admirably sincere and accurate analysis" of the racial complex and inner hatred of the protagonist depicts the quest for identity in any divided soul.

1044   Vigo, René.   "Regards sur l'Amérique: Les franges du romanesque." *L'Est-Eclair* (July 31, 1967).
The article contains a review of *The Flagellants* by Carlene Polite. "She is devoured by a secret fire ... and nothing could suit negritude better than a Miller-like novel." Extracts from p. 143 of the novel are quoted.   The reviewer finds Polite's story and style enthralling: "terrible visions of the black ghetto" convey the everlasting quest for the absolute in this pitiless fight between reality and imagination; it is "a book so haunting, so rich in thoughts, sensations, so well located in a poetic chiaroscuro that one can savor its ineffaceable harshness." Reading the book requires some effort but it is "deep and fascinating, rich in sensations" and situated in "poetic chiaroscuro."

1045   Wagner, Jean.   "Granby Blackwood, *Un Sang mal mêlé*; Carlene Polite, *Les Flagellants* in "Trois romanciers noirs." *La Quinzaine littéraire* No. 19 (January 1-15, 1967), p. 6.
Un Sang mal mêlé by Granby Blackwood is constructed around the brother/enemy relationship.   One is black, the other white.   "The author takes the protagonist to an undefined spot and the tragedy ends in blood." The reviewer finds the hero's amnesia unnecessary and too elaborate because he manages to remain in the foreground as the narrative unravels. "As a result, what could have been a tragic and forceful work is only a "well-made and well-written book" which could have been "a powerful and tragic work."
In Polite's *Les Flagellants*, "beyond the drops in tempo, the blanks and the useless chapters, a brittle style establishes itself in which words reach beyond words and any concrete situation is translated into another language ... in a universe where pain is the lot of everyone." (The third book, by Melvin Van Peebles, is reviewed by Geneviève Serreau, q.v.)

1046 Wagner, Jean. "Théâtre noir." *La Quinzaine littéraire* No. 31 (July 1-15, 1967), p. 7.
A favorable review of *Dutchman* and *The Slave*. The plays are exemplary as political drama. "Jones breaks away from the tradition of Negro theater to join the core of American theater:" instead of the

Bible and Africa, Richard Wagner is at the root of the inspiration in *Dutchman*, together with the fantastic and lyrical naturalism one finds in Edward Albee. He has deliberately opted for an extreme solution --terrorism-- in order to push toward less extreme ones which, he is sure, do exist. An interview of Jones by Pierre Dommergues is quoted.

1047 Zand, Nicole. "J.W. Johnson et la réhabilitation du folklore nègre." *Le Monde* No. 6960 (May 31, 1967), p. 15.
Mention of a preview of "Trumpets of the Lord" which consists of seven black sermons in verse directly inspired from the Bible, from slave songs, and preacher's performances. "Trumpets" contributes to "rehabilitating black folklore" and making the songs of the black community better known. A long retrospect of James Weldon Johnson's career and a history of the show follow.

1968

1048 Anon. "A la vitrine du libraire: *Jubilee* de Margaret Walker." Bastia *Le Petit Bastiais* (November 19 , 1968).
A brief review which "does not want to hamper the sales" of this novel which only belongs to "charming literature." Its well-contrived plot will bring some "romance to the cloudy skies of everyday routine."

1049 Anon. "*Face á l'homme blanc* par James Baldwin." *Notes bibliographiques* (December 1968), p. 1086.
Baldwin's birthplace, Harlem, and his religious background give these eight stories their "authenticity" and their "religious sentiment." The talented Baldwin demonstrates a "profound humanism" in *Going to Meet the Man*.

1050 Anon.[?] "*Jubilee* de Margaret Walker." *Le Journal du Dimanche* (August 4, 1968).
A short review of a novel which evokes the "other side of American slavery" hitherto depicted essentially by *Gone with the Wind*. It lacks the epic spirit of the "white" novel. Not a masterpiece it seems to have evinced much interest, however.

1051 Anon.[?] "*La prochaine fois, le feu* par James Baldwin." *La Gazette littéraire* (August 17-18, 1968).

Brief comment; *The Fire Next Time* is a manifesto for the Blacks of today who are demanding their civil rights.

1052 Anon. "Lectures: *Jubilee* de Margaret Walker." *Femme pratique* (October 1968), pp. 21-22.
Brief notice of a novel taking place during the Civil War and whose protagonist, Viry, a bastard daughter of the plantation owner is cruelly hated by her mistress. The novel is "redolent of *Gone with the Wind*."

1053 Anon. *"Les Rues de la violence* par Bryant Rollins; *Les Vignes sauvages* par Hal Bennett." *La Quinzaine littéraire* No. 47 (March 15-31, 1968), p.4.
Mentions the publication of Bryant Rollins's *Danger Song* and Hal Bennett's *A Wilderness of Vines* in French. "Violent in tone, inspired by the internal problems of the United States, these novels achieve a sort of ludicrous parody of Southern society and of the black ghetto in Boston."

1054 Anon. "Littérature américaine: *Jubilee* de Margaret Walker; *Face à l'homme blanc* par James Baldwin." *Clartés encyclopédique*s No. 14 (1968).
The plot of Walker's novel and the story of Viry are dealt with in some detail. In this historical novel of adventure and love one also finds the modern debate about racial coexistence. The most extraordinary of the eight short stories in *Going to Meet the Man* is the title story. The reader is allowed to share the "anguish" of the black protagonists and what being black must mean in the United States.

1055 Anon. "Nouveautés: *Jubilee* de Margaret Walker." *Revue de la mercerie* (November 1968), p. 7.
A brief evaluation of the novel, summing up its argument and establishing the circumstances of its writing. "It is a chant of love, hope and freedom."

1056 Anon.[?] "D'autres romans: *Jubilee* de Margaret Walker." *Pourquoi?* (November 1968), pp. 87-88.
A long review of "a beautiful book, a great book" retraces the destiny of Viry and the background of slavery after evoking Margaret Walker's career. Viry is compared to Vietnamese patriots who cannot hate their invaders. "The book has undeniable literary

qualities and expresses a superior kind of humanism. It is a thoroughly enthralling story at the same time."

1057   Anon. [?] "*Face á l'homme blanc* par James Baldwin." Brussels *Le Soir* (September 11, 1968), p. 22.
For Baldwin in *Going to Meet the Man*, the stereotypical image of Blacks belongs to another era. The theme of the Negro pushed to suicide appears throughout Baldwin's works, including "The Rock" and "The Outing." In other stories the situations tend to be too exemplary and only "*Going to Met the Man* escapes banal prose. By contrast in Baldwin's essays the writing is "so beautiful, so pure, so inspired." Often "his vision extends to universal dimensions," to existential anguish, and to the difficulty of being and of communicating.

1058   Anon. "*Face à l'homme blanc* par James Baldwin." *La Vie catholique* (August 21-27, 1968), p. 42.
Summarizes the title story of *Going to Meet the Man* and comments positively on the deft and elaborate style of the collection.

1059   Anon. "*Face à l'homme blanc* par James Baldwin." *Notre Epoque* (November 1968).
Baldwin's world reputation was established by *The Fire Next Time*. In *Going to Meet the Man,* his latest work, he pursues the same theme as in his earlier works: the difficulty of living in the United States if your skin is not white. Baldwin describes the lasting effect on a child who has witnessed a lynching. "Unexpected motivations" are disclosed by Baldwin who knows how to "dig deep." The short stories based on childhood recollections possess a "marvelous sadness" and charm. The volume is an "admirable" work.

1060   Anon.[?] "*Face à l'homme blanc* par James Baldwin." *Le Nouvel Observateur* (November 11, 1968), p. 43-44.
The "very, very beautiful" "Sonny's Blues" is one of five outstanding short stories in this collection of eight. *Going to Meet the Man* presents "slices of Black life in the United States." "Sonny's Blues" is especially revealing about the life of jazz musicians.

1061   Anon. "*Fishbelly* de Richard Wright." *Dictionnaire des oeuvres contemporaines de tous les pays.* Paris: Société d'édition des dictionnaires et encyclopédies, 1968.
Plot summary of *The Long Dream* by Richard Wright.

1062 Anon.[?] *"Jubilee* de Margaret Walker."   *L'Humanité-Dimanche* (October 27, 1968), p. 38.
A rather long review of the "dark and burning story of the novelist's great-grandmother."   The blacks play the major role in this new version of *Gone with the Wind* and everything that surrounds Viry, the protagonist who might appear to be too easily resigned, becomes the basis for the growth of her people's consciousness.   "The clenched fist of the character in the last sentence announces the clenched fist of black athletes at the Mexico Olympics."

1063 Anon. *"Jubilee* de Margaret Walker" *L'Epicerie française* (November 16, 1968).
Detailed review of a "novel written by the great grand-daughter of the heroin, always ready to forgive those who wronged her." The plot is summed up. "A very beautiful book ... quite different from Margaret Mitchell's."

1064 Anon. *"Jubilee* de Margaret Walker." *Revue des Cercles d'études d'Angers* 4, 7 (1968-1969), p. 57.
A long review of the novel, including a summary of the plot. The author thus "celebrates with intelligence and dignity the centennial of her own grandmother's Emancipation. Walker has a lot of talent and the translation keeps "the quaint flavor of nineteenth century Negro speech." Recommended to Catholic librarians.

1065 Anon. *"Jubilee.* Le roman des esclaves noirs d'Amérique." *Bingo* No. 189 (October, 1968) p. 77.
Favorable review of Margaret Walker's novel.   "Never does she allow herself to be carried away by a topic about which, due to her origins," she is particularly sensitive: she controls the theme from beginning to end.

1066 Anon. *"Jubilee* par Margaret Walker." *Jours de France* (October 5, 1968).
The reviewer for this popular, conservative magazine depicts *Jubilee* as an "imaginary tale" and is mostly struck by the musical quality of the Negro spirituals and the religious propensities of the author.

1067 Anon. *"La prochaine fois, le feu* et *Personne ne sait mon nom* par James Baldwin." *Eléments de bibliographie* (1968), p. 25.
The Fire Next Time and *Nobody Knows My Name* by Baldwin as well as *The Only Revolution* by Martin Luther King, Jr. help to

sensitize the reader to the racial drama of the United States. The horizon of these works "extends beyond the typical racial problem."

1068 Anon. [?] *"La prochaine fois, le feu." Le Point* No. 1 (1968).
Six years after the publication of *The Fire Next Time,* Baldwin's prophetic work, the United States is living out its prediction. Although he is not "preaching violence," his words are incendiary. Albert Memmi is right to point out in the preface to the book that "neither submission, nor hate, nor economic success, nor religion" have offered lasting solutions to the problem of racism.

1069 Anon. *"La prochaine fois, le feu* par James Baldwin." *Combat* (September 12, 1968), p. 9.
Baldwin uses threatening language in *The Fire Next Time,* published in 1963, but he is nonetheless a supporter of moderation and integration.

1070 Anon. *"Les Enfants de l'oncle Tom* de Richard Wright." In *Dictionnaire des oeuvres contemporaines de tous les pays.* Paris: Société d'édition de dictionnaires et encyclopédies, 1968.
Plot summary of the five stories in *Uncle Tom's Children* on p. 222.

1071 Anon.[?] "Le livre du mois: *Jubilee* par Margaret Walker." *La Vie catholique* (September 4, 1968).
In this long review, *Jubilee* is said to reveal, through the fate of the novelist's ancestor, "an unknown side of slavery in America." The heroine, "shaped by suffering," responds to hatred with love only. "She is no Scarlett because she is made of flesh and blood." The book can be seen as a long black complaint, something "like a spiritual."

1072 Anon.[?] "Margaret Walker: *Jubilee.*" *Les Echos* (August 23, 1968).
The novel is called a "black *Gone with the Wind,*" the writing is seen as lively and zesty, filled with Negro spirituals and fine descriptions of the beautiful land of Georgia. A fine book for the summer.

1073 Anon.[?] "Problème noir aux Etats-Unis." *Afrique contemporaine* No. 37 (May-June 1968), pp. 37-38.
Contains a favorable notice of Richard Wright's *Lawd Today.* The

style is that of a first novel but the translation is lively and those twenty-four hours in the life of Jake Jackson are exciting.

1074 Anon. "*Puissance noire* de Richard Wright." *Dictionnaire des oeuvres contemporaines de tous les pays*. Paris: S.E.D.E., 1968, pp. 600--01.
Summary of *Black Power* with a photograph of Wright.

1075 Anon. "*Un Enfant du pays* de Richard Wright." In *Dictionnaire des oeuvres contemporaines de tous les pays*. Paris: Société d'édition des dictionnaires et encyclopédies, 1968.
Plot summary of Wright's novel *Native Son* with a photograph from the film on p. 221.

1076 Anon. "Wright (Richard)." In *Dictionnaire des littératures*. Edited by Philippe Van Tieghem. Paris: Presses Universitaires de France, 1968.
Biographical notice on pp. 4201-02.

1077 Arnothy, Christine. "Un roman-fleuve: *Jubilee* de Margaret Walker." *L'Oise-Matin* and *Le Parisien libéré* (August 20, 1968).
Mixed review. Too much suffering and too many details and adventures give the novel "a melodramatic aspect." It makes good reading for people who tend to be bored when on vacation qui distribuait dans les corridor.

1078 B., J. "*Jubilee* par Margaret Walker." *Syndicats* (October 19, 1968).
Jacqueline Barde, the author of this rather long review, sums up the plot of the novel and notes the hopeful ending. A book constructed and written with great firmness of style and purpose. This story of the times of slavery illuminates the present plight of blacks in the U.S.

1079 Barde, Jacqueline. "La descente de Moïse." *Les Nouvelles littéraires* No. 2134 (August 15, 1968), p. 7.
A favorable review of Margaret Walker's *Jubilee*, comparing the novel to McKinley Kantor's *Andersonville*, to Kyle Onstott's *Mandingo* and to the film "Green Pastures." The title is explained in historical and biblical terms. The reviewer emphasizes the birth of a new literary character: the free black. Such a novel "warms your

heart and makes your blood run faster." [Sections of this review also appeared in *Elle* (August 5, 1968).]

1080 Barde, Jacqueline. "Margaret Walker: *Jubilee.*" *Le Papetier de France* (September 1968).
A favorable review of the novel assessed in historical and literary terms. The reviewer compares it to "the great historical series" of a Henri Troyat, dealing with Russian serfdom and revolution. She emphasizes the "freshness of the tone" and places the book in the same line as the spirituals. "The novel should be sold with *Fleuve profond, sombre rivière* by Marguerite Yourcenar and *Le Cahier* by Henri Troyat."

1081 Berger, Daniel. "LeRoi Jones et la révolte noire." *Cahiers du jazz* No. 16-17 (1968), pp. 86-96.
This essay places Jones's career in its political setting; his major works, mostly drama and poetry, are mentioned. The author met Jones in 1965 at "The Free Jazz Society" and recalls his negative reactions: Jones is obsessed with the humiliations suffered by Blacks and his own desire for symbolic, if not real, revenge. In spite of these ideological reservations, one must wish Jones a wider audience, as the strength of Black Power stems from a deepening of the contempt of negritude.

1082 Berger, Yves. "Splendeurs et misères du Sud: *Jubilee* de Margaret Walker." *Le Monde des livres* No. 7732 (August 10, 1968) p. III.
Jubilee is something other than a novel --a document, a source of knowledge. The review emphasizes the role of the Bible in Black liberation and the militancy of the Negro church. Viry is seen as a complex character, "one of the greatest characters in American literature."

1083 Beyssade, Pierre. "*La prochaine fois, le feu,* par James Baldwin." *Livres et Lectures* No. 522 (November 1968).
A review *The Fire Next Time*, in which the radical problem of racism receives a 'lucid' treatment by the talented Baldwin. Political solutions alone will not suffice to solve this complex issue.

1084 Bloch-Michel, Jean. "Autour du problème noir. *Jubilee* de Margaret Walker." *La Gazette de Lausanne* (?, 1968) pp. 1-2.
The review emphasizes the timelessness of racial problems and the

historical dimension of the social conflict evoked in Jubilee in the light of the report of the National Advisory Commission on Civil Disorders.

1085 Bondy, François. "Négritude." *Preuves* No. 213 (December 1968), pp. 66-71.
In this study of the relationship between negritude and miscegenation, the author recalls that negritude did not originate in Africa, but in Harlem, Guyana, and Paris. "The first to speak about it were blacks poets like Claude McKay and Langston Hughes and a few West Indians."

1086 Bouville, Eude. "L'*Autant en emporte le vent* des noirs américains: *Jubilee* de Margaret Walker." *L'Echo de la mode*; (October 27, 1968).
A lengthy summary of the novel precedes praise of this "long love story accompanied by the deep song of spirituals." Beyond daily troubles and occurrences, it conjures up "nostalgia for a lost paradise and the hope for a better world."

1087 Buhet, Gil. "*Jubilee*." [Lyons] *Résonances* No. 630 (November 1968).
Although he does not like to review best-sellers, Buhet is enthusiastic about Margaret Walker's novel. "Its style is not extraordinary, its topic not exceptional, yet something very poignant grips your heart like the spirituals of which each page of the novel is an echo."

1088 Bussang, Françoise. "*Jubilee* de Margaret Walker." *Mobilier et Décoration* (December 1968).
Long, favorable review of "a book to be read by the whole family since it is never an indictment." Viry's "Forgive them, they know not what they do" seems authentic. The protagonist's equanimity and her simple tone, devoid of exaggerated lyricism, serves the cause of racial justice more efficiently than violence.

1089 C., J-P. "*Jubilee* de Margaret Walker." *Le Cri du monde* (November 1968), p. 55.
Very brief review of "a thick novel" which relates the Civil war and the life of a mulatto woman, who is "vaccinating because of her optimism and faith." Tenderness and passion, truth and unhappiness mingle in this book which young people should read.

1090 Cahen, Pierre. *La littérature américaine*. Paris: Presses Universitaires de France, "Que-sais-je?" (5th ed.), 1968.
Only includes Wright and Ellison and mentions a few Blacks in a list of authors.

1091 Chapsal, Madeleine. "Mélodies noires." *L'Express* No. 875 (March 25, 1968), pp. 119-120.
Detailed review of LeRoi Jones's *Blues People*, praising his balanced treatment of the musical genre both in regard to a black aesthetic and as a manifestation of cultural survival and endurance against the odds of racism and oppression.

1092 Chrestien, Michel. "*La prochaine fois le feu* par James Baldwin." *Carrefour* No. 17 (December 16, 1968).
In *The Fire Next Time*, James Baldwin sees moderation as the only answer to racism. Will either race accept integration? Will anyone hear his "cry of alarm"?

1093 D'Aubarède, Gabriel. "*Jubilee* par Margaret Walker." *Livres et Lectures* (November 1968).
Jubilee is a historical novel of the Civil War as well as a moving family story The novel is superior to *Gone with the Wind* because of its historical authenticity. The heroin is caught in the frightful drama of racism whose throes and implications are not yet over.

1094 D'Aubarède, Gabriel. "Un grand drame du racisme, *Jubilee*." *Le Monde et la Vie* (September 1968), p. 69.
Margaret Walker's *Jubilee* is seen as a historical novel into which a moving family chronicle is woven. The outlook is partly moral. "It may be possible to dream about a certain fundamental gentleness of the black man in spite of his hatred in comparison with the implacable resentment of the persecuted Jew." The literary quality of the novel is superior to that of *Gone with the Wind*.

1095 D., M. "La musique dans le dernier Baldwin." *Feuille d'avis de Lausanne* (November 23-24, 1968).
The theme of segregation links the eight pieces in *Going to Meet the Man*. James Baldwin "who loves jazz," makes numerous references to Afro-American music. A column of quotations illustrates the "marvelous richness of images" in Baldwin's descriptions of religious ceremony in "The Outing," the "most remarkable" short story in the book.

1096 Dommergues, Pierre. "Les Etats-Unis et les écrivains noirs. Pour LeRoi Jones: Détruire l'Amérique blanche." Montréal *Le Devoir* (April 13, 1968), p. 17.
The author defines LeRoi Jones in contradistinction to both Ralph Ellison and James Baldwin. Jones favors a world-wide race conflict. Afro-American alienation stems from the shedding of African cultural values in order to adopt European ones. A parallel is drawn between the evolution of the societal condition of black people and that of music. According to Jones, the conclusion reads, "the main thing is to go beyond Western rationalism and renew links with tribal man."

1097 Dommergues, Pierre. "Le message de LeRoi Jones: Détruire l'Amérique blanche." *Le Monde* No. 7220 (March 30, 1968), p. 8.
This essay contrasts three different Afro-American attitudes regarding the white world: Ellison advocates a kind of cultural integration; Baldwin attempts to cure the whites of their prejudices and terrors; Jones is a staunch advocate of blackness. For him, "Blacks must see the worlds with eyes of blacks, not whites." Black music embodies the survival of African culture; it is a valuable asset which the black man must utilize in order to renew links with "tribal man" even though the price may be the destruction of white American. *Blues People* and *Dutchman* are briefly analyzed.

1098 Dommergues, Pierre. "Le Probléme blanc: les deux visages de James Baldwin." *Le Monde des livres* (August 31, 1968), p. V.
The prophetic voice of Baldwin warned that the violence seething in the ghetto would boil over. In *The Fire Next Time*, he announced vengeance. For Baldwin, the problem of racism is not Black but white.

1099 Dreyfus Gilles. "Le chant de l'oppression." *Droit et Liberté* No. 273 (May, 1968), pp. 29-30.
An enthusiastic review of *Blues People* by LeRoi Jones within the context of the assassination of Martin Luther King and impending black violence. The protest function of the blues is emphasized, and Jones magnificently shows how the music mirrors Black history in the United States. The moderation and balance of Jones's committed writing is surprizing and laudable.

1100 Dupré, Guy. "Livres: *Jubilee*, par Margaret Walker." *Centre-Presse* (September 25, 1968), p. 17.

This epic novel is a genuine *Gone with the Wind* as far as blacks are concerned. It is also a long description of a quest for freedom and a March towards it, as well as the chronicle of Viry's extraordinary love, which she finally transfers to her children.

1101 F., A. "*Jubilee.*" *Nord-Matin* (October 2, 1968).
Briefly mentions the novel by Margaret Walker. "A love song marked by the hatred that still divides America today," the novel evokes images of a paradise disturbed over and over. It "sweats truth." An immense cry of love, *Jubilee* is also a chant of the freedom still to come.

1102 Fabre, Michel. "De l'esclavage au Pouvoir Noir: l'émergence d'un peuple." *Réalités* (July-August 1968), pp. 113-38.
A historical retrospect of the black American struggle for liberation drawing upon, and mentioning a few writers, including Frederick Douglass, W.E.B. Du Bois, Langston Hughes, Richard Wright, etc.

1103 Fauchereau, Serge. "Problèmes de la poésie noire." In his *Lecture de la poésie américaine*. Paris, Editions de Minuit, 1968, pp. 197-202.
The concept of negritude is of no use in understanding the disconcerting work of LeRoi Jones; black poetry only really exists in the 20th century; language is occasionally different but the theme is generally racial oppression, while Africa seems very far away. Jones sees the problem quite clearly; the major weakness of black poetry as represented in anthologies is its lack of complexity. Satire is strong; Bob Kaufman is good at tearing things down in his "Abomunist Manifesto" but he offers no replacement. As for Jones, he creates a strong sense of intertextuality and questioning. Jazz is central to black poetry and so is Langston Hughes's influence. Only Wright, Ellison, and Toomer, however, "appear to be 'real' writers when one does not know Melville."

1104 G., S. "*Jubilee* par Margaret Walker." Saint-Etienne *L'Espoir* (August 20, 1968), p. 6.
In this brief review, the "family saga" of M. Walker is compared to *Gone with the Wind*. "This honest, well-meaning book reads well and is of the right color, in spite of a certain unfinished quality." A "fine big novel for the summer vacation."

1105   Giesberg, Franz-Olivier.   "*Jubilee* de Margaret Walker."
Paris-Normandie (August 16, 1968).
A long, enthusiastic review of the novel, compared to which *Gone with the Wind* is but a pale epic of the Civil War. This black novel, written in words of fire, gives us a slice of life, "a plea against the social system which still survives."   Such a book cannot be read serenely by Europeans, who are also guilty of oppression.

1106   Giesberg, Franz-Olivier.   "Le problème no 1 des U.S.A.: *La prochaine fois, le feu.*"   *Paris-Normandie*   (September 27, 1968), p. 7.
"In view of current events, James Baldwin's *The Fire Next Time*, though outdated, has been republished."   The more vociferous voices of LeRoi Jones, Bob Kaufman, William Kinle, and Eldridge Cleaver say nothing new, but their literary and political actions are significant.   They enlighten the reader on "certain aspects of the Afro-African movement." They eliminate white characters from their novels and denounce integration. Baldwin's *Going to Meet the Man* does not meet current needs. It reads like "embattled literature of the thirties." The prose is "trite," outdated and "commonplace." The reader expected a work reflecting the present conditions.

1107   Gilles, Serge.   "*Face à l'homme blanc.*"   *France nouvelle* (October 30, 1968), p. 17.
The publication in France of *Going to Meet the Man* seemed the opportune time to talk about the "admirable" Black Power salute of Tommie Smith and John Carlos at the 1968 Olympics, which "warmed the hearts of all men of good will."   The publication also allows the reader to make some observations about the evolution of the thought of James Baldwin.   At first James Baldwin was an "aesthete of the highest order" who crucified Richard Wright, and who did not intend to mix politics in his writing.   His first two novels evidence the idea.   In *Giovanni's Room* the hero has blond hair and white skin.   Three short stories in *Going* ... date from the same era.   After living in France, Baldwin began to realize that he was not only an American but a Black American, who had to face up to the reality of racism.   For this reason, he began to participate in the Civil Rights Movement and to work with Martin Luther King, Jr. This development resulted in *Nobody Knows My Name*. Feeling a slight uneasiness about the reality of integration, Baldwin "attempted a last effort." In *The Fire Next Time* he sounded the alarm. The murder of M. L. King, Jr. brought about Baldwin's present militant

position. The last five short stories are the best. And "This Morning, This Evening, So Soon" is the best of these. It explores the fear of a father for his mulatto son as the family prepares to return "to the racial jungle," the United States. Today, Baldwin is a "great writer, lucid and honest." The "weight of the social situation made him surpass himself."

1108   Guissard, Lucien. "Ecrivains noirs américains; Margaret Walker: *Jubilee*; James Baldwin: *Face à l'homme blanc*." *La Croix* (August 4-5, 1968), p. 7.
Walker shares with Margaret Mitchell a never ending preoccupation with Southern History. The blues and spirituals and the underground railroad are emphasized as symbols of the call of, and road to, freedom. Her novel is praiseworthy for its controlled writing whereas the author could have vented anger and hatred. *Going to Meet the Man* by James Baldwin is briefly mentioned as "a collection of moving short stories."

1109 Guyaux, Jacques. "Margaret Walker, une grande romancière noire." *Le Journal de Charleroi* (August 17, 1968).
A very favorable review of *Jubilee*, with considerations on Blacks in America. "When they were slaves, they were despised, now they are hated.... To those who are persuaded of the superiority of one race over another, I'd advise placing *Jubilee* on one side of the literary scales, and all the works of Françoise Sagan on the other. Should the latter be multiplied tenfold, they would still not weigh enough."

1110 Guyot, Charly. "Hurrah the Flag that Makes You Free." *Journal de Genève* (November 30, 1968), pp. 22-23.
An article based on eight works dealing with the racial atmosphere in the United States. Among them are Baldwin's *The Fire Next Time* and *Going to Meet the Man*. Of the eight books, the readers will most appreciate *The Fire Next Time* which appeals for moderation and understanding albeit with a threatening tone. It is weak in novelistic technique. *Going to Meet the Man* accuses American democracy. The review includes a long explanation of the title of Margaret Walker's *Jubilee*, taken from Leviticus 25. It strongly emphasizes the role of religion and the "subdued tone of the spirituals heard throughout the book."

1111 H., J. "Les livres de la semaine: *Bon sang de bonsoir* par

Richard Wright." *Perspectives* (March 19, 1968). n. p. [This mimeographed pamphlet is not the USIS publication.]
This review of *Lawd Today* explains that the publication of the novel was postponed during forty years because of CP advice. The novel deals with Wright's major theme: the condition of black Americans. Like *Black Boy,* it relates the plight of a young black male in the prewar era. The narrative is appallingly bleak, however, and filled with crude episodes. One only feels "repulsion and pity." The protagonist is not stupid but instinctive and violent as he refuses to stay in his "place." Wright's testimony is still valid, as the ideology of the Black Muslims reveals but the reviewer deplores the excessive brutality of the novel.

1112 Jardin, Claudine. "Un *Autant en emporte le vent* noir: *Jubilee* de Margaret Walker." *Le Figaro* (September 4, 1968).
The reviewer parallels the novel with *Gone with the Wind*, which would have been written otherwise had its author, Margaret Kennedy (sic), been black. A summary of the plot insists on runaway slaves and the life of Viry, who loves a free man but whose children belong to her master. "Margaret Walker is no Tolstoy and the characters psychology is overly simple. ... They live and die without delivering a message, without even showing indignation." Nonviolence is probably the best quality of her novel.

1113 Gros, L.G. "Liberté, ce mot interdit..." *Le Provençal-Dimanche* (July 14, 1968), p. 11.
The reviewer explains the title of Margaret Walker's *Jubilee*, alluding to the Union war song. The novel is placed in its historical context and the economic causes of the Civil War are emphasized. "A great book rather than a great novel because only its poetic accents save it from the facility of popular fiction.... It is no lament upon the past but a reflection, fraught with anguish, on the future of Afro-Americans." *Jubilee* goes further than *Gone with the Wind*.

1114 Jean-Nesmy, Dom Claude. "*Jubilee*, de Margaret Walker." *L'Echo illustré de Genève* (December 7, 1968), p. 39.
The reviewer praises the book as a warning against the manichaean view of American history centering on the Civil War. "Is not the vast amount of mutual mistrust due to ignorance more than to hatred?"

1115 Kanters, Robert. "Mes ancêtres, les Nègres..." *Le Figaro littéraire* No. 1168 (September 23, 1968), p. 18.

A review of *Bound to Violence* by Senegalese novelist Yambo Ouologuem and *Blues People* by LeRoi Jones. The latter book is favorably reviewed, largely on account of its measured tone and the absence of hatred and violence, said to characterize Jones's recent writings.

1116 Kattam, Naïm. "Baldwin s'interroge sur la réalité." Montréal *Le Devoir* (October 23, 1968), p. 2.

World fame has come to the author who disturbed the "American conscience." But reality changes. This causes some of his short stories to be dated. Baldwin "touches us" when he describes present reality. Baldwin is not at his best in *Going to Meet the Man*. There is a summary of each story.

1117   Koechlin, Philippe.   "Pour s'en sortir."   *Le Nouvel Observateur* No. 174 (March 13-19, 1968), p. 41.

A review of *Blues People* by LeRoi Jones. The author of the article is favorable, albeit not overwhelmingly so, to this "study which is based upon a rich culture, and substantiated by numerous references." The topic is new and provides insights into black music and black culture and the African continuum. The writing is dull however.

1118 Langlois, Gérard. "Melvin Van Peebles, premier réalisateur noir américain." *Les Lettres françaises* No. 1228 (April 3, 1968), p. 24.

An interview of Van Peebles about his movie, "La Permission" or "The Three-Day Leave."

1119 Las Vergnas, Raymond. "Ce que n'emporte pas le vent. Lettres américaines. Margaret Walker: *Jubilee*; Hal Bennett: *Les Vignes sauvages*." *Les Nouvelles littéraires* No. 2136 (August 29, 1968), p. 5.

A long, precise summary of *Jubilee* ends with a two-paragraph discussion of this "very feminine novel." Margaret Walker has attempted "to make us feel not only the dark poetry of the South, the melancholy of ruins and sunsets, but also the supremely lyrical impetus of the oppressed." Hal Bennett's novel is found full of interest even though his writing is somewhat undistinguished and his depiction of a black macho character brings him very close to the familiar stereotype of Negro hypersexuality.

1120   Le Bris, Michel.   "*La prochaine fois, le feu* de James Baldwin." *Jazz hot* No. 244 (November 1968), pp. 9, 18.
The reviewer analyzes Baldwin's attitude in *The Fire Next Time*, construed as "opposed to peaceful solutions to the racial problem in the United States."

1121   Le Bris, Michel.   "*Le Peuple du blues* de LeRoi Jones." *Jazz hot*; No. 241 (May-June 1968), pp. 9-13.
A generally favorable review of *Blues People* discussing the history of black music from a social angle and a mostly musicological perspective.

1122   Le Divenah, Patrick.   "De l'esclavage à la liberté: *Jubilee* de Margaret Walker." *Combat* (September 5, 1968), p. 11.
The review analyzes the novel from a historical perspective, then concentrates on the fate and psychology of Viry. "The novelist casts a serene and objective look upon the Civil War and the deep complexities of the racial problem." Walker shuns a manichean outlook as well as hatred. The novel, however, will probably not enjoy the enviable career of *Gone with the Wind*.

1123   Lemaire, Marcel.   "*Jubilee* de Margaret Walker."   Brussels *Le Soir* (August 7, 1968).
A mixed review, which describes most of the characters in the novel as dangerously close to the usual stereotypes and the echoes of Beecher Stowe's *Uncle Tom's Cabin* pervade more than one page. However, Viry, the protagonist, is a well-rounded character. The book lacks the sophistication of *Gone with the Wind* and the author is "often clumsy... [and] devoid of artistic experience." The "texture of the novel remains rather coarse," although the story is moving.

1124   Léna, Arlette.   "La révolution culturelle des noirs américains." *Le Magazine littéraire* No. 23 (November 1968), p. 18-21.
Based on examples taken from black arts, black music, and black writing, this analysis of the cultural predicament of the black community in the United States is largely favorable to the Black Aesthetics Movement as a cultural revolution capable of furthering liberation from neo-colonialism all over the world.

1125   Memmi, Albert.   Preface to *La prochaine fois, le feu* by James Baldwin. Paris, Gallimard, 1968. Pp. vii-xx.
Memmi claims that the American Negro must now be placed in the

category of "the oppressed" together with the symbolic figures of he Poor, the Jew and Woman. He analyzes the effects of racial oppression and its consequences on the black struggle; he explains in his preface to *The Fire Next Time* that "neither submission, nor hate, nor economic success, nor religion and the church" have brought a permanent solution to the problem of racism.

1126 Mespouille, José. "L'univers inconnu, tendre, cruel du Sud esclavagiste. *Jubilee,* par la romanciére noire Margaret Walker." *Vers l'avenir* (August 17, 1968).
A favorable, even compassionate review of the novel, stressing some of the clichés of the Civil War and slavery period. The novel is a revelation: "joy, pain, hope, and hatred take on an unusual echo, one that is so new for a white reader." Also printed in *Le Courrier de Verviers* and *L'Avenir du Luxembourg*.

1127 Neuvéglise, Paule. "Deux grands romans étrangers." *France-Soir* (July 13, 1968).
Jubilee is briefly reviewed, together with *Le Maître et Marguerite*, a novel by Mikhail Boulgakhov. The author's great-grandmother was a light complexioned, fair-haired mulatto; oral tradition has transmitted her tragic and beautiful story to Margaret Walker.

1128 Olivier, Daria. "Lettres étrangères; feuilles d'automne." *Réforme* (September 21, 1968).
Margaret Walker's *Jubilee* is not just another black *Gone with the Wind*, it is a "vast human tragedy ... teeming with people who live and suffer in God's little acre" since skin color determines a person's fate in the Deep South.

1129 P., B. "Revue des livres nouveaux; *Jubilee* de Margaret Walker." Lyons *Le Bulletin des lettres* (October 15, 1968), p. 291.
An extensive review of "a simple story, too cleverly put together" because the characters remain somewhat stereotyped and the situations symbolic in order to illustrate a painful situation (illiteracy, the Ku Klux Klan, etc.) Viry is the "image of the mother of man;" nothing can destroy the children of her people.

1130 P., C. "*Face à l'homme blanc*, par James Baldwin." *Jeune Afrique* (September 23-27, 1968), p. 13.
Rather than a work of anger like *The Fire Next Time, Going to Meet the Man* is a work of "pity" for the "malaise" of the alienated man,

which is expressed with "psychological finesse." There is a brief discussion of "Come out the Wilderness," "Going to Meet the Man," and "This Morning, This Evening, So Soon."

1131 Pache, André. "Une interview de James Baldwin." *La Voix protestante* (August 16, 1968), p. 1, 7.
Baldwin, once a minister, has been invited to speak at the ecumenical council in Upsala, Sweden. He assiduously works to eliminate racism in American society. Reprinted as "Un visiteur inattendu à Upsala: James Baldwin," in the November, 1968 issue of the same publication.

1132 Paret, Pierre. "Chronique littéraire: *Jubilee* de Margaret Walker." *La Dordogne libre* (September 8, 1968).
A long review evokes the setting of the novel, summarizes its plot, and situates it within the history of the United States. The novel should be a lesson for whites. Yet Paret seems to refuse to accept the achievements of blacks and excuse white oppression to a degree. He wonders how the racial situation can change if people's minds don't and if the blacks remain subservient, like Viry. "A sober, earnest, uncompromising novel which is devoid of the obsolete 19th-century charm" of *Gone with the Wind*.

1133 Pélieu, Claude. "Poème-piège pour Bob Kaufman." *Opus international*, No. 7 (June 1968), pp. 26-27.
A tribute to the Abomunist poet, "a black planet which became older with the earth." Composed in San Francisco on January 14, 1968. The same issue carries Ted Joans' poem "Parler noir" [Black Talk].

1134 Peloux, Jean. "Lettres: Cette semaine." *Le Figaro littéraire* No. 1160 (July 29, 1968), p. 18.
A brief notice of *Tell Me How Long the Train's Been Gone* (US edition) by James Baldwin including the gist of its contents.

1135 Pétillon, Pierre-Yves. "Blues pour un mutant." *Critique* No. 257 (October 1968), pp. 855-62.
A perceptive review of Ralph Ellison's *Invisible Man*, alluding to *Shadow and Act* and Ellison's cultural and political stance. "Black identity is a new frontier and as long as the 'I' remains at an embryonic stage, not only is the Negro reduced to a minority status but America is deprived of one dimension of its identity," which only

the Black perspective can contribute as well as decipher.

1136 Phillot, A. "Livres, *Jubilee* par Margaret Walker." *Eaux vives* (November 1968).
A long, rather lyrical review of Walker's novel compares it to *Un plat de porc anx bananes vertes* by Simone and André Schwartz-Bart. Walker's picture is not devoid of violence but her universe retains its human dignity intact. Her faith in man anticipates the influence of Martin Luther King. A long summary of the novel emphasizes its "apparent truthfulness and authenticity as a document on conditions of life in the South a century ago."

1137 Poli, Bernard. "Littérature américaine." In *Encyclopaedia Universalis*. Paris; S.V., 1968.
Baldwin, Bellow, and Malamud have no affinity with the "dialectics of city-country, the tension between past and present" which others have explored (p. 645).

1138 Porquerol, Elisabeth. "Margaret Walker: *Jubilee*." *La Nouvelle Revue française* No. 191 (November 1968), p. 697.
In this brief review, the French novelist finds that *Jubilee* lacks the epic spirit of *Gone with the Wind*. "The spirituals have lost their sonorousness... The author, an offspring of black slaves, is a teacher of literature --is this an explanation?"

1139 Prévost, Claude. "Des romans policiers." *La Nouvelle Critique* No. 18 (October 1968), pp. 30-31.
The reviewer mentions the appearance of the well-known Himes' Harlem Domestic novels in the "Poche noire" series. The stories all take place in the Harlem ghetto and their tone is wry and somber humor. He commends Himes for a fine example of "critical realism."

1140 Rivet, Auguste. "*Jubilee*, les travaux et les joies des noirs américains au XIXéme siécle." Le Puy *L'Eveil de la Haute-Loire* (December 16, 1968), p. 4.
A favorable review, not exempt of paternalistic prejudice. "We wonder whether the easy, and for some happy, acceptance of their condition by the black slaves did not correspond to the confused intuition they had of the needs of the plantation system." The novel is more than a documentary: it compares favorably with *Gone with the Wind* and Walker's characters are well rounded and convincing.

Christian faith supports their lives.

1141 Rossi, Paul-Louis. "Thêâtre: *Le Métro fantôme; L'Esclave.*"
Cahiers du jazz No. 16-17 (1968), pp. 145-50.
This review criticizes French drama critics for having unduly
emphasized the ideology in *Dutchman* and *The Slave,* to the
detriment of theatrical aesthetics. The plots are summed up in an
attempt to reveal structure. *Dutchman* is a fine psychodrama but its
ideological content is rather weak. LeRoi Jones's theater is a good
illustration of Antonin Artaud's "theatre of cruelty."

1142 Roussot, Yves. *"Face à l'homme blanc* par James Baldwin."
Centre protestant d'études et de documentation (1968).
Will racial conflict have its final day? Baldwin paints a picture of the
difficult relations of Blacks and whites in *Going to Meet the Man.*
This review also includes summaries of "Going to Meet the Man,"
"Blues for Sonny," and "This Morning, This Evening, So Soon."

1143 Rudel, Yves-Marie. "Lectures: *Jubilee* de Margaret Walker."
Ouest-France (July 3, 1968), p. 6.
This "thick novel by a young novelist" who tells the story of her
great-grandmother during the Civil War will be "enjoyable reading
during the Summer vacation."

1144 Sourillan, José. "Le vieux Sud en négatif." *Minute*
(September 12-18, 1968), p. 20.
A review of Margaret Walker's *Jubilee*, excellently translated. The
novel is compared to *Gone With the Wind.* Walker expresses
reservations about the possible reconciliation of blacks and whites
"through the idyllic and Christian-like solution of integration."

1145 Theis, E.[douard] *"La prochaine fois, le feu* par James
Baldwin." *Centre protestant d'études et de documentation* (1968), p.
4.
This rather favorable review includes a summary of *The Fire Next
Time.*

1146 Thompson, James, Raphael Lennox and Steve Cannon.
"Ralph Ellison: la parole est à l'homme invisible." *Informations et
Documents* No. 250 (March 15, 1968), p. 22-26.
Extracts from interviews originally published as "A Very Stern

Discipline" in *Harper's Magazine*, March 1967.

1147 Valogne, Catherine. "Quatre romans d'auteurs 'colored': la parole est aux noirs." *La Tribune de Genève* (September 1, 1968).
Recent works by Bryant Rollins (*Danger Song*), Kyle Onstott, Margaret Walker (*Jubilee*), and James Baldwin describe the "tragic world of Blacks" more effectively than news reports. In spite of the bland translation, Baldwin's style "explodes from the first lines" in *Going To Meet the Man*. His works have enabled the Kennedys to "understand with insight the truncated world" of Black people.

1148 Verval, J. *"Face à l'homme blanc*, par James Baldwin." *Fiches bibliographiques* (1968).
"Sonny's Blues," the best of the short stories in *Going to Meet the Man*, captures the "depth of the relations of two brothers." Brief comments on some of the other stories.

1969

1149 Alante-Lima, Willy. *"Jubilee." Présence africaine* No. 72 (4th trimester 1969), p. 226-28.
Favorable review of Margaret Walker's novel, "completed exactly one century after the emancipation of her ancestor." The role of religion is emphasized and the actuality of the theme: "we have the impression we are deciphering the currents of today's America ... with only a change in accessories." The book is alive, devoid of artificiality and "builds up an edifice of unique simplicity."

1150 Anon. *"Jubilee* de Margaret Walker." *Heures claires* No. 164 (January 1969), p. 36.
A brief review of the love story of Viry, "the first novel of a young (sic) Afro-American woman." A fine book, captivating and deeply human.

1151 Anon. *"Jubilee* de Margaret Walker." *Informations dieppoises* (March 7, 1969).
A brief, lyrical review of a novel which reveals an "unsuspected side of American slavery." The heroine has been "molded by suffering but answers hatred with forgiveness." She has no time to waste with hating.

1152   Anon.   "Vient de paraître: Ralph Ellison, *Homme invisible, pour qui chantes-tu?*"   *Le Monde des livres* (May 31, 1969), p. II.
Publication notice of a new translation of *Invisible Man* by Robert and Magali Merle.

1153   Anon.   "Aux éditions Christian Bourgois: *Camétude* par Art [sic] Leroi Bibbs."   *Bulletin critique du livre français*   (September 1969).
Brief notice.   "A novel by an Afro-American--in slang, a black man tells the woman with whom he is living about his obsession: drug addiction, women, Black Power, etc. Deep misery results from it."

1154   Anon.   "*Face à l'homme blanc* par James Baldwin."   *Le Bibliothécaire* (1969).
The realism of *Going To Meet the Man* is painful but its value is in its documentary quality.   A brief discussion of the title story follows.

1155   Anon.   "*Face à l'homme blanc* par James Baldwin."   *Le Nouveau Monde* (February 1969).
The difficult existence of Black people in the United States is the central theme of the short stories in *Going to Meet the Man*. Baldwin's directness is lucid and sometimes painful.   Summary of the title story and "This Morning So Soon."

1156   Anon.   "*L'Autant en emporte le vent* des Noirs."   *La Nouvelle Critique* No. 21 (February 1969), p. 58.
Brief review of *Jubilee* by Margaret Walker, herself the "great grand-daughter of black slaves."   The novel is compared to Margaret Mitchell's *Gone with The Wind* and called the black counterversion of that example of pro-Southern propaganda.

1157   Anon.   "La *NC* signale... un très grand roman américain;"   *La Nouvelle Critique* No. 27 (October 1969), p. 63.
Mentions the publication of *Invisible Man* by Ralph Ellison under the title *Homme invisible, pour qui chantes-tu?*   Quotes Pierre Dommergues who speaks of "a prophetic book," unique in its intention of rendering a unique culture, and unique in the transcending of black reality to which it nevertheless remains faithful.

1158   Anon.   "Le griot surréaliste, Ted Joans."   *Jazz hot*: No. 35

(July-August 1969), 22-23.
Ted Joans is introduced to the reader as a jazzman who writes poems on bebop rhythms. His career began in New York with the help of disk jockey Dan Burley. He associated with musicians and beat poets while doing surrealistic paintings. This short essay is followed by poems by Joans: "Jazz is my Religion," "Two Worlds," "Did You Know?" "I Am," "For Pianoman and Afroamerica," "New Names," "They Forget Too Fast," "There are Those," and "Get It," together with a few collages. (pp. 24-25)

1159 Anon. "Margaret Walker, *Jubilee.*" *Le Prêtre de Saint-François de Salles* (January 1969), p. 26.
The reviewer advises reading the book as a means of understanding the Negro problem in the U.S. The novel is all the more fascinating in that it renders the climate of hatred and contempt that prevailed in slavery times without bombast nor lyrical indignation. It ends on a note of hope to the chords of Negro spirituals.

1160 Anon. " 'Black People', poème de LeRoi Jones." *Vie du Tiers-Monde* Nos. 1-2 (January-April 1969), pp 40-42.
An analysis of Jones's poem within its socio-political context shows that it embodies the spirit of protest which started the "long hot summers." It reveals among the disinherited ghetto dwellers the birth of class consciousness. A detailed retrospect of Jones's literary and political career recalls his imprisonment. He is quoted, as a conclusion: "We must create our black world, create a world in which our children will grow."

1161 Barrière, Françoise. "Ralph Ellison: *Homme Invisible, pour qui chantes-tu?* " *Les Lettres françaises* No. 1291 (July 9, 1969), p. 4.
Very favorable review of *Invisible Man* featuring several criteria and evaluating the novel for its contribution to clarifying the issue of black and American cultures.

1162 Boileau-Narcejac. "Les romans policiers: *Dare-dare* de Himes." *Les Nouvelles littéraires* No. 2196 (October 18, 1969), p. 5.
Two accomplished French writers of thrillers carefully review *Run Man Run*. They praise Himes for his colorful and original style. They note that the improbable plot in no way detracts from the reader's interest.

1163   Bonnefoy, Claude. "*La Mort d'Horatio Alger*, par LeRoi Jones." *Le Nouvel Observateur* No. 234 (May 5-11, 1969), p. 43.
The reviewer of *Tales* seems mostly impressed by the iconoclastic and critical tone of these stories; the book heralds "the demise of the classical novel." Writing "assumes the values of a spiritual murder." The author notes the possible influences of Jean Genet, Louis-Ferdinand Céline, and the beat poets on Jones.

1164   Bonnet, Melchior. "La vie littéraire: *Jubilee*, roman de Margaret Walker" *La Nouvelle République du Centre-Ouest*; (January 10, 1969).
This love story could have become a melodramatic saga had not the author made it into a humanistic one, by showing the Negro side of American society at the time of *Gone with the Wind*. The documentary interest of the novel is emphasized; but is Walker an authentic interpreter of the Black life under slavery? She shows neither hatred nor anger in the face of social injustice.

1165   Bourniquel, Camille.   "Librairie du mois. Ralph Ellison: *Homme invisible, pour qui chantes-tu?*" *Esprit* 37, No. 384 (September 1969), p. 368-70.
A favorable review of *Invisible Man*, alluding to a conference given by Ellison at the International Harvard Symposium organized by Henry Kissinger in 1961. Ellison wants to be universal and thinks that a great book is not necessarily political. He defines the Negro as a zombie among men, a living embodiment of the negative. The novel evinces "a desire to be lucid which, rejecting political opportunism, seems to reconcile the racial groups by balancing their cynicism and blindness."

1166   Brodin, Pierre.   {James Baldwin} In his *Présences contemporaines: écrivains américains d'aujourd'hui - les années soixante*. Paris: Nouvelles Editions Debresse, 1969.
Simply notes that since Baldwin has not written anything which adds to his reputation in the last five years, he will be excluded from the present work.

1167   Brodin, Pierre.   "LeRoi Jones." In his *Présences contemporaines: écrivains américains d'aujourd'hui - les années soixante*. Paris: Nouvelles Editions Debresse, 1969.
Several of Jones's works are summarized: the musical criticism in *Blues People* is judged less important than his dramatic impact with

Dutchman, The Slave, The Baptism and *The Toilet.* The stories collected in *Tales* help understand his evolution and present stand. Comparing Jones with other black writers shows how he has become the champion of the most intransigent kind of negritude. He is a disturbing writer who pours out his hatred in brutal, sometimes obscene language, diametrically opposed to the bygone spirituals, Uncle Toms, or plantation dialects.

1168 Bruls, J. "De l'esclavage au Black Power." *Eglise vivante* (1969), pp. 66-68.
Baldwin's *Going to Meet the Man* is discussed along with Margaret Walker's *Jubilee*, Hubert Gerbeau's *Martin Luther King, Jr.*, O. Willane's *Pasteur King*, and Yves Loyer's *Black Power.* Of the two books by black Americans only *Going to Meet The Man* explores "violent racism." One can scarcely have more than a "platonic" sympathy for *Jubilee* while Baldwin leads us to a radical confrontation with American society.

1169 Bueges, Jean. "Ralph Ellison: *Homme invisible, pour qui chantes-tu?*" *Paris-Match* No. 1063 (September 20, 1969), p. 25.
A brief evaluation of *Invisible Man*, mostly from a thematic angle.

1170 Copperman, A.[nnie]. "Ralph Ellison: *Homme invisible, pour qui chantes-tu?*" *Les Echos* (June 27, 1969), p. 16.
The plot of *Invisible Man* is summarized, but not quite accurately. The review focuses on the hero's attempt at self-realization and his difficulties in achieving a viable relationship with his black and white environment. The artistry and balanced writing of Ellison are highly praised.

1171 Cabau, Jacques. "Nous sommes tous des nègres." *L'Express* No. 936 (June 16, 1969), pp.56-57.
A detailed review of *Invisible Man* stresses the universal relevance of the novel, based upon the narrator's final claim that he speaks for the reader "on the lower frequencies." Ellison's craft is supreme and the thematic development of the protagonist's evolution well-achieved. A major American, not only Afro-American novel.

1172 Cham, M.H. "*Homme Invisible* de Ralph Ellison." *Etudes* No. 331 (December 1969), p. 773.
A brief, highly favorable review of *Invisible Man* which "ranks among the most important works of American literature."

1173 Chedel, A. "*Face à l'homme blanc*, par James Baldwin." *L'Impartial* (April 30, 1969).
Baldwin's book of short stories, *Going to Meet the Man*, sounds political but it is above all literary. The stories are "cruel but lucid."

1174 Constant, Denis. "Les voix noires de la libération." *Témoignage chrétien* No. 1287 (March 13, 1969), p. 32.
A long essay on the different means black Americans can resort to in order to convey and express their grievances and rebellion. The author concludes that the black revolutionary movement is irreversible. A poem by Ted Joans is quoted: "the time has come to swing now."

1175 Cote, Michèle. "Entre deux mondes hostiles." *La Quinzaine littéraire* No. 78 (September 1-15, 1969), pp. 8-9.
The reviewer contrasts the failure of the first edition of *Invisible Man* in France and the success it immediately had in the United States. The analysis emphasizes the "blues" technique of writing and the humanistic message of the novel which, "expressing Ellison's belief in cultural integration as opposed to violence, is closer to a political statement." Its strength lies in avoiding both regionalism and marginalization.

1176 Coudert, Marie-Louise. "Martha Foley: *Cinquante ans de nouvelles américaines*." *Europe* Nos. 478-479 (February-March 1969), p. 340.
A very favorable account of "Bright and Morning Star" by Richard Wright in an otherwise rather negative review of the collection.

1177 Cousin, P. "*La prochaine fois, le feu*." *Livres et Lectures* (November 1969), p. 539.
Of the different phases and strategies of the Civil Rights Movement in the United States, James Baldwin chose nonviolence in spite of his fiery rhetoric in *The Fire Next Time*.

1178 Cousty, Paulette. "*Jubilee* de Margaret Walker: Un *Pain noir* américain." *Le Populaire du Centre* (May 22, 1969), p. 6.
The novel, a portrayal of destitution, reminds the reviewer of *Pain noir* [Poor people's brown bread] by Georges-Emmanuel Clancier. The role of religion is examined, particularly the use of the Bible to justify slavery: "great iniquities need a reassuring mask." Each chapter is a chronicle of plantation life, with blacks struggling to

survive and whites comforted in their righteousness by reading the Bible.

1179 Deransart, M. "Un livre par mois: *Jubilee* de Margaret Walker." *L'Illustré protestant* (January 1969), p. 15.
Emphasizes the documentary aspect of the novel, written by the great-granddaughter of the protagonist. Walker insists on the Christian-like qualities of whites and blacks who find in the Bible food to sustain their view of the situation. Viry's long struggle is retraced. "A beautiful book and a splendid lesson in Christian humanity."

1180 Dommergues, Pierre. "Etude: Ralph Ellison et la culture noire; un livre prophétique." *Le Monde des livres* No. 7594 (June 14, 1969), pp. IV-V.
Includes the two essays "Un livre prophétique" and "L'homme invisible à la recherche de son identité," as well as long contrasting quotations from Ellison, Baldwin, and Jones dealing with their definitions of the Black man, their views on Afro-American and American culture, on integration and negritude, the role of the black artist, and the relation between race, art, religion, and politics. *Invisible Man* is a "prophetic book" which announces the two trends in Negro thinking: integration and the movement towards national liberation. The views of Baldwin, Jones, and Ellison are contrasted, and Ellison's presented as favoring the mixture of black and white culture and black integration into American culture. A biographical note is included under the title "From Huck Finn to Raskolnikov."

1181 Dommergues, Pierre. "*La Mort d'Horatio Alger* et *Home* de LeRoi Jones." *Le Monde des livres* No. 7570 (May 17, 1969), p. VII.
Review of *Tales* and *Home* from a thematic angle. The books accurately represent Jones's major objectives: to bring down the ghetto walls and attack the police; to transform into a national consciousness the specificity of the black experience racially, nationally, and culturally; to fight white-oriented culture and regain the African heritage. Jones's ideological itinerary is retraced from *Blues People* and his early plays up to the final essays in *Home*.

1182 Dommergues, Pierre. *Les Etats-Unis par les textes*. Paris: Armand Colin, 1969.

Baldwin's name is briefly mentioned in this anthology as one who
states that the radical problem is primarily white America's problem.
Excerpt: "Black Boy looks at White Boy."

1183 Ducornet, Guy. Review of *Invisible Man* by Ralph Ellison.
Les Langues modernes, 63 , 4 (July 1969), pp. 394-401.
A detailed academic study of *Invisible Man.* Not seen.

1184 Dupeyron, G. "*Le Temps noir.*" *Europe* No. 478-479
(February-March 1969), p. 354.
Favorable review of William Wilson's novel, which is analyzed as a
document on the behavior of two American police officers, one
white, one black. The author however, sees no solution to the
racism he exposes.

1185 Fabre, Michel. "La désobéissance civile." *Europe* No. 477
(January 1969), pp. 214-17.
A review of a new translation of Thoreau's *Civil Disobedience*
mentions William Kelley's use of the concept of civil disobedience in
A Different Drummer and Martin Luther King and Malcolm X's
approaches to political dissent.

1186 Fleury, Claude. "L'Amérique invisible." *Le Républicain
lorrain* (June 7, 1969).
A detailed evaluation of Ellison's *Invisible Man.* The novel brings to
the European audience largely unknown psychological traumas and
hidden aspects of cultural as well as human conflits between the raes
in the United States. The protagonist's quest makes this an epic
novel; it is strikingly conceived and superbly written.

1187 Freustié, Jean. "Le Noir invisible." *Le Nouvel Observateur*
No. 243 (July 7, 1969), pp. 32-33.
A favorable review of *Invisible Man* in which Ralph Ellison, who
"has often been accused of sparing the whites, is merciless about
them." More than the very beautiful symbolism at work in the novel
it is the novelist's impressive intellectual and poetic vision which is
praiseworthy. He "foresaw the rift which was going to divide liberal
and radical Negro intellectuals." The book is "a most beautiful
lyrical masterpiece."

1188 Galey, Mathieu. "Unique livre d'un noir américain de 55 ans,

un roman prophétique reparaît en France après 15 ans de succés aux USA." *Paris-Presse* (May 29, 1969), p. 21.
Stresses the "prophetic value" of *Invisible Man* and Ralph Ellison's relevance to the intellectual community through his attempt at a sort of lucidity that transcends ideological commitment.

1189 Garavito, J. "Notes de lecture: *Anthologie de la littérature négro-américaine* (Vol.II)." *Europe* Nos. 480-481 (April-May 1969), pp. 401-02.
Favorable review of an anthology prepared by Léonard Sainville and published by Présence africaine. Together with James Baldwin, Peter Abrahams, William Conton, and George Lamming, the author mentions Arna Bontemps, Charles Wright, Herbert Simmons, and Saunders Redding, "all four of them from the United States," as among the future successors to Richard Wright and Langston Hughes. [As a matter of fact, Sainville's anthology is full of inaccurate information and badly balanced.]

1190 Gérard, Albert. *Les Tambours du néant: le problème existentiel dans le roman américain.* Brussels: La Renaissance du Livre, 1969.
A whole chapter is devoted to "The sons of Ham" (pp. 148-191). The neo-primitivism of white intellectuals is seen as an incentive to the Harlem Renaissance. "Big Boy Leaves Home," *Native Son*, and above all *The Outsider*, are studied as revealing Wright's existential positions. Ellison's *Invisible Man* is analyzed at length; it typifies a double sort of alienation but ends with communion between narrator and the reader. Baldwins *Go Tell It On the Mountain* poses the problem of individual responsibility, while *Another Country* sets up an opposition between love and alienation. It "realizes the fundamental ambition of the Afro-American novel. For the first time, the condition of the black man appears as a modality of the condition of man." A thoughtful, well balanced, and thoroughgoing study.

1191 Grandmaison, Jacqueline de. "Les livres: *Jubilee* de Margaret Walker." *La Semaine de Provence* (January 17, 1969).
This brief review compares *Jubilee* to *Gone with the Wind* and *Uncle Tom's Cabin*; it is a "vast epic pregnant with violence." More than a chronicle of the Civil War, it proves to be a reflection of the sorrowful hope and Christian love of a torn race. "It should be read earnestly, just like one listens to the spirituals."

1192 K., J-L. "*Camétude*, de Art (sic) LeRoi Bibbs." *La Tribune de Lausanne* (December 11, 1969).
How can we call this a book? It is a manifesto, "a tract denouncing everything, whose initial victim is language."   This is no revolutionary text but rather the testimony of a drug addict which speaks of a double kind of alienation. It offers no analysis of the consequences of evil. Only one thing is certain and that is the narrator's hatred for those who tyrannize him.

1193 K., M. "A propos de *Proposition pour un manifeste Black Power.*" *Le Magazine littéraire* (June 1969), p. 56.
Favorable mention of Ted Joans' collection of "Black Power" poems.

1194 Kyria, Pierre. "Chant de mémoire et blues de l'homme noir." *Combat* (June 12, 1969), p. 7.
A favorable review of *Invisible Man* by Ralph Ellison, emphasizing its thematic contents as well as its aesthetic concerns, over and above its ever-present relevance to the racial situation in the United States.

1195 Las Vergnas, Raymond. "La Nuit noire." *Les Nouvelles littéraires* No. 2179 (June 26, 1969), p. 5.
A long essay devoted to a review of LeRoi Jones' *Tales* and Ralph Ellison's *Invisible Man*. The two works are summarized, analyzed, and contrasted: Jones is presented as the spokesman for black separatism on the cultural level.   Ellison's view is more comprehensive and favorable considering the intricate cultural connections between blacks and whites.

1196 Lemaire, Marcel. "*Homme invisible, pour qui chantes-tu?*" Brussels *Le Soir* (October 22, 1969).
This review focuses primarily on the literary value of Ralph Ellison's *Invisible Man* --the symbolism, the writing, the variations on a theme. The sociological contents come second.

1197 Léna, Arlette. "Révolution culturelle à Harlem." *Jazz hot* No. 35 (April 1969), pp. 17-21.
This well-documented report on the cultural situation in Harlem shows how jazz music can help the black community to become more autonomous culturally. Malcolm X, Frantz Fanon, and LeRoi Jones are quoted in an examination of the three "levels of negritude" i.e. color, culture, consciousness, and of the possible role of the

"cultural weapon" which the demand for Black studies seems to articulate.

1198 Louit, Robert. "Ralph Ellison, LeRoi Jones: de la révolte à la révolution." *Le Magazine littéraire* No. 31 (August, 1969), p. 35-37.
Although the review of *Invisible Man* is full of praise for Ellison's aesthetic achievement, it is felt that his "integrationist" position is no longer valid in comparison with LeRoi Jones's more militant writing. Black authors have evolved in their attitudes towards their white readership: from trying to win it over they have moved onto trying to antagonize it.

1199 Maillard, Lucien. "Rencontre avec Hart Leroy Bibbs: Aujourd'hui la drogue..., demain, le style." *Combat* (October 30, 1969), p. 9.
An interview on the publication of *Camétude* by Editions Christian Bourgois , the English version of which, "A Dietbook for Junkies," had not yet appeared in the United States. Bibbs talks about his life and concludes with his hopes for the advent of Black Power.

1200 Masselot, Félix. "Voici des livres: *Jubilee* de Margaret Walker." *L'Hopital* (June 1969).
The plot is briefly summarized. The reviewer concludes that, although the black situation is well-known, the novel as a documentary is worthy because of the "serenity of its tone." It tells much about the peculiar psychology of blacks which their songs eloquently translate.

1201 Merle, Robert. Preface to *Homme invisible pour qui chantes-tu?* by Ralph Ellison. Paris: Grasset,1969.
Emphasizes Ellison's "faithfulness to traditional narrative schemes in Anglo-Saxon literature and to the book's more specifically American theme." This picturesque novel embodies several responses to the dilemma of the "invisible" black in the United States, from nationalism to a rather cautious approach to integration. The literary merits and intertextuality of the novel are nicely explored by the translator of the novel, a well-known novelist and academic.

1202 Mignon, Paul-Louis. *Le Théâtre contemporain*. Paris: Hachette, 1969.
Brief mention of James Baldwin and LeRoi Jones as playwrights of

a "literature of denunciation and combat." (p. 163)

1203 Pélieu, Claude. Preface to *Camétude* by Hart Leroi Bibbs. Paris: Christian Bourgois, 1969.
The French beat poet commends Bibbs' book for being more than fiction, a long, nearly surrealistic prose poem haltingly giving his readers the best of the excruciating experience of drug addiction. Bibbs provides all junkies some advice but mostly he subverts all regular modes of writing. These qualities make it an important work.

1204 Pool, Rosey E. "What is Africa to me?" *Présence africaine* Special issue 'Mélanges' (3rd trimester 1969), pp. 32-36.
This essay notes that the books published by Présence africaine and the important works of Alain Locke were instrumental in helping black Americans discover their African roots. The author, a Dutch Africanist, mentions a conversation she had with Léopold Senghor, Samuel Allen, and Wilfred Cartey during a USIS-organised TV program in Washington, D.C.

1205 Prévot-Laygonie, M-F. "Le livre du mois: *Jubilee* de Margaret Walker." *Educatrices paroissiales* (March-April 1969), p. 12 [?].
A short description of "this very fine novel/poem to freedom" which retraces the story of the author's own grandmother. It is a "book for young people because of its quest for happiness" and a book for Christians "with its Evangelical spirit, a psalm surprisingly full of truth."

1206 Recht, Jean-Jacques. "Actualité de W.E.B. DuBois." *Présence africaine* No. 70 (June 1969), pp. 181-89.
This retrospect on Du Bois' career does not neglect his poetry ("A Litany at Atlanta") and his literary action and achievements during the Harlem Renaissance. The problems raised by Du Bois in *The Souls of Black Folk* are examined in the light of more recent events in the United States and the world.

1207 Sabatier, Robert. "Les Caps de la désespérance." *Le Figaro littéraire* No. 1209 (July 21, 1969), p. 24.
Favorable review of *Tales*, a collection of short stories by LeRoi Jones. Jones is praised for his writing only, and his ideological stance and racial protest are not taken into consideration. The author suggests that "American Negritude might have found its *Chants de*

Maldoror [Lautréamont's innovative surrealistic masterpiece] with this book."

1208 Thinesse, Anne. "Est-il autre chose qu'un Oncle Tom qui a réussi?" *Le Figaro littéraire* No. 1212 (August 11-17, 1969), p. 28.
The reviewer claims that, although Ellison feels he is an embattled writer, he is an integrationist, "an Uncle Tom who has made it." *Invisible Man* is "not an autobiography" since the novelist has always found a way of making himself visible. An interview of Ralph Ellison by John Corry, originally published in the *New York Times Book Review* (November 20, 1966), is quoted at length.

1970

1209 Anon. "Introduction aux poètes de la beat generation." In "41 poètes américains d'aujourd'hui." Special issue of *Les Lettres nouvelles* (December 1970-January 1971).
Biographical notice on LeRoi Jones whose " A Poem for Neutrals" is printed on pp. 128-31 with a translation by Serge Fauchereau.

1210 Anon. "James Baldwin: *L'Homme qui meurt.*" *Paris-Match* No. 1126 (December 5, 1970), p. 122.
Tell Me How Long... is briefly summarized. It is "a sensitive, sincere novel" which cuts across the intertwining destinies of its protagonists and "makes clear to us the contradictions of American society."

1211 Anon. "Chester Himes: *L'Aveugle au pistolet.*" *Le Drapeau rouge* (November 27, 1970).
A brief review of *Blind Man with a Pistol* in this anarchist paper takes note that Himes depicts the disorganization and lack of solidarity among the black characters during their ineffectual revolt against white injustice. Himes is comparing this undirected violence to the actions of the blind man and his revolver. Although the story is an entertaining one, he says, it cannot be seriously considered as a political parable.

1212 Anon.[?] "Chester Himes: *L'Aveugle au pistolet.*" *La Libre Belgique* (November 22, 1970), 5.
In this favorable appraisal of *Blind Man with a Pistol,* the reviewer

calls Himes "the author who gets closest to the problems of Harlem."
He further notes that in Harlem "sun, sweat, the smell of skin, dirt
and sins" are symbolic of a milieu where confusion runs rampant.

1213 Anon. "Chester Himes: *La Reine des pommes.*" *Bulletin de la
Guilde du livre* (November 1970), pp. 6-7.
A biographical note about Himes and a summary of *For Love of
Imabelle* precede a very favorable evaluation of the book. Noted is
the fact that this is a new title (No. 835) in a thriller series called "La
Guilde du mystère."

1214 Anon. "*L'Aveugle au pistolet* par Chester Himes." *France
nouvelle* No. 1304 (November 30, 1970).
The reviewer lauds Himes' latest detective tale, *Blind Man with a
Pistol*, although he feels that this is too limited a designation for
writing that appeals more to the heart than to the mind. He sees
Himes' Harlem as "a microcosm that foreshadows a world of the
future; overpopulated, underfed, desperate, but possessed of a rage
to live."

1215 Anon. "*L'homme qui meurt* par James Baldwin." *Syndicats*
(November 7, 1970).
A summary of *Tell Me How Long...* precedes the conclusion: it is a
vast accusation launched against an unjust, undemocratic society
where racism dominates all in the eyes of a black man. Baldwin is
rejected by the black Panthers and extremist groups, yet he fights for
black liberation with "firmness and great independence."

1216 Anon. "La *NC* signale... un roman de James Baldwin." *La
Nouvelle Critique* No. 39 (December 1970), p. 78.
Mentions the publication of a novel by Baldwin by Gallimard. The
title is given as "L'Enfant de Harlem" and it "deals with the
contradictions of American society." [No book was published in
French under this title, and the allusion probably is to *Tell Me How
Long the Train's Been Gone*."]

1217 Anon. "Lettres: pas en temps, mais en lieu." *Informations et
Documents* (January 1, 1970), p. 44.
Mentions the first publication of *The Chosen Place, the Timeless
People* by Paule Marshall. She is one of "the most gifted Afro-
American women writers" and very knowledgeable about the
situation in the Caribbean. Her book is set in Barbados but the

protagonists are white, a trio of experts for economic development whose narrowness of spirit and selfishness opposes to a revolutionary figure, an old black woman. Marshall confirms the qualities which had made the success of *Brown Girl, Brownstones* and *Soul, Clap Hands and Sing.* Also mentions the new publication of the anthology, *The Negro Caravan* by Sterling Brown and others.

1218 Anon.[?] *"Le Système de l'Enfer de Dante* de LeRoi Jones."
Le Nouvel Observateur No. 310 (October 19-25, 1970), p. 3.
Brief comment about *The System of Dante's Hell* under a photograph of LeRoi Jones. "This novel by the great Negro writer is the work of a poet. Its lyrical mode reminds one both of Henry Miller and John Dos Passos."

1219 Anon. "Romans étrangers: *L'Homme qui meurt* par James Baldwin; *L'Aveugle au pistolet* par Chester Himes." *Sélection des libraires de France* (December 1970).
Two African American novelists react almost similarly to the racial situation but their voices are original and different. Baldwin's novel is "a cry" [or a shout], Himes's reaction is "a burst of laughter" yet both of these "mingle into the same anguish." Baldwin also embodies "impetuous élan and a grating lucidity."

1220 Anon. "Une nuit et un jour à Harlem." *La Nouvelle Critique* No. 38 (November 1970), p.101.
On the occasion of the French publication of *Blind Man with a Pistol,* Himes is hailed as "the great black writer." The plot is analyzed and seen as a pretext for Himes' symbolic vision of the future of the race problem in the United States.

1221 B., M-L. *"Camétude*... le monologue d'un poéte du jazz et de la négritude." *Jazz Magazine* (March 1970).
Hart Leroy Bibbs is well-known and admired by all jazz musicians among whom he lives in Paris. His book is at the same time a "novel, a monologue, a prose poem" supposedly giving his readers and all junkies some advice and recipes. It subverts all modes of writing. "Its cruelty, tenderness, delirium, the announcement of unknown worlds and then nostalgia of lost paradise... make it an essential work."

1222 Bott, François. "Comment être nègre?" *Le Monde des livres* (October 30, 1970), pp. 15-16.

Contains a long quotation about the terror which seizes Leo when, still a youngster, he meets with white power: this serves to introduce *Tell Me How Long the Train's Been Gone*, by James Baldwin, translated as *L'Homme qui meurt.* Frantz Fanon is also mentioned in order to explain "the vile, viscous and creeping feeling of existential anguish" created by seeing oneself mirrored and defined radically as the Other in someone else's eyes.

1223   Constant, Denis.   "*Musique Noire* par LeRoi Jones." *Témoignage chrétien* No. 1375 (November 12, 1970), p. 29.
A brief review of *Black Music*, whose "publication in French translation now completes that of *Blues People*."

1224   Copans, Simon.   "L'héritage africain dans la musique des Américains." *Connaissance de l'Afrique* No. 34 (June 1970), pp. 17-20.
In a discursive essay on African influences in Afro-American music and poetry, mention is made of Harlem Renaissance poets like Countee Cullen, Claude McKay, Langston Hughes and their relationship to Africa; Charlotte Forten's memories of Blacks dancing on Africa rhythms are recalled. James Weldon Johnson and W.E.B. Du Bois exerted a definite influence towards the preservation of black folk lyrics. Two paragraphs review *Black Music* and *Blues People* by LeRoi Jones.

1225 Copperman, Annie. "Chester Himes: *L'Aveugle au pistolet*." *Les Echos* (November 20, 1970), p. 17.
Copperman reviews *Blind Man with a Pistol*, summarizing the plot and commenting on its qualities. She believes that in this and in his previous novels, Himes is the writer who most accurately and explicitly reflects the persistent barriers between American blacks and whites.

1226   D., J.-M.   "Chester Himes: *L'Aveugle au pistolet*." *Le Monde des livres* (November 13, 1970), p. 20.
This review of *Blind Man with a Pistol* concentrates on Himes' depiction of episodes from Harlem's life and his description of the tensions in a ghetto about to explode with racial unrest.

1227 D., J.-M. "Etude." *Le Monde des livres* (November 13, 1970), p. 20.
In an introduction to the two-page spread entitled "Chester Himes et

la saga de Harlem," the critic describes Himes' evolution as a writer and provides a capsule biography. He also discusses the themes in *Blind Man with a Pistol* and gives a chronology of Himes' life.

1228 Daridan, Pierre. "Chester Himes: *L'Aveugle au pistolet.*" Lille *Nord-Matin* (October 15, 1970), p. 5.
The critic primarily spends his review discussing the plot of *Blind Man with a Pistol*. He concludes that Himes "depicts violence and lawlessness in Harlem almost with nostalgia."

1229 Decock, J. "Lettre des Etats-Unis: Plus de noir que de nu." *La Quinzaine littéraire* no. 97 (June 16-30, 1970), pp. 25- 26.
Concerning the situation of drama in New York City, the author makes references to *A Raisin in the Sun* by Lorraine Hansberry and to "Great Goodness of Life" by LeRoi Jones.

1230 Depestre, René. "Les métamorphoses de la négritude en Amérique." *Présence africaine* No. 75 (3rd trimester 1970), pp. 19- 33.
The Haitian poet proposes a scheme for the exploration of the origins and evolution of the African Renaissance movement. After Haitian "indigenism," its second stage was represented by the New Negro Movement in the U.S. The role of W.E.B. Du Bois and Marcus Garvey is emphasized; also the contribution of Hughes, McKay and Cullen prior to the works of Richard Wright, James Baldwin and LeRoi Jones. The perspective is comprehensive, international and mostly ideological.

1231 Diagne, Pathé. "*Homme invisible, pour qui chantes-tu?* de Ralph Ellison." *Présence africaine* No. 74 (2nd trimester 1970), pp. 223-25.
This detailed review mentions the success of *Invisible Man* in the U.S., and analyzes its plot in detail. Its "density, internal cohesion and massiveness are remarkable...It certainly belongs to the great tradition of the Anglo-saxon novel...The style is of tremendous scope." The novel is full of epic and lyricism, with "qualities of style which owe more to talent, innate speech habits than to technique... It renders the pulsing and rhythmical life of a world of emotions."

1232 Diagne, Pathé. "*La Mort d'Horatio Alger* par LeRoi Jones." *Présence africaine* No. 74 (2nd trimester 1970), pp. 225-28.

This long review-essay dwells on the style of Jones in the short stories collection, *Tales*, and mostly centers on an analysis of his political and ideological position: Jones differs from Ellison by his belief that the black writer must become a spokesman for his race; to Ellison's "africanness" he opposes the "blackness" of American Negroes. Blackness must be struggled for on the cultural, situational and political levels.

1233 Dommergues, Pierre. "La révolution par les armes et les mots." *Le Monde* (December 11, 1970), p. 17.
An essay on, and interview of LeRoi Jones, focussing on his ideological positions and his aesthetics aims: black American culture is specific; the black man must not be torn between two cultures; black revolution must be organized not exclusively in political terms: it should aim at liberating blacks, at making white American explode, and at developing black consciousness.

1234 Duhamel, Marcel. "Préface." In Chester Himes. *L'Aveugle au pistolet*. Paris: Gallimard, 1970, pp. 1-19.
The preface briefly evokes Himes' literary career and Duhamel's relationship with him. (He was Himes' first translator and then his series editor and friend.) Duhamel stresses the imaginative power of Himes' writing and insists that this last entry in the Harlem series is much more than a detective novel.

1235 Duparc, Christine. "Chester 'Harlem' Himes: Ses livres ressemblent de plus en plus à ceux de Malcolm X." *Le Nouvel Observateur* No. 310 (October 19, 1970), pp. 41-42.
The reviewer discusses Himes' early career as a "bad nigger" and his beginnings as a writer. Duparc describes the teeming world Himes has created and notes that although violence seems to predominate in the plots, this factor is usually balanced by the lead character's determination to fight back against oppression. Himes is quoted as saying that "white Americans only respect strength. We must kill as many of them as we can. Only when we are all united will we be able to defeat them."

1236 Durozoi, Gérard. "*Camétude.*" *Opus International* (March, 1970), p. 38.
The novel by Hart LeRoi Bibbs was not published in the U.S.A. because "it goes too far." Rebellion does not follow expected patterns but destroys language. Such a type of writing, repetitive,

full of obscene insults was needed. Bibbs does not speak to us but to America. It is not true that he shouts to no purpose and for the only pleasure of shouting--his rebellion leads to that of Black Power.

1237 Fabre, Michel. "Ecrire, une initiative pour révèler l'absurdité de la vie." *Le Monde des livres* (November 13, 1970), p. 21.
This interview with Himes focuses on his writing, political beliefs, and career in both the U. S. and France. Himes explains that he consciously writes fiction for self-realization. He also enjoys depicting the element of chance in man's existence.

1238 Fabre, Michel. "Mort du sociologue noir Horace Cayton." *Le Monde* (January 29, 1970), p. 13.
Obituary notice about Horace Cayton, mentioning his relationship with Richard Wright and his writings, notably *Old Long Road* and *Black Metropolis.*

1239 Fabre, Michel. "Péres et fils dans *Go Tell It on the Mountain* de James Baldwin." *Études Anglaises* 23, 1 (April 1970), 47-61.
A detailed analysis of the novel, centering on the protagonists' family and on his relationship to his stepfather. Includes a discussion of Baldwin's own relation to Wright. [Repr. as "Fathers and Sons in *Go Tell It on the Mountain*" in Michael Cooke, ed, *Modern Black Novelists* (Englewood Cliffs, Prentice-Hall, 1971) and in Keneth Kinnamon, ed., *James Baldwin* (Englewood Cliffs, Prentice-Hall, 1974), pp. 120-39]

1240 Fabre, Michel. "Un redoutable argot." *Le Monde des livres* (November 13, 1970), p. 21.
Even in translation, Himes' humor is largely verbal and the result of his artful use of black American slang. His racy flair for language is one of his most important characteristics. Fabre believes that misunderstandings about just what Himes is trying to say have often arisen about his writing among critics and readers. Some examples of the problems inherent in translating Himes's work are provided.

1241 Farès, Nabile. "Avec James Baldwin." *Jeune Afrique* No. 504 (September 1, 1970), pp. 20-24.
A long interview of Baldwin, focusing on the racial situation, also on his writings and their relevance for Africans is preceded by a brief introduction, defining him as "a black American integrationist writer."

1242 Gaugeard, Jean. "Crucifixion en noir." *Les Lettres françaises*
No. 1361 (November 25, 1970), pp. 9, 11.
Detailed thematic and stylistic review of *The System of Dante's Hell*
by LeRoi Jones, considered as "one of the most splendid books
produced by Afro-American literature."

1243 Gilbert, C. "Notes de lecture: *Commandos noirs*, de Julian
Moreau." *Europe*; Nos. 485-87 (September-November 1969), p.
334-35.
A mixed review of Julian Moreau's *The Black Commandos*. The
novel is seen mostly as a mixture of "political fiction" and "science
fiction" centering around a coup taking place in the United States.

1244 Gilles, Serge. "Chester Himes: *L'Aveugle au pistolet.*"
France nouvelle No.1304 (November 4, 1970), 28-29.
Gilles emphasizes the social aspects of *Blind Man with a Pistol* and
explains that the fictional inhabitants of Harlem are deliberately
presented as the victims of an oppressive society.

1245 Gilles, Serge. "James Baldwin: *L'homme qui meurt.*" *France
nouvelle* No.1306 (November 18, 1970), 28-29.
Baldwin has long been a champion of integration and the target of
black nationalists. An honest man, he has realized that integration
was only an electoral ploy. Here he appears only a fine, competent
novelist to tell the story of a black actor, reminiscent of Sidney
Poitier, who cannot cure his many neuroses in spite of his success
with the Establishment. *Tell Me How Long...* is Baldwin's best
novel.

1246 H., J. "*Camétude* de Hart Leroy Bibbs." *Jazz hot* No. 257
(January 1970), p. 29.
Brief, favorable review of a black poet's "junkie prose poems... full
of verbal magic." His "Books of Recipes" vaporizes through the
magic of language the monstrous postulates of racism and reaction...
it denounces prejudice, hypocritical sentimentalism... Its power
forcefully comes out in the translation by Mary Beach, a specialist of
the Beat Generation.

1247 Hérouard, Jean-François. "Une musique de la rupture."
Réforme No. 1294 (January 3, 1970), p. 12.
This article on Free Jazz frequently refers to *Blues People* by LeRoi
Jones.

1248 Jotterand, Frank. *Le Nouveau Théâtre américain*. Paris: Le Seuil. 1970.
Chapter 1, sect. 4, of this study of contemporary American theater deals with black theater and musical comedy in the early 20th century (pp. 24-27) and Chapter 2, Section 10 with "the civic dramas of Martin Luther King" (p. 62). A whole section, devoted to black theater, focuses on LeRoi Jones: his various experiments, and his quest of Black history. His best known plays are mentioned as well as "Great Goodness of Life," "Home on the Range," "Black Mass" which are analyzed. The work of the Free Southern Theater and the New Lafayette with Robert Macbeth and Ed Bullins is studied. Bullins's "Clara's Old Man," *The Electronic Nigger*, "The Gentleman Caller," and *How Do You Do?* are analyzed and Bullins assessed as "a great writer." Ron Milner, Ben Caldwell, Lonne Elder and others are mentioned.

1249 Joubert, Jacques. "Chester Himes: *L'Aveugle au pistolet*." *Le Figaro* (November 9, 1970), p. 16.
Joubert extolls Himes' ruthless depiction of a closed ghetto world, noting that its aimless inhabitants seek refuge in prostitution, gambling, drugs, theft, and murder. In spite of Himes' brutal disruptions of time and place in this novel, it manages to hold the reader's attention because it is "teeming with life, blood, and sexuality."

1250 Juin, Hubert. "*Camétude* par Hart Bibbs." *Combat* (October 30, 1970).
Unfavorable notice. "Bibbs shouts to no purpose, just to shout and maybe to listen to his shouting."

1251 Julien, Claude. "Un monde cocasse, hilare et sanglant." *Le Monde des livres* (November 13, 1970), p. 20-21.
This is one of several articles devoted to Himes in "Chester Himes et la saga de Harlem", a special feature in the literary section of the leading French daily newspaper on the occasion of the French publication of *Blind Man.with a Pistol*.. Julien, a leading journalist and specialist on America, analyzes the social and political conditions of African Americans in a world where "pork chops become the sole compensation that the oppressed can find" and where only murder can restore the black man's dignity.

1252 Kattan, Naïm. "La chronique de Naïm Kattan: *L'homme qui*

meurt de James Baldwin." Montréal *Le Devoir* (December 5, 1970), p. 3.
Baldwin hardly renews himself but this only partly accounts for the uneasiness and dissatisfaction one experiences when reading the book. The topic -black and white relations- is timely and concerns us deeply, yet the characters are shorn of some of their human dimension. How can one write about black people without taking their skin color into account? Ralph Ellison accurately defines and solves that problem in *Invisible Man*, which argues that the white man "creates" the Negro.

1253 Kaye, Jacqueline. "Claude McKay's *Banjo*." *Présence africaine* No. 73 (1st trimester 1970), pp. 165-69.
This long essay, subtitled "Notes towards a mythology of blackness" analyses McKay's novel of black life in Marseilles and praises its bringing into focus the North African problem. "*Banjo* is a sketch of black personality and it spans across a whole range of Blackness" as it seeks to "arrive at the common black denominator, the equivalent of the Negritude to be generated by the poetry of francophone Blacks."

1254 Kotchy, Barthélémy. "Retour aux sources dans la littérature négro-africaine." *Présence africaine* No. 76 (4th trimester 1970), pp. 143-65.
The second part of this essay, "The Pioneers" focuses on the influence of the Harlem Renaissance writers and W.E.B. Du Bois on the Negritude school. Claude McKay's role is especially singled out.

1255 Kyria, Pierre. "James Baldwin: *L'homme qui meurt*."
Combat (October 15, 1970), p. 7.
Review of *Tell Me How Long...* Baldwin is a great storyteller who manages to pose embarrassing questions about the contradictions and social violence of America. Here he focuses on "the thousand shapes and fantasms the human crisis can assume in the loneliness of big cities." "A mixture of anger and tenderness, aggressive vulgarity and passion" endows his style with definite "relief and color."

1256 Las Vergnas, Raymond. "Rapsodie en noir et blanc." *Les Nouvelles littéraires* (November ?, 1970), p. 5.
Review of *Tell Me How Long...* by James Baldwin. Very curiously, it appears as "a love story" rather than as a "platform of

demands." Also discusses *Blind Man with a Pistol* by Chester Himes

1257 Lewis, Ida. "LeRoi Jones." *Jeune Afrique* No. 504 (September 1, 1970), pp. 24-27.
 In this long interview, Jones is quoted on aesthetic and ideological issues. Among other things, he says that "as long as the black man has not become conscious of his political rights it will be useless to try and incite him to revolt."

1258 Louit, Robert. "Baldwin et LeRoi Jones: de la révolte à la révolution." *Le Magazine littéraire* No. 47 (December 1970), pp. 42-45.
This essay on contemporary Afro-American writing retraces its ideological and thematic evolution from James Baldwin's fiery diatribes which are nevertheless addressed to the conscious of white America, to the violent prose of LeRoi Jones who resolutely turns his back on the white West in order to address the black community. Louit confronts Baldwin's *Tell Me How Long...* with Jones's *The System of Dante's Hell*, "which expresses a clear break with the values of white America."

1259 Mayer, Daniel. "Tribune libre: *Jubilee.*" *Combat* (November 19, 1970).
The author of this column uses *Jubilee* to condemn racism in Europe. Margaret Walker's novel is briefly summarized and used mostly to show that, in France, too many colored immigrants suffer from oppression, TB, malnutrition and that social racism is still widely spread.

1260 Mercoeur, Antoine. "Le Changement." *Les Nouvelles littéraires* No. 2251 (November 12, 1970).
It is American society at large which suffers from "the black American syndrome." Hence the slogan "Everything right now," and the desire for change in the racial minority. Baldwin expresses this in *Tell Me How Long...* and concludes that a new morality is required --"a new kind of morality encompassing the whites themselves in order to fight their own."

1261 Monod, Martine. "Chester Himes: *L'Aveugle au pistolet.*" *L'Humanité* (October 26, 1970), p. 11.
A largely ideological consideration of *Blind Man with a Pistol*

concludes that Himes' novel advocates the use of violence to effect political change. Himes' implication that white America understands only the use of force provides the justification for black people to use it in order to shake off the burdens of an unjust political system.

1262 Monod, Martine. "Des livre sur ma table: Parce que je suis noir..." *L'Humanité-Dimanche* (November 22, 1970), p. 40.
Racism wounds a black person so deeply that nothing, not even literary creation allows him to forget it. Since *The Fire Next Time*, Baldwin has reiterated in fiction the same message, relived the same painful experiences. In *Tell Me How Long...*, the hero is Baldwin's *alter ego* and the quasi-autobiographical narrative has "the irreplaceable taste of experience." The dramatic story of Leo Proudhammer tells us that individual freedom is not enough and that the time has come for the collective liberation Angela Davis is fighting for.

1263 N. "Hart LeRoi Bibbs, *Camétude*." Brussels *Nouvelles Techniques* (January 1970).
Bibbs' testimony should have been published in the United States as it is an important item in a present day dossier, that of injustice. Beat literature tends to present theatrical happenings in which the authors vent their frustrations. Language isolates the reader behind a veil of words but he is soon reminded that oppression and injustice exist everywhere.

1264 Noël, Gérard. "La 'Nouvelle chose' en gestation." *Jazz hot* No. 36 (March 1970), p. 15.
A review of *Black Music* The book brings material which makes it possible to concretely reconstruct what had been only theoretically postulated in *Blues People*. Again, LeRoi Jones brings the major prophets and the forgotten ones to life; he does not help the reader appreciate music, but to understand it. His testimony may be brutal but it is sincere as he tries to explain things from an inside view with sensitivity. The "Lexicon of great jazz musicians," added to the French translation, is criticized for being full of errors.

1265 Pinot, Germaine. "Chester Himes: *L'Aveugle au pistolet*." *L'Epicerie française* (December 5, 1970).
Pinot discusses how Himes symbolizes his political philosophy with his picture of black people trapped in the inferno of the ghetto. Himes favors clear-eyed, well-organized violence, Pinot says, and

he uses his book to criticize fellow blacks who react like blind men as they rampage through Harlem.

1266 Reis, Jacques. *"La Mort d'Horatio Alger."* *Europe* No. 489 (January 1970), p. 270.
An enthusiastic review of *Tales*, praising LeRoi Jones equally for his forceful plays and poetry. The variety and artistic achievement of the stories in the volume are emphasized.

1267 Renaud, Tristan. "Notes de lecture." *Les Lettres françaises* No. 1322 (February 18, 1970), p. 10.
A mostly descriptive review of *Blues People* by LeRoi Jones. "The book without doubt be of interest to jazz fans-- but not only to them."

1268 Roubine, J.-J. "LeRoi Jones: *Slaveship.*" *La Nouvelle Revue française* No. 211 (July 1970), p. 151.
A brief review of *Slaveship*, which was performed at the Theatre de la Cité internationale. The performance is praised and an examination of "a theater beyond reality," and "a political theater" is attempted.

1269 Sandier, Gilles. "Le théâtre retrouvé." *La Quinzaine littéraire* No. 96 (June 1-15, 1970), p. 27.
Very favorable review of *Slaveship* by LeRoi Jones, performed at the Recontres internationales at the Théâtre de la Cité internationale in Paris. In this play, which is reduced to gestural, musical, and physical action, reduces the text to a minimum. Everything is violently, and sometimes with unbearable truth, expressed bodily, by songs, and by the Afro-jazz rhythms of Archie Shepp and Gil Moses. Even scraps of spirituals sing the racial revolution instead of God. This is "quintessential black art with its incantatory power...theatrical poetry at its most intense...as fascinating as a religious ritual."

1270 Saporta, Marc. *Histoire du roman américain*. Paris: Seghers, 1970.
Devotes a chapter to black American novelists (pp. 238-257). Among a score of writers representing the period from the Harlem Renaissance to the Black Power era, all the luminaries are mentioned or characterized. Wright's major fiction is analyzed and evaluated on pp. 246-247. Chester Himes is singled out for "the surrealistic

power of his crime novels." Ellison is dealt with on pp. 317-18 and highly commended as the greatest artist. The chronology of American literary events even lists his short story, "Mister Toussan" (1941).

Translations or Original Publications of African-American Literature in France Until 1970

Anderson, Alston. *Le Tombeur*. Paris: Calmann-Lévy, 1964. Adapt. Alain Bosquet (*Lover Man*, 1959).

Baldwin, James, Malcolm X, M.L. King. *Nous, les nègres. Entretiens avec Kenneth Clark*. Paris: Maspero, 1965. Tr. André Chassigneux (*The Negro Protest*, 1963).

Baldwin, James. *Chronique d'un pays natal*. Paris: Gallimard, 1973. Tr. J. A. Tournaire (*Notes of a Native Son*, 1955).

Baldwin, James. *Face à l'homme blanc*. Paris, 1968 (*Going to Meet the Man*, 1965).

Baldwin, James. *Giovanni, mon ami*. La Table Ronde, Paris, 1958. Tr. Claude Messanges (*Giovanni's Room*, 1954).

Baldwin, James. *L'homme qui meurt*. Paris: Gallimard, 1970 (*Tell Me How Long the Train's Been Gone*, 1968).

Baldwin, James. *La prochaine fois, le feu*. Paris: Gallimard, 1963. Tr. Michel Sciama (*The Fire Next Time*, 1963).

Baldwin, James. *Les Elus du Seigneur*. Paris: La Table Ronde, 1957. Tr. Henri Hell and Maud Vidal (*Go Tell It on the Mountain*, 1952).

Baldwin, James. *Personne ne sait mon nom*. Paris: Gallimard, 1963. Tr. Jean Autret (*Nobody Knows My Name*, 1961).

Baldwin, James. *Un autre pays*. Paris: Gallimard, 1964. Tr. Jean Autret (*Another Country*, 1961).

Bennett, Hal. *Les Vignes sauvages*. Paris: Stock, 1968 (*A Wilderness of Vines*, 1966).

Bibbs, Hart Leroy. *Camétude*. Paris: Bourgois, 1969 (Unpublished in English).

Blackwood, Granby. *Un Sang mal mêlé*. Paris: Denoël, 1966.Tr. Jacqueline Bernard (Unpublished in English).

Brown, Claude. *Harlem ou la terre promise*. Paris: Stock.1966 (*Manchild in the Promised Land*, 1965).

Butcher, Margaret Just and Alain Locke. *Les Noirs dans la civilisation américaine*. Paris: Buchet-Chastel, 1958. Tr. Jean Rosenthal (*The Negro in American Culture*, 1956).

Du Bois, William E. B. *Ames noires*. Paris: Présence Africaine, 1959. Tr. Jean-Jacques Fol (*The Souls of Black Folk*, 1903).

Ellison, Ralph. *Au-delà du regard*. Paris, Denoel, 1954 ; *Homme invisible, pour qui chnates-tu?* Paris: Grasset, 1969. Tr. Robert and Magali Merle (*Invisible Man*, 1952).

Hansberry, Lorraine. *Un Raisin au soleil* . Paris: Nouveaux Horizons/ Seghers. 1968. Adapt. Emmanuel Roblès (*A Raisin in the Sun*, 1958).

Himes, Chester. *Couché dans le pain*. Paris: Gallimard (Série noire), 1959. Tr. J. Hérisson and Henri Robillot (*The Crazy Kill*, 1959).

Himes, Chester. *Dare Dare*. Paris: Gallimard (Série noire), 1959. Tr. Pierre Verrier (*Run Man Run*, 1966).

Himes, Chester. *Il pleut des coups durs*. Paris: Gallimard (Série noire), 1958. Tr. Claude Wourgraft (*The Real Cool Killers*, 1959).

Himes, Chester. *Imbroglio negro*. Gallimard (Série noire), 1960. Tr. Jane Fillion (*All Shot Up*, 1960).

Himes, Chester. *L'Aveugle au pistolet*. Paris: Gallimard, 1972. Tr. Henri Robillot (*Blind Man with a Pistol*, 1969).

Himes, Chester. *La Croisade de Lee Gordon*. Paris: Corréa, 1952. Tr. Yves Malartic (*Lonely Crusade*, 1947).

Himes, Chester. *La Fin d' un primitif*. Paris: Gallimard, 1956. Tr. Yves Malartic (*The Primitive*, 1956).

Himes, Chester. *La Reine des pommes*. Paris: Gallimard, 1958. Tr. Minnie Danzas (*For Love of Imabelle*, 1957; *A Rage in Harlem*, 1965).

Himes, Chester. *La Troisième Génération*. Paris: Plon, 1957. Tr. Yves Malartic (*The Third Generation*, 1954).

Himes, Chester. *Mamie Mason*. Paris: Plon. Tr. Henri Collard (*Pinkoes,* 1961).

Himes, Chester. *Ne nous énervons pas*. Paris: Gallimard (Série noire), 1961. Tr. Jane Fillion (*The Heat's On*, 1966).

Himes, Chester. *Retour en Afrique*. Paris: Plon, 1964. Tr. Pierre Sergent (*Cotton Comes to Harlem*,1965).

Himes, Chester. *S'il braille, lache-le*. Paris: Albin Michel, 1949. Tr. Renée Vavasseur and Marcel Duhamel (*If He Hollers Let Him Go,* 1945).

Himes, Chester. *Tout pour plaire*. Paris: Gallimard (Série noire), 1959. Tr. Yves Malartic (*The Big Gold Dream*, 1966).

Himes, Chester. *Une Affaire de viol*. Paris: Les Yeux Ouverts, 1963. Tr. André Mathieu (*A Case of Rape*,1980).

Hughes, Hughes, Langston. *Trésor africain* . Paris: Seghers, 1962 (*An African Treasury*).

Hughes, Langston, ed. *La Poésie afro-américaine*. Paris: Seghers, 1966. [Tr. Sim Copans]. Bilingual edition.

Hughes, Langston. *Histoires de Blancs*. Editions de Minuit, Paris, 1946. Tr Hélène Bokanowski (*The Ways of White Folks,* 1934).

Hughes, Langston. *L'Ingénu de Harlem*. Paris: Laffont , 1961. Tr. F.J. Roy (*The Best of Simple*, 1961).

Hughes, Langston. *Langston Hughes*. Paris: Seghers, 1955. Ed. bilingue. Tr. François Dodat.

Hughes, Langston. *Les Grandes Profondeurs*. Paris: Seghers, 1947 (*The Big Sea*, 1940).

Hughes, Langston. *Sandy*. Paris: Rieder, 1934. Tr. Gabriel Beauroy (*Not without Laughter*, 1930).

Joans Ted. *Proposition pour un manifeste Black Power*. Eric Losfeld, Paris. 1969. Tr Jeannine Ciment and Robert Benayoum (*Black Pow-Wow*, 1969).

Johnson, James Weldon. *God's Trombones; Sermons noirs en vers*. Paris: L'Epi, 1960. Tr. Claude Julien (*God's Trombones,* 1927).

Jones, LeRoi. *La Mort d'Horatio Alger*. Paris: Calmann-Lévy, 1969 (*Tales*, 1967).

Jones, LeRoi. *Le Métro fantôme; L'Esclave*. Paris: Gallimard, 1967. Adapt. Eric Kahane (*Dutchman; The Slave*, 1964).

Jones, LeRoi. *Le Système de l'Enfer de Dante*. Paris: Calmann-Lévy, 1970 (*The System of Dante's Hell*, 1965).

Jones, LeRoi. *Théâtre noir révolutionnaire*; Quatre pièces à la gloire de l'homme noir. Paris: Buchet/Chastel, 1972. Adapt. Nicole Tisserand (*Black Revolutionary Plays*).

Kaufman, Bob. *Sardine dorée*. Bourgois: Paris, 1976. Tr. Claude Pélieu, Mary Beach and Jacques François (*Golden Sardine*, 1967).

Kaufman, Bob. *Solitudes* . Bourgois: Paris,1974. Tr. Claude Pélieu, Mary Beach and Jacques François (*Solitudes Crowded with Loneliness*, 1965).

Kelley, William Melvin. *Un Autre Tambour*. Casterman, Paris, 1965. Tr. Lise Rosenbaum. (*A Different Drummer*, 1962).

Mayfield, Julian. *Un Coup de chance*. Paris: Albin Michel, 1960. Tr. Guy Le Clech (*The Hit*, 1957).

McKay, Claude. *Banjo*. Paris: Rieder, 1930. Tr. Ida Treat and Paul Vaillant-Couturier (*Banjo*, 1929).

McKay, Claude. *Quartier noir*. Paris: Rieder, 1931. Tr. Louis Guilloux (*Home to Harlem*, 1928).

Moreau, Julian. *Commandos noirs*. Paris: Julliard, 1968. Tr. Pierre Alien (*The Black Commandos*, 1967).

Petry, Ann. *La Rue*. Paris: Charlot, 1948 (*The Street*, 1946).

Polite, Carlene Hatcher. *Les Flagellants*. Bourgois, Paris, 1966. Tr. Pierre Alien (*The Flagellants*, 1967).

Rollins, Bryant. *Les Rues de la violence*. Paris (*Danger Song*, 1967).

Séjour, Victor. *André Gérard*. Paris: Michel-Lévy, 1857.

Séjour, Victor. *Compère Guillery*. Paris: Michel-Lévy, 1860.

Séjour, Victor. *Diégarias*. Paris: C. Tresse, 1844.

Séjour, Victor. *L'Argent du diable*. Paris: Michel-Lévy, 1857.

Séjour, Victor. *La Madone des roses*. Paris: Michel-Lévy, 1869.

Séjour, Victor. *La Tireuse de cartes*. Paris: Michel-Lévy, 1860.

Séjour, Victor. *Les Aventuriers*. Paris: Michel-Lévy, 1860.

Séjour, Victor. "Le Comte de Haag." *L'Ordre*, 23 March 1872, p. 3.

Séjour, Victor. *Les Enfants de la louve*. Paris: Michel-Lévy, 1856 (with Théodore Barrière)

Séjour, Victor. *Les Fils de Charles-Quint*. Paris: Michel-Lévy, 1864.

Séjour, Victor. *Le Fils de la nuit*. Paris: Michel-Lévy, 1856.

Séjour, Victor. *Les Grands Vassaux*. Paris: Michel-Lévy, 1869.

Séjour, Victor. *Le Marquis Caporal*. Paris: Michel-Lévy, 1856.

Séjour, Victor. *Le Martyre du coeur*. Paris: Michel-Lévy, 1858 (with Jules Brésil)

Séjour, Victor. *Les Massacres de la Syrie*. Paris: J. Barbre, 1856.

Séjour, Victor. *Les Mystères du temple*. Paris: Michel-Lévy, 1862.

Séjour, Victor. *Les Noces vénitiennes*. Paris: Michel-Lévy, 1855.

Séjour, Victor. *Le Paletot brun*. Paris: Michel-Lévy, 1860.

Séjour, Victor. *Le Retour de Napoléon*. Paris: Dauvin et Fontaines, 1841. 7 p. *La Chute de Séjean*. Paris: Michel-Lévy, 1849.

Séjour, Victor. *Richard III*. La Nouvelle Orléans: A Gaux et L. Dutuit (*La Semaine*), 1853. 44 p.; Paris: Michel-Lévy, 1870.

Séjour, Victor. *Les Volontaires de 1814*. Paris: Michel-Lévy, 1862.

Smith, William Gardner. *Malheur aux justes*. Paris: Club

Français du Livre, 1952; La Table Ronde, 1953. Tr. Jean Rosenthal (*Anger at Inoocence*, 1950).

Van Peebles, Melvin. *La Permission; la Fête à Harlem*. Paris: Jérome Martineau, 1967.

Van Peebles, Melvin. *Le Chinois du XIVeme*. Paris: Jérome Martineau, 1966 (Unpublished in English).

Van Peebles, Melvin. *Un Américain en enfer*. Paris: Denoël, 1965. Tr. Paule Truffert (*The True American*, 1976).

Van Peebles, Melvin. *Un Ours pour le F.B.I.* Paris: Buchet-Chastel, 1967. Tr. Paule Truffert (*A Bear for the FBI*, 1968).

Walker, Margaret. *Jubilee*. Paris: Le Seuil, 1968 (*Jubilee*, 1966).

Washington, Booker T. *L'Autobiographie d'un noir*. Paris: Plon, 1903. Tr. Othon Guerlac (*Up from Slavery*, 1900).

White, Walter. *L'Etincelle*. Paris (*The Fire in the Flint*, 1924).

Wright, Charles. *Le Messager*. Paris, 1963 (*The Messenger*).

Wright, Richard. *Bandoeng, 1.500. 000.000 d'hommes*. Paris: Calmann-Léry, 1955 (*The Color Curtain*, 1955).

Wright, Richard. *Black Boy (Jeunesse noire)*. Paris: Gallimard,1947. Tr. Marcel Duhamel and Andrée Picard (*Black Boy*, 1945).

Wright, Richard. *Bon sang dé bonsoir*. Mercure de France, Paris, 1965. Tr. Hélène Bokanowski (*Lawd Today*, 1963).

Wright, Richard. *Ecoute, homme blanc*. Paris: Calmann-Lévy, 1959. Tr. Dominique Guillet (*White Man, Listen*, 1957).

Wright, Richard. *Espagne païenne*. Paris: Buchet, Chastel, Corréa, 1958 (*Pagan Spain*, 1957).

Wright, Richard. *Fishbelly*. Paris: Julliard, 1960. Tr. Hélène Bokanoswki (*The Long Dream*, 1957).

Wright, Richard. *Huit Hommes*. Paris: Julliard, 1962. Tr. Jacqueline Bernard and Claude-Edmonde Magny (*Eight Men*, 1961).

Wright, Richard. *Le Dieu de mascarade*. Del Duca, Paris, 1955. Tr. Jane Fillion (*Savage Holiday*, 1954).

Wright, Richard. *Les Enfants de l'Oncle Tom*. Paris: Albin Michel, 1946. Tr. Marcel Duhamel and Boris Vian (*Uncle Tom's Children*, 1938; 1940).

Wright, Richard. *Puissance noire*. Paris: Corréa, 1955. Tr. Roger Giroux (*Black Power*, 1954).

Wright, Richard.*Le Transfuge*. Paris: Gallimard, 1955. Tr. Guy de Montlaur (*The Outsider*, 1953).

Wright, Richard. *Un Enfant du pays*. Paris: Albin Michel, 1947. Tr. Hélène Bokanowski and Marcel Duhamel (*Native Son*, 1940).

Yerby, Frank. *La Dynastie des Benton*. Verviers: L'Inter, 1957 (*Benton's Row*, 1954).

Yerby, Frank. *Le Chant du sacrifié*. Paris: Editions de Trévise, 1970 (*Goat Song*, 1967).

Yerby, Frank. *Le Clan des Jarrett*. Paris: Fleuve noir, 1968 (*Jarrett's Jade*, 1959).

Yerby, Frank. *Les Diablesses*. Lausane: Margurat, 1950 (*The Vixens*, 1947).

Yerby, Frank. *Le Dilemme du Dr. Childers*. Paris, Seghers, 1960 (*The Serpent and the Staff*, 1958).

Yerby, Frank. *Pietro, chevalier d'amour*. Paris, 1954 (*The Saracen Blade*).

Index of Authors and Concepts

Index of Titles

Index of Periodicals

About the Compiler

MICHEL FABRE is Professor at the Research Center in African-American Studies at the University of Paris III. His many publications include *Chester Himes: An Annotated Primary and Secondary Bibliography* (Greenwood, 1992).

ISBN 0-313-25368-4

90000>

EAN

9 780313 253683

HARDCOVER BAR CODE